Understanding Urban Poverty in India

Understanding Urban Poverty in India

Experiences from Mumbai

Edited by

Olivier Brito
Aditya Singh

RAWAT PUBLICATIONS

Jaipur • New Delhi • Bangalore • Hyderabad • Guwahati • Kolkata

ISBN 978-81-316-0622-3

Published by
Prem Rawat for **Rawat Publications**
Satyam Apts, Sector 3, Jawahar Nagar, Jaipur 302 004 (India)
Phone: 0141 265 1748 / 7006 Fax: 0141 265 1748
E-mail: info@rawatbooks.com
Website: www.rawatbooks.com

New Delhi Office
4858/24, Ansari Road, Daryaganj, New Delhi 110 002
Phone: 011 2326 3290

Also at *Bangalore, Hyderabad, Guwahati* and *Kolkata*

Typeset by Rawat Computers, Jaipur

Printed at Chaman Enterprises, New Delhi

Contents

Contributors

Abdul Shaban, Professor and Chairperson of International Student Office (ISO), Centre for Public Policy, Habitat and Human Development, School of Development Studies, Tata Institute of Social Sciences, Mumbai, India

Abhishek Kumar, Research Scholar, International Institute for Population Sciences, Mumbai (India)

Aditya Singh, Doctoral Candidate, School of Health Sciences and Social Work, University of Portsmouth, Portsmouth (United Kingdom)

Anisha Thomas, graduated in Development Studies from the Tata Institute of Social Sciences. She is currently with the Sexual Assault Survivors support program at the Majlis Legal Center, Mumbai, India

Atul Jaiswal, Edelgive Fellow, UnLtd India Fellow, Junior Research Fellow, Founder Ananya Foundation for Social Change (TISS – Edelgive Fellowship Project), Tata Institute of Social Sciences, Mumbai, India

Mahesh Nath Singh, Assistant Professor, Tata Institute for Social Sciences, Mumbai (India)

Mohan Guruswamy, Chairman and founder of Centre for Policy Alternatives. He is also Advisor at Ministry of Finance, Non-Resident Senior Fellow at Atlantic Council of the United States and Distinguished Fellow at Observer Research Foundation. He has over three decades of experience in government, industry and academia. He was educated at Osmania University, Hyderabad; John F. Kennedy School of Government, Harvard University; Fletcher School of Law and Diplomacy, Tufts University; and Graduate School of Business, Stanford University.

Olivier Brito, Lecturer in Social Work, Université Paris Ouest Nanterre la Défense, Nanterre, France.

Raj Narayan, Doctoral Fellow, International Institute for Population Sciences, Mumbai (India)

Rajiva Prasad, Professor, Department of Migration & Urban Studies, International Institute for Population Sciences, Mumbai, India.

Ranjana Raghunathan, graduated in Social Work from the Tata Institute of Social Sciences, Mumbai (India). She is currently based in Singapore and working as freelance researcher.

Ronald Joseph Abraham, currently IDinsight's Country Director for India, holds a B.A. (Hons.) in Economics from St. Stephen's College, Delhi University, and a Master in Public Administration (International Development) from Harvard Kennedy School.

Sanjay Rode, Assistant Professor, Department of Economics, S.K. Somaiya College, Mumbai (India).

Shikha Gupta, graduated in Health Administration from the Tata Institute of Social Sciences, Consultant- Secretariat, TRG, National Urban Health Mission, National Health Systems Resource Centre, Ministry of Health and Family Welfare, New Delhi, India

Introduction

Understanding Urban Poverty in India: Experiences from Mumbai

This book proposes to reflect on several key elements of urbanization with the aim of getting a better grasp on some of the actions that could be taken to tackle urban poverty. It is focused on the city of Mumbai, the fifth most populous city in the world in which over half of the population lives in slums or is homeless. By examining urban poverty in the megacity of Mumbai and focusing on how Mumbaikars cope with it, we believe that it is possible to learn about poverty and enhance anti-poverty interventions. In other words, this book is an opportunity to learn more about the complex reality of poverty. This educational purpose requires committing to a set of basic guidelines.

It is first necessary to look beyond the traditional poverty research dichotomy opposing qualitative and quantitative approaches. The limits of positivist research designs that merely focus on income and consumption measurement are well known. The scientific community seems to agree on the fact that poverty should be studied through cross-disciplinary lenses and urges social scientists to engage in what is termed as 'Q-squared' approaches of poverty. It is, however, important to keep in mind that the simple combination of methodologies is also limited and should not be considered as a 'magic' approach of alleviating poverty. Recent research assessing poverty in various developing countries has drawn attention to the fact that different methods can lead to different findings (Chambers, 1997; Laderchi et al., 2003; McGee, 2004; Davis, P., Baulch, B.). The study of poverty should, therefore, not only be multidimensional but also be comprehensive. The topics covered in the book range over a wide spectrum of social sciences, from economics to population studies and feminist epistemology. We have approached poverty from multiple angles and lenses with multiple understandings of urban poverty. Though different papers contained in the book can be considered independent to each other, we believe that the core utility of this book lies in the intersection of these contributions. This consideration reflects our second guideline and can be identified as a dynamic approach of poverty. This book is divided into nine parts, with each chapter looking at a different aspect of poverty in urban slums of Mumbai.

Chapter 1 presents a thorough examination of poverty debate and questions the relevance of simple poverty lines based on caloric measures as a yardstick of poverty in today's India. The paper then moves deeper into the trends of poverty in India and the politics of poverty. It also highlights the major problems with present poverty lines and proposes a 'new and more realistic poverty line that envisages poverty in India in human and humane terms rather than animal life levels of present definition'. Taking current costs of nutritional norms, basic health needs, energy, clothing, education, transport and communication, access to water and shelter and many other miscellaneous items into consideration, the authors estimate a new poverty line which they claim to be more inclusive of basic needs of human life. At the end of the paper, they define a person as poor in India if he or she has a monthly per capita income less than ₹ 840 or does not have an access to either safe drinking water, proper shelter, sanitation, quality secondary education, or an all-weather road with public transport. Taking into consideration the regional diversity, they call for separate poverty line for each state.

Chapter 2 explores the quantity of water used in domestic households vis-à-vis the recommended quantity of water consumption in seven major Indian cities, namely, Delhi, Kanpur, Kolkata, Ahmedabad, Mumbai, Hyderabad and Madurai. The author attempts to find out equity in consumption of water across various socio-economic groups, sources of water supply, perception of households about quality of municipal water and duration of municipal water supply.

Chapter 3 is a qualitative research focusing on the life experiences of the homeless women on the streets of Mumbai. This ethnography delineates the women's experiences of homelessness from a feminist perspective. It is exploratory in nature, with the objective of documenting the women's experiences of homelessness. It draws primarily from in-depth interviews and focused group discussions conducted with homeless women in three different settings – on the streets, in temporary shelters of non-government organizations and in government institutions. This chapter explores the nuances of the meanings of home and homelessness.

Chapter 4 looks at urban poverty and health status and health care utilization in urban India. It basically examines economic inequality in maternal and child health indicators in urban India using the first and third round of the National Family Health Survey conducted during 1992–93 and 2005–06, respectively. Urban poor are also compared with the rural residents. Selected outcome variables are – current contraceptive use, antenatal care, safe delivery, childhood immunization, underweight, stunting, wasting and infant and under-five mortality. Using statistics, concentration index and multivariate techniques, it shows stark differences between urban poor and non-poor in all the selected outcome variables. Moreover, the differences remained stagnate over the period for the child health indicators. Comparison of urban poor with rural population shows that utilization of healthcare services is better among urban poor while health status is better among rural population. Based on the findings, it is suggested that in order to improve the reproductive and child health condition in the country, the attention should be given to the urban poor along with the rural population. It calls for targeted policies to improve the health of urban population in the country.

Chapter 5 examines the contraceptive behaviour among slum and non-slum dwellers in Mumbai using secondary data from a nationally representative survey – National Family Health Survey (NFHS) conducted in 2005–06. Some very interesting pattern of modern contraceptive use was revealed. It was found that there is a very small gap between slum and non-slum dwellers in terms of prevalence of modern contraceptive methods. The findings of multinomial logistic regression are also very interesting. Women in slum areas were more likely to use modern contraceptive methods compared to those living in non-slum areas. Muslim women were more likely to use modern contraceptive methods compared to Hindu women. Authors conclude with some policy implication of their study.

Chapter 6 examines the economic impact of illness on Nepalese community in selected urban slums of Mumbai. The paper provides a brief description of Nepalese diaspora in India and then moves on to the examination of utilization of different health care providers, per capita income and expenditure. It further looks into how much households spend on health or healthcare related expenditures. In cases where health expenditure occurs, the source for funds to pay for such expenditures has also been explored. Authors then try to estimate the proportion of households that have suffered catastrophic expenditure for healthcare. The paper, thus, brings out a new aspect of poverty – healthcare expenditure led poverty in urban slum of Mumbai.

Chapter 7 provides an insight into the lifestyle of youth from urban slums in Mumbai. Using data collected from selected slums in Mumbai, this study also throws light on how young people participate in decision-making within their homes. It uncovers the patterns of lifestyle, especially substance abuse and peer group interactions.

Chapter 8 looks at the employment patterns among informal sector workers in slums of Mumbai. Mumbai, being the epicentre of economic growth in India since the last century or so, has been attracting migrants from different corners. However, this has led to rapid proliferation of urban slums. These slums have been the shelter for new migrants who come to Mumbai in search of employment. These slums have become a major centre for informal sector workers. Using primary data collected from selected urban slums in Mumbai, the paper explores the pattern and characteristics of informal sector workers and throws light on their plight.

Chapter 9 provides an understanding of the barriers in health services utilization in slums of Mumbai from both the clients' and health providers' perspectives. Using the best of both qualitative and quantitative methods (mixed methods approach), this study uncovers several factors affecting healthcare utilization in an urban setting that are generally not possible to cover in quantitative surveys.

Chapter 10 contributes to the quest for an operational definition of begging. In order to illustrate the need for an operational definition of begging, the author has reviewed the legal definition of begging enacted in the Bombay Prevention of Begging Act as well as theoretical definitions of begging. This chapter highlights that researchers and policy makers examining begging suffer from definitional shortcomings. Social scientists generally provide a minimalistic and paradoxical definition of begging. Among law and policy makers, there is no consensus on a definition of begging. Begging can be defined broadly or narrowly, it can be considered as acceptable or be criminalized. This chapter, therefore, proposes an operational definition of begging, distinguishing begging policies, begging strategies and begging techniques.

This book represents the efforts of scholars, social workers and researchers to share their expertise on poverty and reflects our belief that a comprehensive and multidimensional approach of poverty can only deepen the understanding. This book is not meant to be an authoritative statement on urban poverty in Mumbai. The city's diversity and the complexity of poverty make such an endeavour impossible. Yet, this book is a perfect opportunity to modestly contribute to the conceptualization of a dynamic approach of poverty that is generating a debate involving economist, geographers, sociologist, educationist, psychologist and other social scientists.

1 Redefining Poverty

A New Poverty Line for a New India

Mohan Guruswamy and Ronald Joseph Abraham

Poverty: The state or condition of having little or no money, goods, or means of support; condition of being poor; indigence.

Synonyms are penury, destitution, need, want. These words imply a state of privation and lack of necessities. Poverty denotes a serious lack of the means for a proper existence.

Poverty Line: A minimum income level used as an official standard for determining the proportion of population living in poverty.

Webster's Encyclopaedic Unabridged Dictionary of the English language.

'I have learnt to seek my happiness by limiting my desires rather than in attempting to satisfy them.'

—John Stuart Mill

Defining Away the Poor

Poverty is an economic condition. Hunger is a physical condition that often arises out of a severe economic condition. While the definition of hunger in terms of calories can remain constant, the definition of poverty is relative to the prevalent levels of general prosperity. However, in India, when defining poverty, our planners seem to be taking J.S. Mill literally because for decades the Planning Commission of India has followed a rather limited definition of poverty. The present official poverty line is based only on calories and, hence, accounts for little else but the satiation of one's hunger. It would have been more accurate to define this as the starvation line, as that is exactly what it is.

This limited definition has allowed successive governments to claim great achievement in the percentage reduction of poverty, if not absolute reduction in the number of poor. But when you have a more expanded definition by factoring in other basic human needs, minimum living standards and access to public services, we will see that a majority of Indians are, in fact, still extremely poor. Quite clearly how we define poverty will determine the nature and content of public policy relating to its elimination.

The Official Poverty Line is a 'Starvation Line'

The idea of defining poverty in terms of a poverty line was first proposed during the Indian Labour Conference in 1957. A Working Group under the Planning Commission then stipulated a poverty line of ₹ 20 per person per month.[1] They derived this poverty line using consumer expenditure data and a caloric norm. The understanding was that anybody spending less than this amount is poor because he or she does not have the purchasing power to buy enough food that met the caloric norm.

In 1979, a task force was assigned by the Planning Commission to look at this definition of poverty again. After much deliberation, it too fixed a poverty line largely based on calories. It delineated ₹ 49 and ₹ 57 per person per month as rural and urban poverty lines respectively at 1973 prices.[2] In 1999–2000, the poverty lines after adjusting for inflations, which were ₹ 327 and ₹ 454 in rural and urban areas, respectively.[3] As of December 2005, these figures stood at approximately ₹ 368 and ₹ 559 per person per month for rural and urban areas.[4]

These official poverty lines in India are, however, woefully unsatisfactory and should, in fact, be renamed 'starvation lines'. This is because apart from factoring about 650 grams[5] of food grains everyday, this line makes very little provision for the other essentials of life. Is it enough to consume just calories, when state institutions – such as the Indian Council of Medical Research – themselves advocate a nutritious diet? What about drinking water? Shelter and sanitation? Essential clothing? Access to education? Healthcare…

The fact is that an average Indian does not have an access to these basic needs. For a country aiming to join the league of developed nations by 2020, such a plight is embarrassing, to say the least. A true and complete definition of poverty should, therefore, include *all* the basic needs of human life with a modest modicum of quality.

Is Poverty Really Declining?

It is striking to note that despite what is very obviously a conveniently low threshold of poverty, in 1973 nearly 55 per cent of the population or 32.13 crore people were below the poverty line (see Table 1). In 1993, even after 20 years of the state trying to alleviate poverty, the number of poor remained at almost the same level at 32.03 crores. By 2004, the number declined to about 25 crores. However, this is hardly an achievement as the rate of decline of poverty since 1973 has been at a dismal 0.81 per cent per annum.[6] Considering the economy grew at over 5 per cent over the same period, such a low rate of decline of poverty must be deemed unacceptable. It is not surprising that the Planning Commission and the government prefer not to talk about these figures and, instead, dwell on the fact that the percentage of poor has declined to 26 per cent since reforms. Many experts even dispute this claim.

Table 1 *Percentage and Number of Poor in India Since 1973**

Year	*Percentage of Poor*	*Number of Poor (Crores)*	*Annual Real Rate of Decline in the Number of Poor ^*
1973–74	54.9%	32.13	—
1977–78	51.3%	32.89	–0.59%
1983	44.5%	32.29	0.31%
1987–88	38.9%	30.71	1.25%
1993–94	36.0%	32.03	–0.70%
1999–2000	26.1%	26.02	3.40%
2004**	23.6%	24.97	0.82%

* As per the Expert Group Methodology.

^ A negative rate of decline means the number of poor increased.

** Based on the estimated population of 2004 and poverty ratio calculated using the latest National Sample Survey in 2004.

Source: National Institute of Rural Development (2004).

Aiming too Low: A Convenient Poverty Line Helps

If *India Vision 2020*[7] of a developed India is to become a reality, a proper definition of poverty is vital. By that time, the state needs to ensure that every citizen not only gets at least two square and wholesome meals a day but also has an access to all the basic amenities required to lead a modestly comfortable life with dignity. However, the present inadequate definition of poverty has ensured that all the policies aimed at alleviating poverty aim much too low by focussing on eliminating hunger rather than eliminating poverty as a whole.

A good example of this is the present Mahatma Gandhi National Rural Employment Guarantee Scheme (MNREGS), which guarantees one able-bodied member of each family work at a wage of ₹ 60 a day. Therefore, even if this person works on all 30 days of a month, he/she earns only ₹ 1,800. For a typical family of five, that amounts to ₹ 360 per person, which is exactly what the rural poverty line is right now. Therefore, even a scheme released with as much fanfare as the MNREGS at best only ensures that each person in the family consumes a certain quantity of food grains. It guarantees little else. Moreover, the guarantee is only for 100 days in a year, leaving the poor to fend for themselves for the rest of the 265 days. This surely cannot be our vision for 2020!

In fact, the present ceiling on poverty is so low that even if the government were to hand out enough money to each poor family to buy enough food to be just above the official poverty line, it would only cost around ₹ 57,000 crores[8] per year. This amount is only 25 per cent of what it costs to maintain the entire bureaucracy of India[9] (around ₹ 2,27,000 crores every year)[10] or a little over 6.7 per cent of the annual central and state budgets combined (about ₹ 8,47,000 crores)[11] or about 2.1 per cent of the GDP (about ₹ 27,60,000 crores).[12] This is quite telling when you consider that the Central Government spends over ₹ 58,000 crores on salaries and pensions alone and ₹ 47,500 crores on direct subsidies that mainly benefit the already well-off. It is ironical that the elimination of poverty is topmost on the agendas of not only the government, but all political parties.

The sad reality is that despite electoral catchphrases like '*Garibi Hatao*', 'India Shining' and '*Aam Admi*' being campaign platforms during elections, a determined assault on poverty and backwardness has in reality been low on the list of national priorities. From 1973 to 2004, the poverty percentage has reduced by more than half – from 54.9 per cent to 23.6 per cent. This gives one the notion that poverty is declining steadily and soon there will be none of it. However, it is self serving only to look at poverty rates because the decline of the actual number of people below the poverty line has been less than a quarter – from 32 crore people to 25 crore people – or as mentioned above, an annual decline of only 0.81 per cent. Considering that the absolute numbers of those officially deemed poverty stricken has only decreased marginally since 1973, the notion that the problem of poverty is being tackled is an ill-conceived one. When this is considered along with the official notion of what is poverty, it should cause much pondering about the true nature of India.

The Present Poverty Line: Three Major Problems*

Present Poverty Class Does Not Even Meet the Caloric Norm

We have argued, earlier, the definition of poverty based just on the caloric norm is unacceptable. Now, consider this. Many of those who might be relatively better-off in terms of income may in fact be getting less than the stipulated calories each day, either due to ignorance or due to the lack of availability. It is a fact that despite the increase in agricultural production, the per capita availability of cereals is about the same since 1981, whereas the per capita availability of pulses has declined from 37.5 grams in 1981 to 28.2 grams in 2003.[13]

The average person just above the official poverty line from rural India falls short of the caloric norm by about 22 per cent. Similarly, a person just above the poverty line in urban India falls short of the norm by about 9 per cent (see Table 2). Therefore, the present poverty line, which was only supposed to ensure a certain calorie intake, fails even on that single front.

The present official poverty line is based on the norm that the average person in rural India should be able to consume 2,400

* There exist more than just three criticisms to the present poverty line. The three elucidated here have the most bearing on policy issues and, hence, are treated in detail.

calories and the average person in urban India should be able to consume 2,100 calories. In 1979, when the present poverty line was formed, this was the case, i.e., the average person above the poverty line met the caloric norm. However, currently (1999–2000), those people who are just above the official poverty line do not meet this norm.[14] This can clearly be seen in Table 2, where the group just above the poverty line (called the Poverty Line Group or PLG) consumes an average of 1,868 calories in rural areas and 1,912 calories in urban areas. Therefore, these groups fall short of the caloric norm by 22 per cent in rural areas and 9 per cent in urban areas.

Table 2 *Average Per Person Intake of Calories of Groups Below, On and Above the Poverty Line (1999–2000)*

Group	*Per Person Per Day Intake of Calories (kcal)*
Rural	
Below Poverty Line Group	1,614
Poverty Line Group (PLG)	1,868
Above Poverty Line Group	2,386
Urban	
Below Poverty Line Group	1,627
Poverty Line Group (PLG)	1,912
Above Poverty Line Group	2,375

Source: Calculated from Government of India (2001c).

Looking at Only Calories is Not Enough

The current caloric standard is anyway an insufficient nutritional norm; there are two reasons for this. First, the caloric standard set by the Planning Commission is a glaring under-stipulation. The Indian Council of Medical Research (ICMR) prescribes 3,800 calories for an adult male doing heavy activity and 2,925 calories for an adult female carrying out heavy activity.[15] From this, it is amply clear that for the millions of poor unskilled wage labourers in India carrying out heavy manual labour every day, a stipulation of 2,400 (2,100) calories in rural (urban) areas is grossly insufficient.[16] One clear implication of this is that the minimum wages in the various states need to be substantially raised.

Secondly, and more importantly, there exists a need to go beyond a simple caloric standard, as the body also needs proteins, fat, minerals, iron and vitamins.[17] Given below is an excerpt from ICMR's book on dietary guidelines for Indians.[18]

> Man needs a wide range of nutrients to lead a healthy and active life and these are derived through the diet he consumes daily. The components of his diets must be chosen judiciously to provide all the nutrients he needs in adequate amounts and in proper proportions... . The body needs energy (calories are the primary source of this) for maintaining body temperature, metabolic activity, supporting growth and physical work... . Proteins provide amino acids for the synthesis of body... . In the adult, dietary protein is essential to synthesise new proteins... . Fat is a concentrated source of energy... and also helps in the absorption of beta-carotene and other fat-soluble vitamins... . While a minimum amount of fat has to be present in the diet, excess of fat in the diet is considered harmful... . Minerals that are important in human nutrition are calcium, phosphorous and magnesium and the electrolytes, sodium and potassium... . (Iron is important because) iron deficiency anaemia is widespread in our country, the prevalence varying from 45 per cent in male adults to 70 per cent or more in women or children... . Vitamins are accessory food factors, which carry out diverse functions in the body.

Nutrition deficiency is also a leading cause for disease. According to the UNICEF, 'malnutrition limits development and the capacity to learn. It also costs lives: about 50 per cent of all childhood deaths are attributed to malnutrition'.[19] Lack of vitamin C leads to scurvy, a disorder that affects our bones. Vitamin B_1 deficiency leads to mental confusion, muscle weakness and heart disorder. Osteoporosis, or the tendency to lose bone mass, is linked with lack of calcium in our diet. Zinc deficiency in children leads to growth retardation.[20] Therefore, it is amply clear that a nutritious diet is a fundamental need of the human body; this must not be ignored when formulating a poverty line.

Out of all the nutritional requirements mentioned above, the present poverty line only fulfils the minimum protein requirement of 50 gm per day. This is mainly because 75 per cent of the total protein is derived from cereals.[21] However, to ensure adequate consumption of *all* the essential nutrients, a commodity-basket should be formulated that includes a minimum diet of cereals, pulses, oils, vegetables, fruits, etc. Thereafter, the cost of this diet should be calculated and included when constructing the poverty line. This will ensure that if someone is above this renewed poverty line, he or she will have the capability to consume a nutritious diet. This has been elaborated in Section V which attempts to delineate an alternative poverty line.

No Norms for Non-food Basic Needs

The title of the 1974 Hindi movie, *Roti, Kapda aur Makan* (Bread, Clothing and Shelter), captures very well the notion that man does not live by bread alone. The present poverty line not only ignores important nutritional needs but also the other basic needs of life: shelter, clothing, healthcare, sanitation, drinking water and equal opportunity for education.

In 1979, when the present poverty line was defined, the expenditure on non-food items of the group of people who consumed over 2,400 (2,100) calories in rural (urban) areas was calculated. In addition to the total expenditure on calories, this non-food expenditure was also included into the poverty line. However, such a method is akin to suggesting that whatever the poor spend on non-food items, it is 'enough'. Instead, one needs to analyse what is consumed through non-food expenditure and verify whether it meets the basic needs of a human being. For example, as per the latest national sample survey on consumer expenditure, those who are just above the poverty line in rural India spend only around ₹ 8 per month on medical care. Clearly, this is grossly insufficient. It is not as if the Planning Commission has not taken note of the fault in its methodology.[22]

The (Planning Commission Expert) Group recognizes the desirability of defining the normative standard for non-food consumption and its constituents without reference to actual behaviour, but until this is done, the existing basis seems to be the most practical and reasonable.

Despite this apparent 'recognition' by the Commission, no such norms exist in reality. Considering that most of these norms can be derived scientifically, there seems to be no explanation for why this has not taken place? The only plausible explanation can be that since raising the poverty bar higher will only compound the task of our policy makers and economic planners, it remains at a ridiculously low level to enable claims of better achievement and to avoid deployment of resources to areas and people who deserve them more.

Towards a More Realistic Definition of Poverty in India

The aim of this section is to define poverty in India in a manner that visualizes it in more human and humane terms rather than the animal life levels of the present definition. Quite clearly a more reasonable poverty line ought to be based on the cost of all basic needs. Thus, this section details the cost of nutrition, healthcare, clothing, etc. In addition, some needs that cannot be quantified in money terms – such as access to water, education, etc. – are also identified and included.

Nutritional Norms and Cost

Even in this day and age, around one in four Indians are malnourished. The consequences of such a plight are devastating as nutrition is the most important need of a human being after water. Presently, 47 per cent of Indian children below the age of 5 are underweight for their age.[23] The UNICEF reports that one in every three malnourished children in the world is in India.

Table 3 *Balanced Diet for Infants, Children, Adolescents and Adults*

Food Groups	*Infants*	*Years*							*Adult (Heavy Activity)*[24]	
	6–12 Months	*1–3*	*4–6*	*7–9*	*10–12*		*13–18*			
					Girls	*Boys*	*Girls*	*Boys*	*Woman*	*Man*
Cereals & Millets (g)	45	120	210	270	270	330	300	420	480	690
Pulses (g)	15	30	45	60	60	60	60	60	90	90
Toned Milk (ml)	500	500	500	500	500	500	500	500	300	300
Roots & Tubers (g)	50	50	100	100	100	100	100	200	200	200
Green Leafy Vegetables (g)	25	50	50	100	100	100	100	100	100	100
Other Vegetables (g)	25	50	50	100	100	100	100	100	100	100
Fruits (g)	100	100	100	100	100	100	100	100	100	100
Sugar (g)	25	25	30	30	30	35	30	35	45	55
Fats/Oils (visible) (g)	10	20	25	25	25	25	25	25	40	55

Source: Indian Council of Medical Research (2003).

However, it is not as if the government is not in the know about the importance of balanced nutrition because the National Institute of Nutrition (NIN) under the aegis of the ICMR itself recommends what it considers is a nutritious diet for healthy living. The NIN has also published a balanced diet for Indians, reproduced in Table 3. In fact, the apathy of the government is quite evident from the fact that despite having sponsored detailed studies on nutrition in India, it still adopts a norm that only sees poverty in terms of calories.

Given in Table 4 are the prices of these foodstuffs with information on how they have been computed.

Table 4 *Prices of Foodstuffs as of 2005*

Food Product	*Price (₹/kg)*	*Remarks*
Rice	11.23	Result for 2005; average of South and East Zone.
Wheat	8.71	Result for 2005; average of North and West Zone.
Tur (Arhar, Pulses)	28.99	Result for 2005; all-India average.
Mustard Oil	52.98	Result for 2005; average of North and East Zone.
Sugar	19.2	Result for 2005; all-India average.
Vegetables	7.83	Calculated using the weighted average of the rate at which urban and rural India bought vegetables as given in GoI 2001b. The figure is adjusted for inflation.
Fruits	16.59	Calculated using the weighted average of the rate at which urban and rural India bought fruits as given in GoI 2001b. The figure is adjusted for inflation.
Milk	15.00	Using the standard MRP for toned milk.

Source: Government of India (2001b, 2005a), MRP of toned milk.

With the recommended diet given in Table 3 and the prices in Table 4, one can calculate the cost of this diet. This is shown in Table 5.

The last row in Table 5 provides the ideal monthly expenditure on food that enables one to have a complete nutritious diet. Using the age-sex distribution information of the population, one can calculate that the per capita expenditure on food that provides for the recommended balanced diet for the average Indian person should be around ₹ 573 per month. Therefore, for a typical family of five, the total monthly expenditure on just food should be about ₹ 2,900. If the two adult members of a family work for 25 days a month on the officially prescribed minimum wage of ₹ 60 each,[25] they would just about earn ₹ 3,000 between them.

Table 5 *Cost of Diet (in ₹)*

Food Groups	*Infants*	*Years*							*Adult*	
	6–12 Months	*1–3*	*4–6*	*7–9*	*10–12*		*13–18*			
					Girls	*Boys*	*Girls*	*Boys*	*Women*	*Men*
Cereals	0.45	1.2	2.09	2.69	2.69	3.29	2.99	4.19	4.79	6.88
Pulses	0.44	0.87	1.31	1.74	1.74	1.74	1.74	1.74	2.61	2.61
Milk	7.5	7.5	7.5	7.5	7.5	7.5	7.5	7.5	4.5	4.5
Vegetables	0.78	1.17	1.57	2.35	2.35	2.35	2.35	3.13	3.13	3.13
Fruits	1.66	1.66	1.66	1.66	1.66	1.66	1.66	1.66	1.66	1.66
Sugar	0.48	0.48	0.58	0.58	0.58	0.67	0.58	0.67	0.864	1.056
Fats/Oils (visible)	0.53	1.06	1.32	1.32	1.32	1.32	1.32	1.32	2.12	2.91
Total Daily Cost	11.84	13.94	16.03	17.84	17.84	18.53	18.14	20.21	19.67	22.75
Total Monthly Cost	360	424	487	543	543	563	552	615	598	692

Note: Cereals include an average of rice and wheat (₹ 9.97).
Price of Arhar is used for pulses.
Mustard oil is used for calculations on visible fats/oils.

Source: Calculated using Table 3 and 4.

Therefore, in order to have a nutritious diet, nearly all the money that can possibly be earned needs to be spent on food. It must be remembered that daily wage labourers account for over 80 per cent of our workforce of over 422 million.[26] The average number of working days available to agricultural labour has also decreased drastically over the last two decades: from 123 days in 1981 to 72 days in 2003.[27] Two policy implications are very obvious. One is the immediate revision of minimum wages and the other is to greatly expand work opportunities for the least qualified and majority of our work force.

*The Cost of Meeting Basic Health Needs**

India is a signatory to the Alma Ata Declaration during the International Conference on Primary Health Care (ICPHC) in 1978 which

---

* The authors would like to thank Dr Rajeev Ahuja for his personal views on per capita medical expenditure. Mr Ahuja is an expert on Health Insurance.

states, 'A main social target of governments... should be the attainment by all peoples of the world by the year 2000 of a level of health that will permit them to lead a socially and economically productive life'. The declaration further identifies primary healthcare as 'the key to attaining this target'. According to the declaration, primary healthcare 'addresses the main health problems in the community, providing promotive (*sic*), preventive, curative and rehabilitative services accordingly'. Furthermore, the Indian wing of this health movement, championed by the National Human Rights Commission, states that primary healthcare should be provided free of cost.

However, India is a long way away from providing free healthcare to all. According to the present Health Minister's public 'message', only 20 per cent of Indians are covered by public healthcare and the rest take recourse to the private sector.[28] Evidently even many Indians below the official poverty line seek medical care from the private sector. Financing ones own healthcare is clearly a burden for the poor in India. Even where the services are available medicines and drugs are often not available. In addition, implicit and indirect costs of accessing healthcare are often not accounted for; such as loss of wages, cost of travel, etc.[29] These factors make it imperative to calculate the average minimum per capita expenditure on healthcare and include it in the poverty line.

Average monthly per capita healthcare cost can be calculated by multiplying the probability of requiring medical care with the actual cost of such medical care.[30] This is called the 'expected value' of healthcare expenditure. This is exactly the computation undertaken by actuaries while calculating premiums for health insurance. The 'Universal Health Insurance Scheme' is one such scheme targeted at the low-income group. As per this scheme, for a premium of ₹ 365 per annum, an individual can get insured for all in-patient medical care up to a sum of ₹ 30,000.[31]

Therefore, ₹ 365 per annum or ₹ 30 per month per capita is the 'expected value' of health expenditure for the poor in India. Clearly, even this is a small amount, but nonetheless at least this much should be ensured to every citizen of this country.

Access to Water

The minimum water consumption as per the World Health Organization should be about 50 litres a day per person to cover consumption and hygiene needs.[32] However, as per the latest National Family Health Survey of 1999–00, 37.7 per cent of households do not have access to safe water supply within 15 minutes of their home.[33] In a typical family of five, if two persons each fetch a traditional vessel full of water daily, they will be able to bring back at the most 40 litres of water between them. That is about 8 litres of water or approximately 8 mugs of water per person in a family of five. Therefore, at least one in three Indians does not get this basic daily water requirement. This is without any comment on the quality of water.

Access to Shelter and Sanitation

It is only humane that every human being should have a secure shelter with at least basic amenities and comforts. If we were to define minimum housing standards that provide for the bare minimum, the following should be reasonable to expect:

A housing unit with two bedrooms, a kitchen and a covered toilet.

One electric lamp each in all the four rooms
One fan each in the two bedrooms
One tap each in the toilet and kitchen
One septic tank or connection to a sewage
Reinforced cement concrete (RCC) roof[34]
Brick or stone walls reinforced with cement

While there does not exist information on the availability of housing with the above features specifically, information on the percentage of households living in '*pucca*', 'semi-*pucca*' or '*katcha*' houses is available in a nationwide survey on housing done in 2002.[35] *Pucca* house is one which has a roof and walls made of *pucca* materials, such as cement, concrete, oven-burnt bricks, metals, etc. A *katcha* house is one with a roof and walls made of non-*pucca* materials, such as bamboo, mud, grass, etc. A semi-*pucca* house is one which has either a roof or the walls made of *pucca* materials, but not both.

For security and protection against the elements, a dwelling unit should at least be a *pucca* house. In rural and urban areas, 64 per cent and 23 per cent of the households, respectively, do not have a *pucca* house.[36] Thus, a weighted average of 49 per cent of all households do not have shelter that meets our minimum standards. Will we be able to provide this minimum standard of shelter to these households by 2020?

The condition of public sanitation can be seen all along our roads and railway tracks. Even the most basic living standard demands that a dwelling unit should have access to a latrine that is either connected to a sewage line or a septic tank. However, 89 per cent and 37 per cent of rural and urban India, respectively, or a weighted average of 69.5 per cent of Indians do not have access to such a latrine facility.[37]

Cost of Energy

Presently, about 57 per cent of Indian households do not have access to electricity.[38] Even in households that have an electricity connection, the supply of electricity is extremely erratic.[39] Clearly, if India is to be considered a developed country, each household should have an electricity connection and there should be enough electricity available for all at all times.

The basic house described above needs a few basic electrical fittings – four bulbs and two fans – that constitute the bare minimum need for electrical appliances. We assume that each ceiling fan is on for 8 hours during the night and 4 hours during daytime, thus a total of 12 hours. We also take that the two bulbs are turned on for about 4 hours each in the evenings, mainly for reading or cooking purposes. With these minimal fittings and reasonable usage, the monthly cost on electricity comes to ₹ 175 for a household (see Table 6). Considering that there are 4.99 persons to a household in India, the per capita monthly expenditure on electricity comes to ₹ 35.

Electricity is the most expensive and the least preferred energy source for cooking. On the other hand, the widely used low-grade fuels – such as wood, dung, hay, coal – are a significant source of indoor air pollution as per a report by the Indian Council of Medical Research.[40] This report also states that there is a growing evidence linking indoor air pollution and diseases, such as respiratory diseases, tuberculosis, asthma, heart diseases, cataract, etc.

Table 6 *Minimum Electricity Consumption of a Household in a Month*

Appliance	*Wattage (A)*	*Quantity (B)*	*Usage (hours/day) (C)*	*Units/Month (AxBxCx30)/1,000*	*Cost (₹ 2.2 per unit)*
Ceiling Fan	80	2	12	57.6	126.72
Light Bulb	40	2	4	9.6	21.12
Fixed Charges					20.00
Tax*					7.39
Total				67.2	175.23

* 5 per cent tax on variable cost

Source: Rate list printed by BSES Power Ltd., 2005.

However, as Table 7 shows, over 90 per cent of rural India uses these very low-grade fuels indoors! Though urban India performs relatively better, it too has a 30 per cent prevalence of harmful indoor fuels. Clearly, such use of these disease-causing fuels should be minimized.

Table 7 *Main Types of Fuel Used for Cooking in India (%)*

Type of Fuel	*Urban*	*Rural*	*All India*
Wood	23.1	73.1	59.3
Crop Residues	0.5	8.1	6.0
Dung Cakes	1.4	8.4	6.5
Coal/Coke/Lignite/Charcoal	4.9	1.7	2.6
Kerosene	21.5	2.7	7.9
Electricity	0.8	0.2	0.4
LPG	46.9	5.1	16.7
Biogas	0.6	0.5	0.5
Others	0.2	0.2	0.2
Total	100	100	100

Source: International Institute of Population Sciences (IIPS) and ORC Macro (2000).

While LPG is the ideal cooking fuel, its set-up costs are high. It is mainly an urban middle-class fuel (see Table 7). Despite the fact that most people using LPG are not the ones needing financial support from the state, the government continues to subsidize it. Kerosene is a more affordable substitute and can be used more widely by the poor. Moreover, it is a reasonably clean fuel and can be recommended for use over polluting and harmful fuels like wood, dung, coal, etc.[41] However, as Table 8 shows, over the past few years, kerosene has received lesser budgetary support as compared to LPG. In 1993–94, the LPG subsidy was a third of kerosene. However, in 2002–03, it was more than that of kerosene. It would seem that not only has the state been reducing its support towards LPG and kerosene consumption, it has been doing so at the cost of kerosene.

Table 8 *Subsidy on LPG and Kerosene (₹ crore)*

Year	*1993–94*	*1994–95*	*1995–96*	*1998–99*	*1999–00*	*2000–01*	*2001–02*	*2002–03*
Kerosene	3,773	3,740	4,190	5,770	8,151	7,522	5,310	3,018
LPG	1,261	1,410	1,630	2,600	4,493	6,724	5,830	3,691

Source: Government of India (2004a).

Presently, kerosene is sold at a subsidized rate of around ₹ 9 under the public distribution system (PDS). The quota ranges from around 10 to 12 litres per ration card per month.[42] Thus, the consumption norm of kerosene for a typical family of five is around 2.2 litres per head per month. Assuming that such kerosene is available to all, the monthly per capita expenditure on kerosene comes to around ₹ 20. Thus, the total per capita monthly expenditure on cooking fuel (₹ 20) and electricity (₹ 35) should be around ₹ 55.

Clothing Requirement

Clothing is the second part of '*Roti, Kapda aur Makaan*'. It is also the most variably priced as clothing requirements varies considerably according to region, gender, age and culture. To overcome these problems to an extent, this paper suggests the minimum amount of cloth required and its cost for persons by age and gender although seasonal requirements are disregarded for the sake of simplicity (see Table 9).

Table 9 *Minimum Clothing Requirements and Cost*

	Child (Age: 0–4)	Male (Age: 5–17)	Female (Age: 5–17)	Male Adult	Female Adult
Clothing Require-ments		* 3.6 metres of shirt material	* 3.3 metres of shirt material		
	* 1 metre of shirt material	* 2 metres of trouser material	* 1.8 metres of skirt/salwar material	* 1.4 metres of shirt material	* 1 three-metre sari
	* 0.8 metre of trouser material			* 1.2 metres of trouser material	* 1 metre of blouse material
	(includes two pairs of children's wear)	(includes one pair of clothing and two uniform shirts and one uniform shorts/trousers)	(includes one pair of clothing and two pairs of school uniform)	(includes one pair of clothing)	(includes one sari and a blouse)
Cost of Cloth	150.68	267.96	343	190.39	131.07

Price of cloth for shirt, pyjama, cloth, etc.: ₹ 47.85
Price of cloth for coat, trousers, overcoat, etc.: ₹ 102.83
Price of sari (3 m): ₹ 83.22
Prices are calculated using the weighted average of the rate at which urban and rural India bought cloth material as given in Government of India (2001c). The figure is adjusted for inflation.

The weighted average of the total costs shown in the last row is ₹ 207 per annum on clothing. That makes it an approximate per capita monthly expenditure of ₹ 17 on clothing.

The Right to Education

As per the 93rd amendment of the Constitution of India, education is a fundamental right of every citizen.[43] It states: 'The state shall provide free and compulsory education to all children of the age of six to fourteen years in such manner as the state may, by law, determine'. It also stipulates that it is the fundamental duty of 'a parent or guardian to provide opportunities for education to his child or, as the case may be, ward between the age of six and fourteen years.'

It should be the minimum responsibility of the state to ensure that each young citizen has access to cost-free schooling with adequate infrastructure (a stipulated classroom size and physical amenities, including furniture, library, laboratory, etc.) and qualified teachers. Such a school should be able to provide each citizen of this country so as to provide complete and quality education. Moreover, we propose that such an institution should lie within a 2-km radius of each person's home so as to ensure not more than 30 minutes are spent walking to school. Failing this, it should be the responsibility of the state to provide transport to the school.

At present, it is not easy to get information on access to free and high quality education. Data largely shows information on the number of schools without information on the quality of these institutions. However, without delving into the question of quality, we can see what percentage of the population receives their fundamental right to education till the secondary level or standard 10. Those who have turned 15 should ideally have completed their secondary education.

As per the latest National Sample Survey on Education in 1999–00, 71.16 per cent of the people in the 15–19 year age group had not completed a secondary education. Therefore, nearly three-fourths of Indian youngsters have not been able to access their fundamental right of education accorded to them by the Constitution.[44] This clearly shows that establishing rights is of no value if means to achieve them are not simultaneously provided. As of 2002–03, about 85.2 per cent of the nearly 6 lakh villages in India did not have a school providing secondary education.[45]

Access to All-Weather Roads and Public Transport

Connectivity is probably the single most important factor guiding whether people of a particular region are being able to access their basic needs of education, healthcare, shelter, etc. Road connectivity will ensure transfer of not only people to and fro from different regions, but will also ensure trade of goods and services. However, in India it is not uncommon to hear anecdotal stories of villagers from remote parts of the country travelling for hours on end to reach even an all-weather road. Upon reaching such a road, they wait further in hope for a bus that will stop. Such stories are not surprising considering the fact that around 43 per cent of Indian villages or over 2,70,000 villages are not connected by road.[46] Furthermore, around 25 per cent of villages that have a population of over 1,000 are not connected by road.[47]

Miscellaneous Expenditures

Of all the basic needs highlighted above, four of them – nutrition, healthcare, clothing and energy consumption – have been quantified in rupee terms. The total cost of obtaining these needs comes to ₹ 675 per person per month. However, apart from this cost, various other unavoidable expenditures invariably arise that are hard to account for in advance. Moreover, more often than not, such expenditure by the poor is incurred while trying to obtain one's basic needs. For example, obtaining healthcare would often mean spending money travelling to the doctor; obtaining a nutritious diet involves buying utensils to cook in; getting clothes can include stitching costs; etc.

Therefore, while computing a poverty line, we need to factor these miscellaneous expenses. The present official poverty line accounts for miscellaneous expenditure by adding to the poverty line the total non-food expenditure of the group just on the poverty line. This paper follows a variation of this. Instead of including total non-food expenditure, only expenditure under the heads of 'miscellaneous consumer goods', 'miscellaneous consumer services' and 'durable goods' are included. 'Durable goods' are included because items such as utensils, chairs, tables, etc., all come under this head and typically families need to buy some of these items every year. Table 10 shows the amount spent under these heads.

Total non-food expenditure is not used because it includes expenditure on clothing, healthcare, etc., that has already been accounted for above through proposed norms. Additionally, total non-food expenditure also includes expenditure on tobacco, intoxicants, etc., which need not be part of a poverty line. Similarly, our poverty line does not include expenditure on leisure, festivities, all of which are an integral part of society. However, the responsibility of the state does not extend to these, as its primary task is to ensure that each citizen has access to the basic essentials of life. Therefore, a person who is just above the poverty line, as we define it, is only ensured of the most basic needs.

Table 10 *Monthly Per Capita Miscellaneous Expenditure (in ₹, Adjusted for Inflation)*

Item	*Rural*	*Urban*	*Weighted Average*
Miscellaneous Consumer Goods	51.57	67.40	54.14
Miscellaneous Consumer Services	74.86	85.76	74.66
Durable Goods	30.25	22.55	26.23
Total	157	176	164

Source: Government of India (2001a).

Thus, from Table 10, we can see that total monthly miscellaneous expenditure comes to ₹ 164 per person.

What it Really Costs to Live with a Modicum of Dignity?[48]

Summing up minimum costs for nutrition (₹ 573), health (₹ 30), clothing (₹ 17), energy consumption (₹ 55) and miscellaneous expenditure (₹ 164); the poverty line in India should be about ₹ 840 per capita per month.[49]

At this expenditure level, nearly 69 per cent of India's total population is below the poverty line (see Table 11). That is over two-and-a-half times the present official poverty rate of 26.1 per cent. The situation in rural India is much worse with over 84 per cent of the rural populace below this more realistic poverty line.

Table 11 *Poverty Ratio Using a Holistic Poverty Line*

Area	*Percentage*
Rural	84.6
Urban	42.4
Weighted Average	68.8

Source: Calculated using Government of India (2001a, 2005b) and a poverty line of ₹ 840.

Though the poverty line of ₹ 840 per month established above is more inclusive of the basic needs of human life, it still only partially reveals the true state of poverty in India. This is clearly seen in Table 12 which shows that 24.4 per cent of all households above the poverty line of ₹ 840 do not have *pucca* houses. Therefore, a person spending more than ₹ 840 per month does not necessarily have access to all the fundamental needs of life.

Table 12 *Percentage of Households Living in Pucca or Non-Pucca Houses by MPCE* Class*

Monthly Per Capita Expenditure (₹)	*Pucca House*	*Non-Pucca House*	
0–235	23.2	76.8	
235–265	23.6	76.4	
265–320	27.1	72.9	
320–365	29.8	70.2	Weighted average of 61.6 per cent of households below the poverty line of ₹ 840 living in non-*pucca* houses.
365–410	33.3	66.7	
410–460	39.2	60.8	
460–520	43.6	56.4	
520–605	48.4	51.6	
605–730	56.4	43.6	
730–980 (PLG**)	64.4	35.6	Weighted average of 24.4 per cent of households above the poverty line of ₹ 840 living in non-*pucca* houses.
980–1,285	78.4	21.6	
1,285 or more	91.0	9.0	

* MPCE: Monthly Per Capita Expenditure

** PLG: Poverty Level Group

Source: Government of India (2004b).

Therefore, in addition to the poverty line, a proper definition of who is poor should also include 'access parameters' that measure access to drinking water, shelter, etc. To sum up what we saw earlier, listed below are basic needs and the percentage of households that do not have access to them:

> 37.7 per cent of Indian households do not have access to a nearby water source
> 49 per cent do not have a proper shelter
> 69.5 per cent do not have access to suitable toilets
> 85.2 per cent of Indian villages do not have a secondary school
> 43 per cent of Indian villages do not have an all-weather road connecting them.

The realistic poverty line that we propose along with these access parameters will provide a real, more inclusive and clear picture of poverty in India. Quite clearly, this is the most important tool for the task of poverty alleviation. Therefore, as we define it, a person is poor in India if he or she has a monthly per capita expenditure lesser than ₹ 840 or does not have access to either drinking water, proper shelter, sanitation, quality secondary education, or an all-weather road with public transport.

Getting it Right: Redefining the Poverty Line

Clearly, the present official definition of poverty grossly misrepresents the real situation. It is entirely inappropriate to have a simple caloric measure as the yardstick of poverty. The responsibility of the state exceeds this manifold. We need to upgrade the concept of food security to that of nutritious food security. In addition, it should also be the right of every Indian citizen to have access to safe shelter, sanitation, healthcare, education and clothing. Therefore, when we aim policy for the poor, these benchmarks should be our target. Only worrying about each citizen's food grain intake is clearly aiming too low.

This poverty line should be calculated for each state separately to account for regional differences in taste, clothing requirement, housing requirement, etc. It is also important to understand that norms of basic needs and what can be constituted as luxuries evolve over time. For example, presently one tap in the bathroom is considered a minimum norm. However, in a few years as more and more households fulfil this norm, the norm may be upgraded to include a flush toilet in each bathroom. Similarly, by 2020, piped gas for cooking and heating may even become the norm.

To account for such changes in established norms, the poverty line should be updated every five years. The present poverty line is updated only to account for increases in prices. In the long run, however, this distorts the picture of poverty. For example, as shown earlier, even those just above the poverty line do not consume the requisite amount of calories. However, one of the most frequent arguments used against updating the poverty line – except for with the inflation index – is the fact that over-time comparisons become untenable.

However, this argument is unjustified as you can always compute a 'food expenditure level' which can be increased every year based on inflation. This can be used to see what percentage of the population is below this expenditure line and how it has changed over time. The international one-dollar-a-day and two-dollars-a-day lines are such similar thresholds.

Conclusion

By now it is quite clear that the Indian State needs to revisit its concept of poverty. The present unrealistically low poverty line only serves the purpose of making the government and its development efforts – or the lack of it – look good. If the state is as committed to the task of ridding the country from the ills of poverty as it claims, it should start by redefining the current poverty line. This will ensure that the government gets its priorities straight and is able to target policy effectively.

Based on our proposed poverty line of ₹ 840 per month, the state should try to ensure that a typical household of five people is able to earn around ₹ 50,000 per year, or about ₹ 4,200 per month. This household should have access to a *pucca* house with basic amenities such as a toilet connected to a sewage system and electrical fittings. Access to water to a household should be within 10 to 15 metres if not within the dwelling unit, which would be ideal. The children of the household should be able to access their fundamental constitutional right to education. Moreover, the state needs to go beyond just offering an accessible school but should also ensure that the schooling guarantees each student equal opportunities in life.

Such a household with its most fundamental of needs met should be the ideal that the state aims towards. This calls for a paradigm shift in the sphere of development policy in this country. A shift that is imperative if we truly wish for a new India.

Notes

1. Government of India (1979). *Report of the Task Force on Projections of Minimum Needs and Effective Consumption Demand*. Perspective Planning Division, Planning Commission, New Delhi, p. 8.
2. The present poverty line is largely based on the work of this taskforce. For a detailed description of the present poverty line, refer to Government of India (1993). *Report of the Expert Group on Estimation of Proportion and Number of Poor.* Perspective Planning Division, Planning Commission, New Delhi. This report and the above mentioned report are available on the Commission's website, www.planningcommission.nic.in.
3. N.C. Saxena (2001). 'Poverty Estimates for 1999–2000'. Planning Commission, New Delhi.

4. These figures are arrived at by indexing the rural poverty line with the Consumer Price Index for Agricultural Labourers and the urban poverty line with the Consumer Price Index for Industrial Workers. Both are available from the Labour Bureau, Government of India. These are the indices recommended by the Planning Commission (Government of India, 1993). However, further sophistications such as adjusting the data to state-wise price indices, etc., have not been carried out.
5. This is calculated from caloric norm and the nutrition chart given in Government of India (2001c). *NSS Report No. 471: Nutritional Intake in India, 1999–2000*. National Sample Survey Organization, New Delhi.
6. Calculated using the compound growth formula. Rate of decline in Table 1 also calculated using the same formula.
7. *India Vision 2020* is an official document prepared by the Planning Commission (Government of India, 2002c). It is meant to be 'an articulation of the desired end results in (broad) terms' of development activity by 2020.
8. This figure is also referred to as the 'poverty gap'. It denotes the amount of total money required to bring everybody just above the poverty line assuming that the money is handed out without any distribution costs. Here, the amount is approximated with the assumption that the population is normally distributed across expenditure classes.
9. This bureaucracy accounts for only about 1 per cent of the total population of India according to Government of India (2001). *Government of India's Pensionary Liability*. Ministry of Finance, New Delhi.
10. Government of India (2005c). *National Accounts Statistics 2005*. Central Statistical Organisation, Ministry of Statistics and Programme Implementation, p. 65.
11. Government of India (2005e). *Indian Public Finance Statistics, 2004–05*. Ministry of Finance, Department of Economic Affairs, New Delhi.
12. This figure includes the total salaries of Central, State and Local Government employees. Source: Government of India (2005c). *National Accounts Statistics 2005*. Central Statistical Organisation, Ministry of Statistics and Programme Implementation, p. 62.
13. Tata Services Limited (2005). *Statistical Outline of India 2004–05*. Department of Economics and Statistics, Mumbai, p. 45.
14. Pronab Sen (2005) gives a counter argument to this by suggesting that this fall in calorie intake reflects a choice on the part of the consumer

and his capability to buy food is still intact as it was before. He shows that if the Poverty Line Group (PLG) buys calories (food) at the same rate (prices) as those below the PLG, then they can reach the prescribed caloric standard. This is, however, an untenable and tautological argument. First, calories bought by people below the poverty line are cheaper because of its lower quality. It is, therefore, unreasonable to ask the PLG class to consume a basket of food of lower quality than they deemed fit as revealed by their preference. Secondly, and more importantly, if this argument was valid, then the Planning Commission, while calculating the poverty line in 1979, should have used the cheapest rate of calories to calculate the poverty line. If it had done so, the poverty line would have been even lower than it is today.

15. Indian Council of Medical Research (2004). *Nutrient Requirements and Recommended Dietary Allowances for Indians*. National Institute of Nutrition, Hyderabad.
16. The Planning Commission reached these figures after looking at the caloric need of the whole population based on their age, sex and occupations. This ensures a conveniently low caloric standard because it includes the well-off members of society who do not physically exert themselves and therefore do not need as many calories as someone who is doing manual labour. Instead, while stipulating a caloric standard for the poor in India, it should be taken for granted that adults are carrying out manual labour and thus doing heavy activity. Taking this into consideration and the age and gender of the population, the prescribed caloric standard should be 2,700 calories per day. This is 300 (600) calories more than the Commission's recommendation for those in rural (urban) areas.
17. Indian Council of Medical Research (2004). *Nutrient Requirements and Recommended Dietary Allowances for Indians*. National Institute of Nutrition, Hyderabad.
18. Ibid.
19. United Nations International Children's Emergency Fund (2005). 'Nutrition: The Picture in India'. Collected from the UNICEF website: www.unicef.org/india/nutrition.
20. Information on the impact of nutrition deficiency from MSN Encarta Encyclopedia (2005).
21. Government of India (2001c). *NSS Report No. 471: Nutritional Intake in India, 1999–2000*. National Sample Survey Organisation, New Delhi.
22. Government of India (1993). *Report of the Expert Group on Estimation of Proportion and Number of Poor.* Perspective Planning Division, Planning Commission, New Delhi.

23. United Nations Development Programme (2005). *Human Development Report 2005*. UNDP, New York.
24. To calculate the nutritional requirement of adults, it is assumed that they undertake heavy activity, and not moderate or sedentary activity. This is because the poor in India are invariably carrying out unskilled manual labour.
25. We use ₹ 60 here for our calculation as that is the prescribed minimum wage as per the National Rural Employment Guarantee Scheme which takes into account the range of minimum wages prescribed in India.
26. Government of India (2001e). *Census of India 2001*. Ministry of Home Affairs, New Delhi.
27. B. Sivaraman (2006). 'Contours of the Deepening Agrarian Crisis'. *Liberation*, January.
28. Anbumani Ramadoss (2004). 'National Rural Health Mission'. Ministry of Health and Family Welfare, New Delhi.
29. Rajeev Ahuja (2005). Personal Communication on 29 December.
30. While one can use the average expenditure on health (as reported by the NSSO) for this purpose, it would be tautological to do so for reasons similar to the ones discussed in Section IV.C.
31. Rajeev Ahuja (2004). 'Health Insurance for the Poor in India'. Working Paper No. 123, Indian Council for Research on International Economic Relations.

    There are certain limitations for using this scheme as a proxy. First, it only includes in-patient care and does not cover outpatient costs, i.e., visits to the doctor for minor ailments. This tends to understate the actual expenditure on health. Secondly, insurance premiums include the transaction costs for the insurer and the profit margin. This tends to overstate the actual expenditure. Thirdly, the Universal Health Insurance Scheme is not a tested model and thus the premiums mentioned are still on trial-basis (Ahuja, 2005).
32. Guy Howard (2003). *Domestic Water Quantity, Service Level and Health*. World Health Organization, Geneva.
33. International Institute of Population Sciences (IIPS) and ORC Macro (2000). *National Family Health Survey (NFHS-2), 1998–99*. IIPS, Mumbai.
34. It is important to insist on RCC roofing because asbestos is a major indoor pollutant and hence should not be used for roofing purposes (Medappa, 2001).
35. Government of India (2004b). *NSS Report No. 488: Housing Condition in India, Housing Stock and Constructions, NSS 58th*

Round, July 2002–December 2002. National Sample Survey Organization, New Delhi.

36. Ibid.
37. Ibid.
38. However, according to a National Sample Survey on Housing (Government of India, 2004b), only 46 per cent of Indian households are not electrified. According to this report, a household with external or temporary wiring is also electrified. Source for the figure we use: World Bank (2005). *World Development Indicators 2005*. International Bank for Reconstruction and Development, The World Bank, Washington.
39. Government of India (2003). *Electricity Act, 2003*. Ministry of Power, New Delhi.
40. N. Medappa (Ed.) (2001). 'Indoor Air Pollution: A Major Environmental and Public Health Concern'. *ICMR Bulletin*, 31 (5), May.
41. Gordon Hughes, Meghan Dunleavy and Kseniya Lvovsky (undated). 'The Health Benefits of Clean Fuels in India: A Case Study of Andhra Pradesh'. Accessed from: www.cleanairnet.org.
42. Taken from the distribution quota of Punjab and Karnataka. Information from Department of Food and Supplies, Government of Punjab and Ministry of Food and Civil Supplies, Government of Karnataka.
43. T.K. Rajlakshmi (2001). 'A Regressive Bill'. *Frontline*, 18 (25), 8–21 December.
44. Interestingly, this is in contrast with the Pratham Report on Education (2005), which suggests that 93.1 per cent of kids between the age of 6 and 14 are enrolled in schools. However, the number of people who have completed secondary education (28.84% as per the survey) is a much truer indicator about the effectiveness of schooling in India. Pratham's own finding proves this that over 50 per cent of the 'enrolled' students could not read a standard II level simple story. In addition, it has been repeatedly argued that low access to education is a major problem in India. See Shariff and Husain (2006).
45. Department of Secondary and Higher Education, Ministry of Human Resource Development, Government of India.
46. Lok Sabha Starred Question No. 238, dated 13.03.2001.
47. Government of India (2002b). *National Human Development Report*. Planning Commission, New Delhi.
48. Denis Goulet (1979) summed up the 'meaning of development' as the three core values of sustenance, self-esteem and freedom from

servitude. These three values also highlight the need to define poverty in terms of human dignity.

49. The actual sum is ₹ 839; we round it off for convenience.

References

Abusaleh, S. and H. Zakir (2006). 'Stuck in Shallow Waters'. *Times of India*, 26 January.

Ahuja, R. (2004). 'Health Insurance for the Poor in India'. Working Paper No. 123, Indian Council for Research on International Economic Relations.

——. (2005). Personal Communication on 29 December. Mr Ahuja is an expert on Health Insurance and is presently with the World Bank and was formerly with ICRIER.

Basu, K. (2005). 'New Empirical Development Economics: Remarks on its Philosophical Foundations'. *Economic and Political Weekly*, XL (40), 1–7 October.

BSES Power Ltd. (2005). Information on Electricity Tariff Rates.

Chishti, I. (2005). Personal Communication on 30 December. Professor Chishti has had 30 years of experience in architecture and is a Professor at the School of Planning and Architecture.

Dubey, M. et al. (undated). *Social Development in India – The Policy Canvas: An Overview of the Last Fifty Years and Emerging Issues for the Twenty-First Century*. New Delhi: Council for Social Development.

Gopalan, C. et al. (2004). *Nutritive Value of Indian Foods*. Hyderabad: Indian Council of Medical Research.

Goulet, D. (1979). *The Cruel Choice: A New Concept in the Theory of Development*. New York: Atheneum.

Government of India (1979). *Report of the Task Force on Projections of Minimum Needs and Effective Consumption Demand*. New Delhi: Perspective Planning Division, Planning Commission.

——. (1993). *Report of the Expert Group on Estimation of Proportion and Number of Poor*. New Delhi: Perspective Planning Division, Planning Commission.

——. (2001). *Government of India's Pensionary Liability*. New Delhi: Ministry of Finance.

——. (2001a). *NSS Report No. 454: Household Consumer Expenditure in India, 1999–2000: Key Results*. New Delhi: National Sample Survey Organization.

——. (2001b). *NSS Report No. 461: Consumption of Some Important Commodities in India, 1999–2000*. New Delhi: National Sample Survey Organization.

——. (2001c). *NSS Report No. 471: Nutritional Intake in India, 1999–2000*. New Delhi: National Sample Survey Organization.

——. (2001d). *NSS Report No. 473: Literacy and Levels of Education in India, 1999–2000*. New Delhi: National Sample Survey Organization.

——. (2001e). *Census of India 2001*. New Delhi: Ministry of Home Affairs.

——. (2002a). *Tenth Five-Year Plan, Volume III: State Plans, Trends, Concerns and Strategies*. New Delhi: Planning Commission.

——. (2002b). *National Human Development Report*. New Delhi: Planning Commission.

——. (2002c). *India Vision 2020*. Chairperson: S.P. Gupta, December, New Delhi: Planning Commission.

——. (2003). *Electricity Act 2003*. New Delhi: Ministry of Power.

——. (2004a). *Central Government Subsidies in India*. New Delhi: Ministry of Finance, Department of Economic Affairs.

——. (2004b). *NSS Report No. 488: Housing Condition in India, Housing Stock and Constructions, NSS 58th Round, July 2002–December 2002*. New Delhi: National Sample Survey Organization.

——. (2004c). *NSS Report No. 505: Household Consumer Expenditure in India, 2004*. New Delhi: National Sample Survey Organization.

——. (2005a). *Prices of Food Stuffs from Department of Consumer Affairs*. New Delhi: Ministry of Consumer Affairs, Food and Public Distribution.

——. (2005b). *Statistics, Index Numbers*. New Delhi: Labour Bureau.

——. (2005c). *National Accounts Statistics 2005*. New Delhi: Central Statistical Organisation.

——. (2005d). *Union Budget of India 2005–06*. New Delhi: Ministry of Finance.

——. (2005e). *Indian Public Finance Statistics, 2004–05*. New Delhi: Ministry of Finance, Department of Economic Affairs.

Howard, G. (2003). *Domestic Water Quantity, Service Level and Health*. Geneva: WHO.

Hughes, Gordon, Meghan Dunleavy and Kseniya Lvovsky (undated). 'The Health Benefits of Clean Fuels in India: A Case Study of Andhra Pradesh'. Accessed from: www.cleanairnet.org.

Indian Council of Medical Research (2003). *Dietary Guidelines for Indians: A Manual*. Hyderabad: National Institute of Nutrition.

——. (2004). *Nutrient Requirements and Recommended Dietary Allowances for Indians*. Hyderabad: National Institute of Nutrition.

International Conference on Primary Health Care (1978). *Alma Ata Declaration*. September, USSR.

——. (undated). *Indian People's Health Charter*.

International Institute of Population Sciences (IIPS) and ORC Macro (2000). *National Family Health Survey (NFHS-2), 1998–99*. Mumbai: IIPS.

Medappa, N. (Ed.) (2001). 'Indoor Air Pollution: A Major Environmental and Public Health Concern'. *ICMR Bulletin*, 31 (5), May.

MSN Encarta Encyclopedia (2005). 'Human Nutrition'. Accessed from: www.encarta.msn.com.

National Institute of Rural Development (2004). *Rural Development Statistics, 2002–03*. New Delhi: NIRD.

Pratham (2006). *Annual Status of Education Report 2005*. New Delhi: Pratham.

Ramadoss, A. (2004). *National Rural Health Mission*. New Delhi: Ministry of Health and Family Welfare.

Rajlakshmi, T.K. (2001). 'A Regressive Bill'. *Frontline*, 18 (25), 8–21 December.

Ravallion, Martin (undated). 'Poverty Lines in Theory and Practice'. LSMS Working Paper No. 133, Washington, DC: The World Bank.

Reserve Bank of India (2004). *State Finances: A Study of Budgets of 2004–05*. Mumbai: RBI.

Sainath, P. (2006). 'The Health of Nations: Seeking a Way Forward'. *The Hindu*, 4 January.

Saxena, N. (2001). *Poverty Estimates for 1999–2000*. New Delhi: Planning Commission.

Sen, P. (2005). 'Of Calories and Things: Reflections on Nutritional Norms, Poverty Lines and Consumption Behaviour in India'. *Economic and Political Weekly*, XL (43), 22–28 October.

Sivaraman, B. (2006). 'Contours of the Deepening Agrarian Crisis'. *Liberation*, January.

Tata Services Limited (2005). *Statistical Outline of India 2004–05*. Mumbai: Department of Economics and Statistics.

Twelfth Finance Commission (2004). *Report of the Twelfth Finance Commission, 2005–10*. New Delhi: Ministry of Finance, Government of India.

United Nations Development Programme (2005). *Human Development Report 2004*. New York: UNDP.

United Nations International Children's Emergency Fund (2005). 'Nutrition, the Picture in India'. Collected from the UNICEF website: www.unicef.org/india/nutrition.

World Bank (2005). *World Development Indicators 2005*. International Bank for Reconstruction and Development, Washington, DC: The World Bank.

2 Water Scarcity in Major Cities in India

Abdul Shaban

In years to come, water, the need of life, is possibly to pose greatest challenge on account of its increased demand and shrinking supplies due to over exploitation and pollution. In India, with development, the demand of water is increasing both in urban and rural areas. This may create increased tension and dispute between these areas for sharing and command of water resources. The emerging scarcity of water has also raised a host of issues related to sustainability of present kind of economic development. The present paper explores the quantity of water used in domestic households vis-à-vis the recommended quantity of water consumption in seven major Indian cities, namely, Delhi, Kanpur, Kolkata, Ahmedabad, Mumbai, Hyderabad and Madurai. The paper also attempts to find out equity in consumption of water across various socio-economic groups, sources of water supply, perception of households about quality of municipal water and duration of municipal water supply. The organization of the rest of the study is as follows: the next section deals with methods used for data collection and analysis, which is followed by the recommendations of various agencies about the per capita need of water in urban areas. Then, results are presented and the last section offers summary and conclusions of the study.

Materials and Methods

The household survey, to find out the consumption, availability, access and methods adopted for conservation of water in domestic households in seven major Indian cities, Delhi, Greater Mumbai, Kolkata, Hyderabad, Kanpur, Ahmedabad and Madurai, was conducted in March 2005. As per the Census of India 2001, these cities, except Madurai (Municipal Corporation) are among 27 municipal corporations with million-plus population, and their respective populations was 9.8, 11.9, 4.6, 3.5, 2.5, 3.5 and 0.92 million, respectively, in 2001. The number of sample households selected from each of these cities was 507 in Delhi, 500 in Mumbai, 400 in Kolkata, 398 in Hyderabad, 303 in Kanpur, 361 in Ahmedabad and 265 in Madurai. Thus, a total of 2,734 households were interviewed in these seven cities. Each of these cities were categorized in five different areas: (i) high income group (HIG) areas with well-planned buildings, (ii) middle income group (MIG) areas with well-planned buildings, (iii) low income group (LIG) areas with well-planned buildings, (iv) slum areas, and (v) the mixed areas. Within these identified clusters, random sampling of households from electoral role was done. In each of these cities, several clusters of the same kinds of areas can be found and, therefore, from each cluster at least eight interviews were conducted. The data was collected through a structured schedule and target respondents were the housewives. The volume of vessels in which households used to store water was measured and the number of vessels of water used in different activities was ascertained. Where running tap or piped water was used in some activities, the duration for which the tap remained open was arrived at and the quantity of water per minute coming out from the tap was measured. By multiplying the time with the quantity of water per minute, the amount of water used through running taps was arrived at. The amount of water used in toilet was assessed by volume of bucket used and flush tank capacity. The assessment of quantity of water used in various activities was a difficult task, but all the efforts were put in to assure the accuracy of data.

Asset score has been used to classify households in various economic classes, such as the 'very poor', 'poor', 'lower', 'middle' and 'upper' classes. We assigned certain weights to the assets possessed by households and by summing up the scores for each asset, 'asset score' for a household was arrived at. The assets for which data were collected and weights assigned to them, are as follows: four-wheeler/car (weight 5.0), refrigerator (2.0), washing machine (2.0), microwave oven (2.0) three/two-wheeler (1.5), colour-television (1.5), computer/laptop (1.0), music devices like cd/dvd/vcd/MP3 player (0.5), internet connection (0.5), black and white television (0.5), mobile phone (0.5), cable for television (0.25), and radio/tape recorder (0.25). The following ranges of asset scores were used to classify the households in the above mentioned economic/asset classes: (a) very poor class: asset score 0.00 (has no assets on which data is collected); (b) poor class: asset score between 0.01 to 0.99 (at least has radio/tape recorder and/or black and white television); (c) lower class: asset score between 1.00 to 4.99 (at least has black & white television, radio/tape recorder, cable, mobile phone, or some of them with other assets); (d) middle class: asset score between 5.00 to 9.99 (at least has colour-television, refrigerator, washing machine or some of them with other assets); and (e) upper class: asset score 10.00 and above (at least has four-wheeler, refrigerator, washing machine and colour television, or some of them with other assets). Annual income data of households was also collected. The Pearson correlation coefficient between the household asset score and the income was found to be 0.722 (p-value 0.0001). However, we have used household assets score rather than monthly income for classifying households in various economic categories, as there is a greater possibility of under or over reporting of income. Besides categorizing households on the basis of asset score, we have also classified the households in five socio-economic classes (SEC) based on education and occupation of the main wage earner of the household. These five SEC classes are SEC-A, SEC-B, SEC-C, SEC-D and SEC-E (Shaban and Sharma, 2007).

The importance of supply/availability of clean water in economic and health spheres has been the main motivating factor for the present study. It is estimated that about 70 per cent of diseases in human being are due to consumption of uncleaned water. The access to water also has huge cost on educational attainments and incomes of individuals/households. A large share of

Figure 1 *A Deterministic Relationship between Water Availability, Health, Educational Attainments and Earnings*

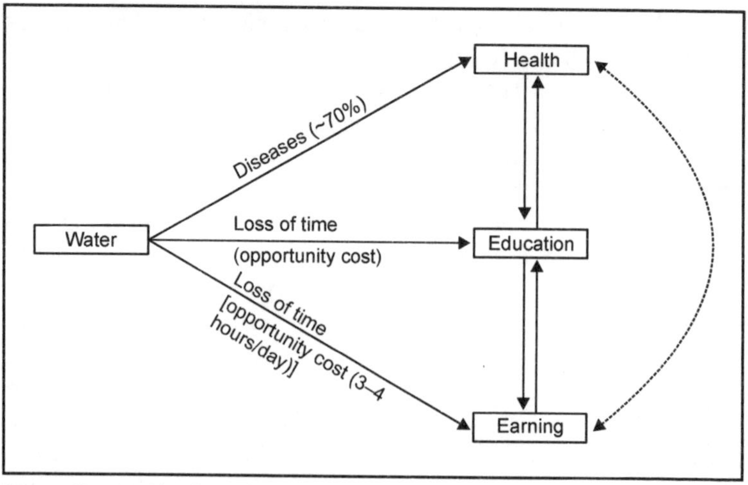

Source: Prepared by the author.

population from the poorer section of the society (both in rural and urban areas) loses their precious time collecting water for their daily needs. This deprives them from daily wages crucial for their economic sustenance (see Figure 1). Further, recurring health expenditures due to consumption of uncleaned water and low wages due to lower skills keep them in vicious circle of poverty. While education helps to improve their earnings, the health expenditures and loss of time/wages due to illness keep them in poverty and penury (see Figure 2). Clean, adequate and regular water supply, therefore, are extremely important in countries of South Asia, more so in India where a large section of population lives in poverty and consumes uncleaned water, to help sizeable proportion of the population move above poverty line.

Quantity of Water Required for Different Activities

A number of factors like climate, culture, food habits, work and working conditions, level and type of development and physiology determine the requirement of water. As per the Bureau of Indian Standards, IS: 1172–1993, minimum water supply of 200 litres per capita per day (lpcd) should be provided for domestic consumption in cities with full flushing systems. IS: 1172–1993 also mentions

Figure 2 *The Making and Unmaking of Poverty*

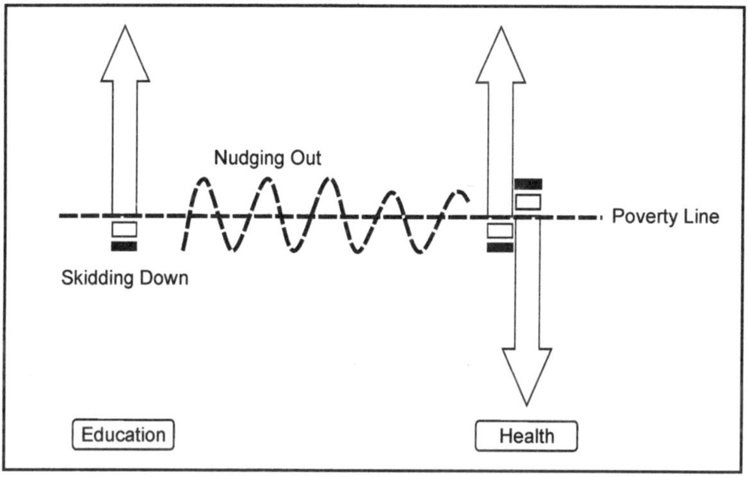

Source: Prepared by the author.

that the amount of water supply may be reduced to 135 lpcd for the LIG and the economically weaker sections (EWS) of the society and in small towns (Modi, 1998).

Besides domestic requirement, water is also demanded for commercial, industrial and civic or public use. The IS: 1172–1993 gives the total requirement of water in industrial and commercial towns with full-flushing system as 280 lpcd. The Ninth Plan (1997–2002) had advocated the requirements of water in urban areas as 125 lpcd in cities with the planned sewerage systems; 70 lpcd in cities without planned sewerage system; and 40 lpcd for those collecting water from public stand-posts. However, in the Tenth Plan (2002–07), the cities with planned sewerage system are classified into two groups based on population, i.e., metropolitan or megacities and non-metropolitan cities. In the former, the recommended minimum water supply level is 150 lpcd and in the latter 135 lpcd (Government of India, 1997, 2002). The National Commission on Urbanisation (1988) recommended that a per capita water supply of 90–100 litres per day is needed to lead a hygienic existence and emphasized that this level of water supply must be ensured to all citizens (quoted in Ramachandraiah, 2001).

The World Health Organization (WHO) classifies the supply and access to water in four service categories. These categories are:

(1) no access (water available below 5 lpcd), (2) basic access (average approximately 20 lpcd), (3) inter-mediate access (average approximately 50 lpcd), and (4) optimal access (average of 100–200 lpcd) (WHO, 2003; see also Bartram, 2003). Considering the fact that various agencies recommend different quantities of requirement of water for domestic use, we have taken 100 lpcd consumption (an indication of availability, as consumption is determined by the availability) of water as benchmark for finding out water deficient households. It must be noted here that there is no strong basis for this 100 litres bench mark but it is some kind of average requirement one must get in order to live with minimum health and hygiene.

Results and Discussion

Domestic Consumption of Water

It is important to note here, and this will be amply clear later, that the quantity of water consumed in most of the Indian cities is not determined by the demand but the supply. People attempt to adjust to the quantity (as well as quality) of water supplied. The 54th round National Sample Survey Organization (NSSO) data reveal that 80 per cent of the households in urban India, across different segments, consider that they have sufficient water supply (Bajpai and Bhandari, 2001), while the present study finds that about 71 per cent of the households in these seven cities consider water supply as adequate. The share of households considering water supply adequate to their need is 73 per cent in Delhi, 77 per cent each in Mumbai and Kolkata, 49 per cent in Hyderabad, 75 per cent in Kanpur, 63 per cent in Ahmedabad and 82 per cent in Madurai. In fact, this shows nothing but adjustment of people to the supply so much that they do not feel that more water is required. This in turn creates hygiene and sanitation problems resulting in several health consequences.

Table 1 shows per household as well as per capita consumption of water in seven major cities in the country. It is very obvious from the Table that in all the cities, the consumption (indication of availability) of water per capita is much lower than what is recommended by the Bureau of Indian Standard, IS: 1722–1993,

Table 1 *Domestic Water Consumption Per Household and Per Capita Per Day (in litres)*

Cities	Per Household		Per Capita	
	Mean	Std. Deviation	Mean	Std. Deviation
Delhi	377.7	256.8	78.0	49.9
Mumbai	406.8	158.6	90.4	32.6
Kolkata	443.2	233.6	115.6	64.9
Hyderabad	391.8	172.0	96.2	43.8
Kanpur	383.7	286.2	77.1	58.2
Ahmedabad	410.9	224.1	95.0	54.6
Madurai	363.1	182.1	88.2	44.4
Total	398.3	220.20	91.56	51.51

Source: Calculated using data from 'field survey'.

and the Tenth Five-Year Plan. Moreover, it is even lower than the recommended level for LIG colonies and weaker section households. The data is also an indication for the lower public hygiene and sanitation conditions in Indian cities. The average per capita water consumption in domestic households for all the seven cities is about 92 lpcd. The highest consumption is in Kolkata (116 lpcd), followed by Hyderabad (96 lpcd), Ahmedabad (95 lpcd), Mumbai (90 lpcd), Madurai (88 lpcd), Delhi (78 lpcd) and Kanpur (77 lpcd). It is surprising to find that in Delhi water consumption is so low when Delhi Jal Board claims supplying, on an average, 211 lpcd per household. Similarly, the Brihan-Mumbai Municipal Corporation (BMC) claims of supplying 198 lpcd (total water supply to the city 2,950 million litres per day – less than 20% losses), but the consumption in Mumbai, as mentioned above, is only about 92 lpcd. In terms of international comparison, the Indian cities have far less consumption of water. For example, domestic water consumption in Munich is 130 lpcd, and in Amsterdam it is 156 lpcd. In Singapore, Hong Kong, Sydney and Tokyo, the consumptions are 162 lpcd, 203 lpcd, 254 lpcd, and 268 lpcd, respectively (Down to Earth, 2005). Overall, in terms of per capita consumption of water, the condition in two North Indian cities, Delhi and Kanpur, seems to be worse. The dispersion statistics (standard deviation) shows that wide variations in per capita consumption of water also exist in North Indian cities. Besides, having the highest level of water consumption, Kolkata also has wide variation in consumption of water per capita. In terms of the variation, Kanpur, Ahmedabad and Delhi follow Kolkata. In these seven cities, a very small proportion of population consumes water above 100 lpcd. As shown in Table 2, only about 35 per cent of the total population in the cities consumes water above 100 lpcd. There also exist wide variations in proportion of household in different cities consuming water above 100 lpcd. For example, in Kolkata 52.9 per cent of the households consume water above 100 lpcd, but in Kanpur only 24.7 per cent consume water above 100 lpcd. Likewise, Ahmedabad (37.9% of the households), Hyderabad (37%), Mumbai (31%) and Madurai (30.7%) follow Kolkata in terms of the consumption of water above 100 lpcd.

Table 2 *Water Consumption: Category-wise Distribution of Households (%)*

Litres/capita /day	*All 7 Cities*	*Cities*						
		Delhi	*Mumbai*	*Kolkata*	*Hyderabad*	*Kanpur*	*Ahmedabad*	*Madurai*
Below 50	17.5	29.8	5.4	11.8	9.0	33.7	19.4	17.0
50 to 75	22.6	22.1	29.4	13.5	21.6	24.4	20.8	26.4
75 to 100	25.3	20.7	34.2	22.0	32.4	17.2	21.9	26.0
100 to 135	20.2	17.2	23.6	24.3	23.4	14.2	18.8	17.4
135 to 175	8.7	5.3	5.0	15.0	8.3	6.9	12.7	10.2
175 to 200	2.2	2.2	1.4	4.8	2.3	1.3	2.2	.8
Above 200	3.4	2.8	1.0	8.8	3.0	2.3	4.2	2.3
Total	100	100.0	100.0	100.0	100.0	100.0	100.0	100.0

Source: As for Table 1.

Kanpur has a dubious distinction among the cities under focus. In this city, more than one-third of population uses water below 50 lpcd. And, in this respect, Kanpur is followed by Ahmedabad (19.4% of population consuming water below 50 lpcd), Madurai (17.0%), Kolkata (11.8%), Hyderabad (9.0%) and Mumbai (5.4%). The water consumption among different areas in a city is not very different from one another, except that the model class of consumption for HIG, MIG and LIG areas is formed by the consumption class of 75–100 lpcd and in the case of slums and mixed areas, it is 50–75 lpcd (Table 3). However, where 23.4 per cent of the population in HIG areas uses water above 135 lpcd, in slum areas only 9.6 per cent of population uses water above 135 lpcd. The consumption of water by various socio-economic classes shows that although a sizeable proportion of households in all the classes consume water below 50 lpcd, it is in the case of SEC-E where the consumption is very low. More than one-quarter of households in this class consumes water below 50 lpcd (Table 4). Also, as compared to 23.3 per cent of the SEC-A consuming above 135 lpcd, it is only 8.1 per cent of the population in SEC-E which consumes water above this limit. The consumptions by socio-economic classes do largely correspond with the consumptions based on the asset classes. Whereas 25.7 per cent of the population in SEC-E has the consumption below 50 lpcd, 28.1 per cent of the population in 'very poor' category consumes water below this limit (Table 5). Similar to HIG, MIG and the LIG areas, the model class of consumption for 'upper', 'middle' and 'lower' categories of households, based on the asset score, is also 75–100 litres per capita per day.

Inadequate water supply in Indian cities seems to be a rule rather than an exception. Even if we take 100 litres per capita per day as the criterion for defining water deficient and sufficient households, 65 per cent of the sample households remain water deficient. The proportion of deficient households is the highest in Kanpur (75.2%), followed by Delhi (72.6%). In fact, except Kolkata, in all the other cities, the water deficient households are above 60 per cent. Analysis shows that households with monthly income up to ₹ 3,000 suffer the most as about 72 per cent of such households are found to be water deficient (Figure 3). Area-wise classification of water deficient households (Table 6) shows that, as expected, these are slum areas which have maximum percentage of water deficient households in all the cities. In Ahmedabad and Kanpur, the percentages of water deficient slum households are as high as 86.1 per cent and 82.1 per cent, respectively, while it ranges between 70 per cent to 75 per cent in case of Delhi, Mumbai and Hyderabad. Among the cities, the least percentage of water deficient households are found in Kolkata (47.3%). Per capita water consumption in different areas, asset-classes and SECs of households are highly correlated with each other, as they have very similar percentages of water deficient/sufficient households (see Tables 3, 4 and 5).

Table 3 *Area and Consumption: Category-wise Distribution of Households (%)*

Litres/capita/day	*High income group area with well-planned building*	*Middle income group area with well-planned building*	*Area low income group area with well-planned building*	*Slum area*	*Others (a mixed area)*
Below 50	19.8	17.7	13.2	21.3	15.5
50 to 75	16.3	20.5	23.4	27.0	26.2
75 to 100	21.2	26.4	31.0	24.2	23.8
100 to 135	19.2	20.0	21.4	17.9	22.5
135 to 175	12.9	8.4	7.6	6.2	8.5
175 to 200	3.8	2.1	1.4	2.3	1.3
Above 200	6.7	4.9	2.0	1.1	2.3
Total	100.0	100.0	100.0	100.0	100.0

Source: As for Table 1.

Table 4 *Socio-economic and Consumption: Category-wise Distribution of Households (%)*

Litres/Capita/Day	*Socio-economic Category*				
	SEC-A	*SEC-B*	*SEC-C*	*SEC-D*	*SEC-E*
Below 50	18.0	17.7	14.1	15.2	25.7
50 to 75	17.7	19.3	25.5	27.5	26.6
75 to 100	22.2	24.9	27.8	29.1	22.7
100 to 135	18.8	21.9	21.6	20.0	16.9
135 to 175	13.1	9.6	7.6	5.4	5.1
175 to 200	2.8	3.4	1.1	1.1	2.1
Above 200	7.4	3.2	2.3	1.7	.9
Total	100.0	100.0	100.0	100.0	100.0

Source: As for Table 1.

Inadequate water supply in Indian cities seems to be a rule rather than an exception. Even if we take 100 litres per capita per day as the criterion for defining water deficient and sufficient households, 65 per cent of the sample households remain water deficient. The proportion of deficient with households is the highest in Kanpur (75.2%), followed by Delhi with very similar percentages of water deficient/sufficient households (see Tables 3, 4, and 5).

Table 5 *Asset and Consumption: Category-wise Distribution of Households (%)*

Litres/Capita/Day	*Asset Class*				
	Very Poor	*Poor*	*Lower*	*Middle*	*Upper*
Below 50	28.1	16.7	13.1	21.5	21.7
50 to 75	23.1	25.9	25.3	18.8	15.8
75 to 100	24.0	28.4	25.9	24.1	22.2
100 to 135	15.7	19.5	22.6	18.8	16.3
135 to 175	5.0	6.2	8.6	9.5	13.1
175 to 200	1.7	1.7	1.9	2.6	3.6
Above 200	2.5	1.5	2.6	4.8	7.2
Total	100.0	100.0	100.0	100.0	100.0

Source: As for Table 1.

Table 6 *Percentage of Water Deficient Households in Different Areas (consuming below 100 lpcd)*

Areas	*All 7 Cities*	*Delhi*	*Mumbai*	*Kolkata*	*Hyderabad*	*Kanpur*	*Ahmedabad*	*Madurai*
HIG Areas	57.3	68.4	48.8	39.8	64.6	75.0	42.5	66.7
MIG Areas	64.6	78.1	69.2	42.1	61.7	66.1	56.3	76.8
LIG Areas	67.4	71.7	76.2	55.7	61.7	70.2	69.2	66.7
Slum Areas	72.5	72.4	74.1	58.1	65.4	82.1	86.1	70.0
Mixed Areas	65.5	72.0	73.1	40.5	62.0	82.8	57.8	67.3
Total	65.4	72.6	69.0	47.3	63.1	75.2	62.0	69.4

Source: As for Table 1.

Activity-wise Consumption of Water

At household level, bathing consumes highest amount of water. Together, in all the seven cities, it consumes about 28 per cent of the total water at household level (Table 7). Consumption in toilets (20.0%), washing clothes (18.6%) and washing utensils (16.3%) follow the consumption in bathing. On an average, less than 10 per cent of the total water in a household is used for drinking and cooking.

Figure 3 *Monthly Income-wise Distribution of Households in Various Water Consumption Categories in Seven Major Cities in India*

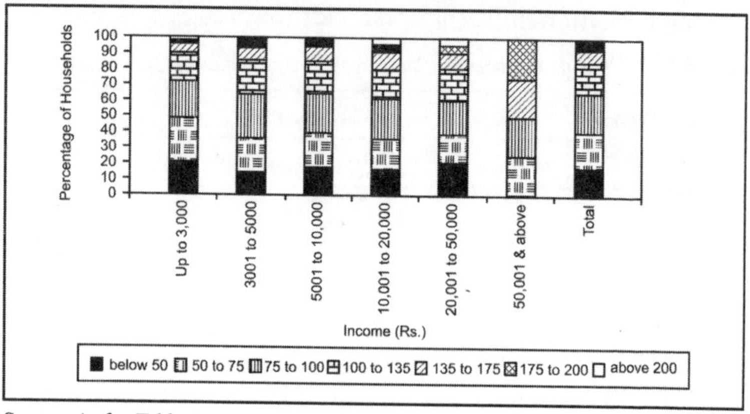

Source: As for Table 1.

Table 7 *Activity-wise Distribution of Water Consumption in Cities (% of total consumption by households/day)*

Activity	*All 7 Cities*	*Delhi*	*Mumbai*	*Kolkata*	*Hyderabad*	*Kanpur*	*Ahmedabad*	*Madurai*
Bathing	28.2	31.7	23.7	37.1	25.6	29.1	22.8	26.6
Washing Clothes	18.6	14.2	24.3	14.0	20.9	16.3	21.4	18.9
Drinking	4.2	5.0	4.2	2.6	4.3	3.8	4.9	4.9
Cooking	3.0	3.7	1.7	2.3	3.1	3.2	3.3	4.2
Toilets	20.0	16.5	21.6	15.9	24.1	20.1	19.1	25.7
Cleaning House	7.3	7.0	6.6	11.7	3.5	5.7	12.4	1.9
Washing Utensils	16.3	16.5	17.4	16.1	16.5	15.4	15.2	16.1
Others	2.4	5.6	0.5	0.3	2.0	6.3	0.9	1.7
Total	10	0.0	100.0	100.0	100.0	100.0	100.0	100.0

Source: As for Table 1.

Among the cities, households (37.1%) in Kolkata consume the highest proportion of total water in bathing. Delhi (31.7%), Kanpur (29.1%), Madurai (26.6%) and Hyderabad (25.6%) follow Kolkata in this regard. Toilet consumes 15–26 per cent of the water at household level in these cities, the highest being in Madurai (25.7%) and the least in Kolkata (15.9%). Washing clothes also accounts for about 14–22 per cent of the total water consumption at household level, and it is the highest in Mumbai (24.3%), followed by Hyderabad (20.9), and Ahmedabad (21.4%). Interestingly, North Indian cities Delhi, Kanpur and even Kolkata use less proportion of water in washing clothes than other cities.

Sources and Perception about Safety of Water

A majority of households in major cities in India depend on the municipal water supply for their daily needs. The 54th round NSSO data show that 70.1 per cent of the households in urban India depend on tap water (municipal supply), 21.4 per cent on tube wells, 6.7 per cent on wells/open wells and the rest on other sources (Bajpai and Bhandari, 2001). However, the present study shows that as high as 92 per cent of the households in the seven major Indian cities under focus are using municipal water supply (tap water). Of this 92 per cent of the population, 9.5 per cent are dependent on community taps and the rest (90.5%) on their own private taps provided by municipalities (Table 8). The proportion of households using community tap water is lower than the 54th round figures of NSSO mainly because it covered all the urban areas in the country, while the present study covers only seven major cities having relatively developed water-infrastructures. The Table 8 also shows that some households are not using water from only one source but from multiple sources. It is noteworthy that although, as mentioned above, about 92 per cent of the households use municipal tap water supply, the proportion of the households dependent only on this source is significantly lower in all the cities, except in Mumbai. The gap between the share of households using municipal tap water and the share of households dependent only on this source is very high in Madurai, Hyderabad, Kanpur, Ahmedabad and Kolkata. This indicates the lack of reliability, regularity and sufficiency of water supply through municipal taps. Mumbai seems to be the only exception among the seven cities, as in this city only about 5.6 per cent of the total households are dependent on sources other than municipal tap water supply. In comparison to Mumbai, the dependence of households on sources other than municipal tap water supply in other cities is significantly high. It is as high as 84.5 per cent in Kanpur, 82.3 per cent in Madurai, 60.3 per cent in Hyderabad, 31.5 per cent Kolkata and

28.6 per cent in Delhi. Thus, except Mumbai, in other cities a sizeable proportion of households use water from other sources (non-municipal tap). In Delhi, 24.5 per cent of the households use tube wells, 0.2 per cent wells/open well, 2 per cent tankers, 2.2 per cent packaged/mineral water, and 0.2 per cent other sources. Overall, 7.5 per cent of the households in Delhi depend only on groundwater. In Kanpur, tube well serves almost 80 per cent of the households and the share of the households dependent only on groundwater in the city is about 41 per cent. In Ahmedabad and Hyderabad, the proportion of households utilizing the tube well water is 38.5 per cent and 48.5 per cent, respectively, while 5 per cent and 0.3 per cent of the households in these two cities, respectively, depend only on groundwater. Overall, in all these seven cities, about two-fifth of the households is using groundwater and about 7 per cent are solely dependent on this source. Thus, the second largest source of water for a majority of households in major cities in the country is groundwater. The rapid increase of population in these cities is making people more dependent on it leading to rapid decline in groundwater table. Delhi, Hyderabad and Kanpur are suitable examples in this regard (see also Soni, 2003).

Households in these cities also face wide seasonal fluctuations in municipal tap water supply. More than 85 per cent of the households in these cities say that shortage in water supply becomes acute during summer. The seasonal variations in municipal tap water supply leads to use of ground water by households as it is seen as the easiest, fastest and to an extent durable 'solution' to the water crisis. And, as mentioned above, this is resulting in groundwater depletion in and around the cities. The overuse of groundwater resources has led to increase in arsenic concentration in many wards in Kolkata and similarly fluoride concentration in majority of cities and towns in Rajasthan and Gujarat.

About 11 per cent of the households in Hyderabad are dependent on tanker water supply. Out of this, 46 per cent are dependent on private tankers. This indicates that private vendors have their hey-day in the city. About 2 per cent of the households in Delhi and 1.1 per cent in Madurai are also using tanker water supply. The packaged/mineral water, particularly for drinking purpose, is also making inroad to urban households. This is

Table 8 *Dependence of Household (%) on Various Sources of Water (multi-source possible)*

Source	*All 7 cities*	*Delhi*	*Mumbai*	*Kolkata*	*Hyderabad*	*Kanpur*	*Ahmedabad*	*Madurai*
1. Municipal Tap Water	92.0	91.9	98.6	98.8	99.7	54.1	94.2	98.5
– of which community tap	9.5	8.1	1.5	1.9	0.3	45.9	20.0	1.5
Depend only on Municipal Tap water	57.6	71.4	94.4	68.5	39.7	15.5	59.6	17.7
2. Groundwater								
(a) Tube well/hand-pumps	38.1	24.5	3.6	27.8	48.5	79.2	38.5	81.1
– of which private tube-well/hand-pumps	24.0	6.3	3.6	1.0	41.8	36.4	37.2	76.7
(b) Well/Open Well	1.0	0.2	0.6	2.8	3.3			
Depend only on Groundwater	6.9	7.5		1.3	0.3	40.6	5.0	1.5
3. Tanker	2.1	2.0		0.5	10.6			1.1
– of which municipal tankers	59.3	60.0		100.0	54.5			100.0
4. River/Canal/Tank	0.4			2.8				
5. Packaged/Mineral Water	0.8	2.2	1.0		0.5	0.3	0.2	1.5
6. Others (Railways supply, broken pipes, mill compounds, etc.	1.1	0.2	0.6			5.3	2.5	

Source: As for Table 1.

supported by the fact that 2.2 per cent of the households in Delhi, 1 per cent in Mumbai and 1.5 per cent in Madurai use packaged water. Kolkata seems to be an exception as none of the surveyed households in the city has reported using packaged water for drinking purpose. It is interesting to note that although about 10 per cent of the households in Kolkata say that water is 'not so safe' and 'not safe at all', and further about 26 per cent express their inability to say anything about the quality of tap water supplied by municipal corporation, still none of these households report using packaged/mineral water (Table 9). Ideological orientation of the population, largely supporting communist ideology and having reservations about multinationals and private companies, may be playing a big role in this regard. Table 9 also shows that only about 40 per cent of the households in Kolkata view municipal water 'quite safe' or 'very safe'. In Madurai, Mumbai and Delhi, about 74 per cent, 65 per cent and 52 per cent of the households, respectively, view municipal water supply 'quite safe' and 'very safe', but in the case of Kanpur, only about 11 per cent say so. Thus, one finds that a sizeable share of households do not consider the municipal tap water as 'safe' or 'very safe' for drinking.

Table 9 *Perception of Households (%) about the Quality of Water from Municipal Taps*

Cities	*All 7*	*Delhi*	*Mumbai*	*Kolkata*	*Hyderabad*	*Kanpur*	*Ahmedabad*	*Madurai*
Safety level								
Not safe at all	2.9	2.96	.20	3.25	2.76	9.90	1.11	1.89
Not so safe	5.0	6.71	2.40	6.50	3.02	12.54	2.49	1.89
Somewhat safe	21.5	30.97	28.40	24.25	12.06	20.46	7.20	21.13
Quite safe	28.6	30.97	31.80	15.50	22.36	10.23	43.49	47.55
Very safe	25.6	20.51	33.60	24.25	57.04	.99	9.14	26.04
Cannot say	16.8	7.89	3.60	26.25	2.76	45.87	36.57	1.51
Total	100	100.00	100.00	100.00	100.00	100.00	100.00	100.00

Source: As for Table 1.

Contamination of municipal tap water has been a common problem, particularly in slums, in Indian cities. The data from

Municipal Corporation of Greater Mumbai (MCGM) shows that 8–10 per cent of the samples taken at consumer taps in 1997 and 1998 were contaminated by coliform bacteria and unfit for consumption (MCGM, 1999). However, the present study reveals that about 46 per cent of the households in slums 'feel' that municipal tap water supply is 'somewhat safe'. In comparison to Mumbai, about 37 per cent in Delhi and only 10 per cent in Kolkata considered that piped water is 'somewhat safe'. As opposed to Mumbai, where none of the households living in slum areas state that the Municipal tap water is 'unsafe', 2 per cent slum households in Delhi and 2.7 per cent in Kolkata consider the water 'not safe at all'. In Kolkata, about 49 per cent of the slum households were unable to say anything about the quality of the municipal water, while in Delhi and Mumbai, the percentages of slum households expressing similar views were 26 per cent and 8 per cent, respectively. A study by Karn et al. (2003) in some selected slums in Mumbai shows that the percentage of households boiling water before consumption varies from slum to slum: highest being 14 per cent and the lowest 5 per cent. However, the present study shows that about 12 per cent of the slum households boil water before consumption, 80 per cent filter it by cloth and the remaining 8 per cent do not use any purification method before consumption. In Delhi's slums, about 9 per cent of the households filter the water before its consumption, 6 per cent boil it and 85 per cent use no purification methods. In Kolkata, about 78 per cent of the slum households use no purification method. In Kanpur, none of the households in slum areas reported using any water purification methods.

Duration of Water Supply and Distance of Source of Water

Cleanliness of municipal water in Indian cities is not the only issue, the supply is also very erratic and for a very limited duration. A basic need and service like water on tap for 24 hours a day has been unheard of for decades in most Indian towns (ADB, 1993). As the supply is highly erratic and for a very limited duration, the households and housing societies store water in their tanks and drums. In the seven cities, about 18 per cent of the households, who reported using municipal tap water supply, stated that the water supply on tap was available for 24 hours, while about 25 per cent and 27 per cent claimed that it was available for a few hours (less than 4 hours) twice a day and once in a day, respectively (Table 10). About 21 per cent of the households in these cities report that water on tap comes for a few hours in two days. Among the seven cities, only in the case of Ahmedabad and Kolkata, about a half of the total households report that the water on tap is available for 24 hours. But, in case of Mumbai, Delhi, Kanpur and Madurai, only 5 per cent, 14 per cent, 6 per cent and 3 per cent, respectively, of the total households report so. In Hyderabad, hardly any household reports the supply of water for 24 hours. More than 80 per cent of the total households in Mumbai get water on tap for a few hours once in a day, while about two-thirds of the Delhi residents report that they get the supply twice a day for a few hours. Hyderabad has dubious distinction among the cities as about 90 per cent of households in the city state that the water on tap is supplied only for a few hours once in two days. In Kanpur, the situation is more pathetic, where more than two-fifths of the households inform that the supply of municipal tap water is not predictable at all.

Table 10 *Availability of Tap Water to Households (%) in Indian Cities*

Supply	*All 7 Cities*	*Delhi*	*Mumbai*	*Kolkata*	*Hyderabad*	*Kanpur*	*Ahmedabad*	*Madurai*
24 hours/round the clock	17.9	13.6	5.0	47.3	0.3	5.6	50.1	2.6
For a few hours once in a day	27.0	15.4	84.4	2.8	7.0	7.3	38.5	14.7
For a few hours twice a day	24.9	64.3	7.4	39.3		44.2	6.4	1.5
Once in two days	20.7		0.2		88.9		2.2	77.0
Once in four days	0.0							0.4
Once in a week	0.2							3.4
Not predictable	1.8	3.7	2.8	0.5	2.0	1.7		
Cannot say	7.3	3.0	0.2	10.3	1.8	41.3	2.8	0.4
Total	100.0	100.0	100.0	100.0	100.0	100.0	100.0	100.0

Source: As for Table 1.

Only about 68 per cent of the total population in the seven cities under focus have source of water supply within their premises. The 54th round NSSO data also reveals that a total 65.7 per cent of the households in urban India have source of water supply within their dwelling or premises (Bajpai and Bhandari, 2001). There is a wide variation among the cities in terms of location of the source of water. Where about 62 per cent and 50 per cent of the households have the source of water outside the dwelling and premises in Kanpur and Kolkata, respectively, in Mumbai, only about 13 per cent of the households have the source of water outside their premises. In Ahmedabad and Delhi, about one-fifth and one-fourth, respectively, of the total households collect water from outside their house premises.

Expenditure and Determinants of Domestic Water Consumption

Available data on slum households in Mumbai show that poorer households spend a large share of their income on water. These are households with monthly income of ₹ 3,000 (below poverty line) or less who suffer the most (Figure 4). Figure 5 shows that about 5 per cent of such households spend more than 2 per cent of their income on water. Thus, water which should have otherwise been a human right, takes precious shares of income of the poor.

Figure 4 *Relationship between Household Income and Expenditure on Water of Slum Households in Mumbai*

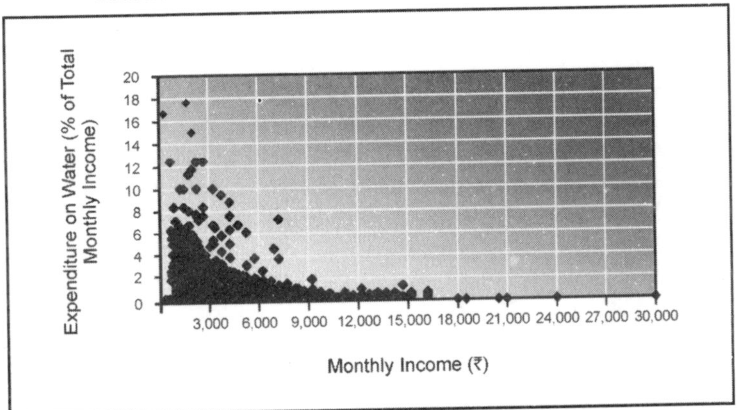

Note: No. of households = 13,148; Data relate to the MUTP affected slum households, 1996–2002.

Source: Based on data from Mumbai Metropolitan Region Development Authority (MMRDA).

Figure 5 *Slum Households and their Expenditure on Water as Percentage to Total Income*

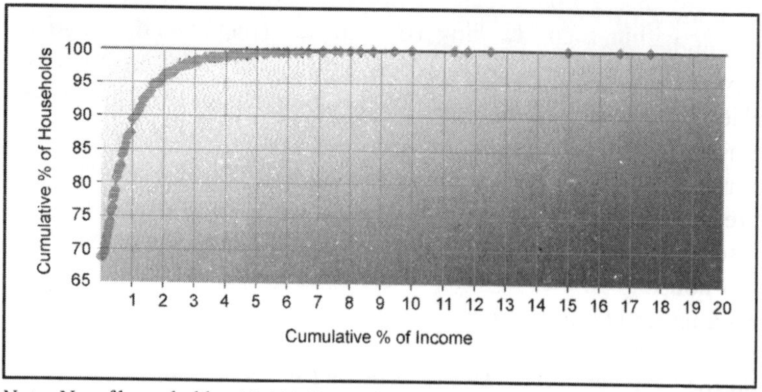

Note: No. of households = 13,148; Data relate to the MUTP affected slum households, 1996–2002. Source: Based on data from Mumbai Metropolitan Region Development Authority (MMRDA).

Table 11 *Determinants of Consumption of Water in Domestic Households*

Determinants	*Regression Coefficients*	*t-values*	*P=Values*
Intercept (α_0)	93.240	15.005	0.000
Mumbai (α_1)	22.399	2.811	0.005
Kolkata (α_2)	58.971	7.319	0.000
Hyderabad (α_3)	29.043	3.685	0.000
Kanpur (α_4)	11.093	1.144	0.253
Ahmedabad (α_5)	42.674	4.575	0.000
Madurai (α_6)	34.421	3.311	0.001
No of family members (ϕ_0)	–5.343	–5.104	0.000
Family Members Mumbai (ϕ_1)	–1.721	–1.157	0.247
Family Members Kolkata (ϕ_2)	–7.171	–4.569	0.000
Family Members Hyderabad (ϕ_3)	–2.539	–1.682	0.093
Family Members Kanpur (ϕ_4)	–1.332	–0.772	0.440
Family Members Ahmedabad (ϕ_5)	–7.194	–4.032	0.000
Family Members Madurai (ϕ_6)	–5.384	–2.538	0.011
Asset Score (β)	.716	3.007	0.003
Year of Schooling of Housewife (λ)	.359	1.736	0.083
24 hrs Tap Water Availability (π)	19.392	7.083	0.000
$R^2 = 0.444$			
$f = 41.750$			0.000

Note: α_1 to α_6 are slope shifters dummies while ϕ_1 to ϕ_6 are slope shifter variables.

Source: Computed using field survey data.

The analysis of determinants of water consumption has always been of special interest to academics and policy makers. Although, it is known that water consumption is supply constrained in the cities under focus, we have attempted to find out the determinants of even this limited supply/consumption of water. As shown in Table 11, there are considerable variations among the cities in terms of per capita water consumption and the greatest similarity emerges only between Kanpur and Delhi. As expected, with increase in family members in a household, per capita water consumption declines (more so in Kolkata). The richer households and households with higher education level have higher consumption of water. Importantly, it is found that the households which have 24 hours of water supply consume about 20 lpcd more than the households not having 24 hours water supply. This again shows that water consumption in domestic households in Indian cities is supply constrained.

Conclusions

Although recycled by the nature, the fresh water is a limited resource. The high water consuming economic activities and population explosion are responsible for declining per capita water availability. To consume more is emerging to be the main goal of societies, more so of the 'privileged', thus putting further pressure on this diminishing natural resource. Indian cities have been appropriating water resources traditionally meant for 'subsistence' in rural areas. This process stands accelerated due to high degree of migration of the rural people to large cities in search of livelihood. The major observations drawn from the paper are: (a) It is observed that water consumption in Indian cities (more so in large cities) is far lower than the norms laid down by Bureau of Indian Standards. Not to mention, in comparison to other major cities in the world, the consumption in Indian cities is also far deficient. The lower consumption results mainly because the water supply is not keeping pace with population growth and increasing needs of users. (b) It is interesting to observe that though a majority of households consume water below the specified norms, they, by and large, show satisfaction with the available supply. This is mainly because they have delimited their aspiration and requirements of water in relation to available supply from the concerned municipalities or water authorities. (c) Some household activities, like washing clothes, bathing, use in toilets and washing dishes and utensils are the most water consuming activities in the cities under focus. It has also been found that in these cities, a majority of the households perceive the above activities as most water wasting activities. This shows that given appropriate and affordable technologies to save water in specified activities, the households would be willing to adopt them. In fact, there exists a large scope for reducing water consumption in washing clothes by adopting appropriate soap/detergent and machines; and in toilets by changing and modifying the flushing system. An awareness campaign about the best practices in these activities can play a big role in saving precious water. (d) As expected, the availability and mode of use of water varies across the socio-economic classes within the cities. But, surprisingly, the difference is not very high. On an average, about 20 litres of consumption is higher among the higher classes. (e) City-wise variations in the supply and quality of water are very much visible. Water supply in cities like Kolkata and Hyderabad is far better, while Kanpur and Delhi perform the worst. Though it is also true that water supply in Hyderabad is a mix of adequacies and inadequacies, where multiple agencies pitch in to meet the needs. The municipal corporation supplies water to majority of households once in two days. Water tankers and bore-wells compensate the deficiency of municipal water in this city. (f) Twenty four hour water supply on municipal taps is a dream for a majority of households in the large cities in the country. The study reveals that only about 18 per cent of the total households in these cities get 24 hours municipal water supply. The erratic and limited duration of supply of water has become a common phenomenon in these cities. This has forced the households, in majority of the cities, to depend on groundwater and other sources of water, like the private vendors who supply water through tankers and drums. These, in turn, are leading to depletion of groundwater due to over withdrawal by the burgeoning population and emerging water markets. In fact, during the summer season private water vendors have their hay-days in these cities. (g) The much talked commodification of water and water services is also making dent into the otherwise role of government departments as the key supplier of water in cities. For instance, in cities like Delhi, Mumbai, Hyderabad, Ahmedabad and Madurai, some households have started using packaged water for drinking purposes. It is also true that so far none of these cities have permanently handed over the task of supplying to their citizens (NGOs) or the private sector.

To conclude, it can be stated that the supply of water in large cities of India is going to be a big challenge in future. The rapid increase in population in these cities, depleting water resources and enhanced consumer needs are going to create a difficult situation. The market oriented development is creating new needs in sectors like entertainment industry and tourism, building industry, adapted new technologies is pushing up water needs, more supply in shopping malls, and so on. Simultaneously, the alarming rise in pollution levels in surface water bodies and even in groundwater is going to add to the situation. Therefore, an urgent need is felt for a comprehensive water policy for cities which is suitable and satisfactory to growing needs of citizens. The prevailing ad-hocism in protecting, enhancing and conserving water needs to be done away with.

Note: This paper partly draws from the paper 'Water Consumption Pattern in Domestic Households in Major Indian Cities' by Abdul Shaban and R.N. Sharma, published in *Economic and Political Weekly*, 9 June 2007.

References

ADB (1993). *Service Level and the Urban Poor: Managing Water Resources to Meet Megacity Need*. Manila: Asian Development Bank.

Bajpai, P. and L. Bhandari (2001). 'Ensuring Access to Water in Urban Households'. *Economic and Political Weekly*, September 29: 3774–78.

Bartram, H. (2003). *Domestic Water Quantity: Service Level and Health*. Geneva: WHO.

Down to Earth (2005). 'Fact Sheet: Fresh Water Up for Grab'. *Down to Earth*, 5 March.

Government of India (1997). *Ninth Five-Year Plan 1997–2002*. Vol. II, New Delhi: Planning Commission.

——. (2002). *Tenth Five-Year Plan 2002–2007*. Vol. II, New Delhi: Planning Commission.

Karn, S. et al. (2003). 'Living Environment and Health of Urban Poor: A Study in Mumbai'. *Economic and Political Weekly,* August 23: 3575–86.

MCGM (1999). *Health Profile 1997 and 1998.* Mumbai: Metropolitan Corporation of Greater Mumbai.

Modi, P. (1998). *Water Supply Engineering.* New Delhi: Standard Book House.

Ramachandraiah, C. (2001). 'Drinking Water as a Fundamental Right'. *Economic and Political Weekly,* February 24: 619–21.

Shaban, A. and N. Sharma (2007). 'Water Consumption Pattern in Domestic Households in Major Indian Cities'. *Economic and Political Weekly,* June 9: 2190–97.

Soni, V. (2003). 'Water and Carrying Capacity of a City – Delhi'. *Economic and Political Weekly,* November 8: 4745–50.

WHO (2003). *The Right to Water.* Geneva: WHO.

3 Street Diaries

Gender, Poverty and Homelessness in Mumbai

Ranjana Raghunathan

Diary of a Feminist Ethnographer

It is the morning of July 6 in 2009; I visit the Beggars' Home in Chembur, along with some of my classmates in the masters programme. The vast open spaces inside the campus, the monsoon breeze and the lush green leaves still wet from the rains welcome me as I enter through the opening in the large Iron Gate. As I walk through the campus towards one of the 'cells', I deliberately avert the gaze of many women squatting in isolation, scattered across the place on wet mud and grass. I feel a pang of guilt throbbing occasionally through my disbelief, shock and intense sadness. I cannot help but wonder what I was doing there as a 'student visitor' on an institutional visit, if I was just a voyeur invading the solitude of the women, solitude in the wide-open prison open to our gaze. All their heads are shaven and they wear pall, shapeless robes that hang from their bodies like shrouds concealing morbidity. Some of them are tattered and some have spots of colour on them – menstrual blood and stains of grass. The still silence of the space screams many questions, and the questions are unrelenting and straight like the vacant eyes of the 'inmates', questions with no easy answers.

I walk through the grass patches, past abandoned cell rooms and their suffocating darkness to the office of *Koshish* – a project of Tata Institute of Social Sciences. The abandoned rooms with rusty metal fetters on the floor echo an oppressive silence and metal clinks of chains on the inmates' feet. The present inmates are free of wearing the metal chains, a victory after an arduous battle I am told. But in a curious way they feel no different to me. They are prisoners of a different order. No chains on their ankles, no darkness to suffocate them in, they have the wide open sky, monsoon breeze and lush green; but they cannot roam wherever they wish. They are arrested for being on the streets in tattered clothes, for looking shabby and unkempt, for appearing to have mental illnesses or for not having a 'safer' shelter option. They are abandoned by their families for their stint on the streets, because 'what good family would want a woman who has been tainted by the filth of the streets?'

Koshish works on three key issues of homelessness, beggary and destitution. We – students of the master's programme, Koshish staff and faculty – discuss several key topics: the Bombay Prevention of Begging Act (1959) and how it criminalizes 'beggars', the vicious cycle that trap the 'inmates' in unemployment, the court procedure after 'beggars' are arrested by the police, the social mores that lead to their abandonment and the acute shortage of safe spaces for women in the city. Words are exchanged in the room with shock, sympathy, anger, hopelessness and a sense of purpose, but my mind wanders outside the window with thick iron bars, where all I see are the vacant gazes of the women and all I hear are their muffled sounds uttered through unintelligible words. Words hang heavy in the room, like the intense humidity of the monsoon cloud and I squirm with the use of certain words – inmate, beggars' home. I recall being told that 'many women are here not because they are beggars or arrested for the act of begging, but because they have nowhere else to go. They are destitute or homeless, and many are mentally ill'. That is not just a statement of fact, but a barrage of questions that explains the gaze of the inmates' eyes. That marks the beginning of my two-year-long journey in Mumbai – on the streets, in shelters, in beggars' home, among activists and women.

18 August 2009, Mahalaxmi

Late one evening, I walk through the streets of an office area in South Mumbai to meet my friend. I see a woman taking her bath on the very pavement. She is not clothed except at the waist, and without a batting of an eyelid, she goes about her business as the blaring traffic speeds past the concrete road in the busy part of the city. She has soaped herself and she dips a plastic mug into a bucket of water, brings it out and pours water on herself. She repeats a few times, and I look away in shame after a few moments. I look down, I look up, I stare at the traffic and feel drowned in the noise of the honking cars. Water with white soap is right under my feet. There are some women who cook their meals on aluminium pots over a fire and stones, men are busy playing cards with a stack of 10 rupee notes on the side and children play their imaginary games shouting excited remarks at each other, pushing each other and laughing. The pavement is a melting pot for the private and public aspects of the city life. My friend once wrote eloquently '… it seems like these public spaces have become their private domains, and their personal/private bodies are open to public gaze, as they sleep, eat and feed their younger ones'. At least six young children, all in shorts and brown, rough hair come to me. They see me talking to my friend on my mobile phone and want to see the phone. They ask if it had a camera and radio, if they could have their picture taken and if they could listen to the latest *Hindi* song. We listen to a couple of *Hindi* songs, share some laughter and I walk on to meet my friend at the street corner with the song playing in my head long after – 'Dhan da Dhaaaaan' from *Kaminey*.

Galat Aurat (Wrong Woman, Prostitute, Someone who Deserves to be Sexually Punished)

I spoke to many women, in different locations – outside a temple, in a tea shop, on the pavement at a shop entrance, outside a court-house. I was chased away along with them, from all the places by a priest, tea shop owner, the shopkeeper and a policeman. I always asked 'why?' I retorted to the teashop owner 'We are here, we are paying for the tea, just like everyone else, why are you chasing us away?' He replies casually 'such women are not allowed to sit here.' I received similar responses from the priest and the shopkeeper, but the policeman said 'it is illegal!' Who are 'such women'? It became clear to me that it was not just about being treated with suspicion by society, but it came with heavy connotations of morality. An unaccommodated woman in a public space then automatically became a '*galat aurat*/wrong woman'.

'They keep chasing us away like garbage',

'Shopkeepers complain to the police against us',

'When we use the public toilet, the people complain against us and so nowadays they don't allow us to use this public toilet' (a public toilet in a prominent location which is also a tourist attraction in Mumbai),

'Rich people (*Seth log*) say that they want to give food for the poor, but all they really want to do is chase us away, they also beat us. I know the pain of being poor, they just know money and they chase us away.'

A young girl shared 'life on the streets is purely that of exploitation.' She vented out in anger:

'... this is wrong, that is wrong... . I tell you, nothing is wrong. Wrong is all the people, you people who do wrong to us. You tell the girl that you will give her a job and then take her into prostitution. Yet she is called the *galat aurat* (wrong woman). Wrong is done by you, not her. They take the girls, sell them in the market. And what does police do? Nothing! Everyone bothers the ones who live on the streets. Even if I sit somewhere for an hour, someone will say get up and leave!'

Yet another girl shared about one of the many instances that random strangers raped her on the streets.

'... three boys misbehaved with me. They beat me... took me to the beach, it was after 5 in the evening. They forced me... . I shouted for help, but no one came! There was another time, when I just beat the man and ran away. I escaped many times like that, but that one night I could not.'

Sometimes 'drunk men just come along, they trouble us, see us in a bad way and talk indecent things about us'. Being a woman on the street makes their bodies open to violent trespassing, by men, apparently for no particular reason except an assumption of their 'wrong status'. It is no wonder that I did not see single women, alone on the streets. They were either married or living with partners or 'families' – their institutions of protection from the violence of the streets, their refuge, their home in their situations of homelessness.

'I got married because men used to always trouble me, look at me in wrong ways... . Men used to forcefully climb on top of me. In the night they would just spread my legs and trouble me... . Once a prostitute trapped me, asked me to have sex with men. If I refused, the men would force into me. The men used to be drunk and they also troubled me… . I used to be very afraid, because I did not have the support of a man… . I have never slept peacefully on the street. I used to sleep with lot of fear, because men used to come and just lay down next to me, or hold me. I used to scream and shout and chase them away, but still sometimes they used to force me…'

Fate, circumstances and laws had wrapped their lives in their coils and thrust them into spaces where love, desire and hope could not enter. However hard I looked, there was neither joy nor hope in the faces before me, even as we sat together and engaged in banter for fun. I could feel my stomach turn inside me in pain and sometimes in deep anger. In one of my visits to the beggars' home, a woman told me '… you see they are not getting what they need most in this world. That is love. No matter what anyone does or gives, if they don't get love, it doesn't make any difference'.

April and May 2010, Various Locations

Despite pockets of excellence, the poor invariably experienced formal institutions (hospitals, schools, ration shops, municipal corporation) as ineffective, inaccessible and disempowering. Recurrent expressions of distrust, humiliation, intimidation, helplessness, hopelessness and often anger emerged. It has worsened in the recent years with increased vigilance and concern about security in the city. A lady sat on the pavement, with her huge bag of toys next to her. She sold them in prominent tourist places and had lived on the streets for many decades. She remarked with nostalgia about how times were changing: 'Now the world has changed. We have also learnt that for everything we need an ID proof to prove our identity. Maybe it is after the bomb blasts that it has become like that and we are seen as a security problem.' But I could not help but wonder why a lack of an 'identity' to prove citizenship became a question of legality of their presence and consequently a presumption of guilt. This then justified repeated demolitions, evictions, violence by state institutions, usurpation of their belongings. The Brinhanmumbai Municipal Corporation (BMC) and the police were their deepest causes of anxiety, fear and terror.

'The BMC people and police constantly threaten to kick us out of here. They take away our belongings quite often, we are so afraid. Yes the police also come and they beat us a lot. They want to chase us from there. The police trouble us a lot. Sometimes, they used to stay there throughout the night and once there was police picketing for three consecutive days and they threatened us that they would take us to jail if we stayed there. We had to move to another location…'

'What do we do? We have to pay money to them to sleep here. Sometimes they just come and take 20, 10, 50, sometimes 100 rupees. Whatever money they get after doing their rounds, they take everything. If they don't find any money, they beat us. If they find money during their rounds, they leave us. In the middle of the night they come and wake you up, beat you. You want to know how they hit us? You know the electricity wire? They hit us with that. Once a man died because of that. He was sick and we told the police that he is sick. You know what they did? They hit him with the wire, that man he could barely sit, he was trying to get up and run away…'

Disillusioned with the state institutions and the violence inflicted upon them, they resign to their fate at times and sometimes question them – what gives them the right to beat the citizens? Even if they are 'illegal', what is the need for violence and terror against its people? It is certainly not the police's responsibility to do so, and yet they continue to do so – making their existence a living hell. Roopa sat with me, vented out in anger and disgust and requested me to write the truth about their lives.

'Stop torturing us… because of that wrong things are also increasing on the streets. There are daily waged workers and your police (emphasis added) hits them saying these people are wrong. If someone starts a business here, municipality comes here and takes everything away. We are poor people, how will we live? If we live like this, how can we live? If not beat us, they take us in beggar vans! The third time when my uncle was taken, there was another man with him who has a deaf child. The father had come from the village in Maharashtra for a medical treatment of the child. They took him away that night, and the child got lost. Till today, the child is missing. After 15 days, the child could not be found. We people gave money and brought him out of the beggars home, but the father is still searching for the child. If this is what the government does, what do we do? Will the government bring the deaf child back to the father? How do we search the boy? He is deaf and mute.

How can the child find us? It is the job of the police to make proper enquiries about who he is, what is happening. They just take the people away. They don't understand who they are, why they are here or why he has come from a village. They just take the people away and go. A child is lost. The father had ₹ 3,500 and the police took it all away. He was crying that the child was lost. Now he is just roaming around Mumbai, looking for the child. If the government wants to take away people, it is their job to ask who is standing, why he is eating there, where he is from. Later, if they really see that he is begging, take them and go. But this man's from the village, he came for his son's medical treatment, why did they take him? He didn't understand Hindi, he didn't understand Mumbai's Marathi, he only knows the Marathi spoken in his village. He is now roaming around, like a mad person and what will happen to such people? He will obviously stay on the streets, right? His son is lost, so he has stayed back and lives on the streets now. He cannot go back to the village, they have taken all his money, how will he go? They have made him homeless (emphasis added). He didn't come here to earn money, or work or beg. Who is responsible for this? You have a government, you have the police, but these people do not think before their actions and they don't even take responsibility. They only have greed for money and will take away random people for the ₹ 50 commission they get. Everyday they take away people, who do not even beg, and put them in beggars jail. All for the greed of money, for the commission of ₹ 50 per person. These are people who are working around here. I have gone to the beggars home once too. After that I haven't gone there. Over there a lot of injustice happens with women. A lot of wrong happens, I have seen it with my own eyes. Officers take the women and abuse them sexually. That is why I said we are not wrong, wrong is being done to us. No one takes a wrong path on purpose. You people force us to take the wrong path.'

14 May 2010, Beggars' Home, Chembur

I am there during lunch time, food is served on the floor, outside the 'cells', under the shade of the trees. It is a hot and humid summer day, no breeze, just the unbearable heat of the noon sun. It seemed as if the beggars' home had changed too, since my first visit, like the seasons. A pall of silence and suffocating heaviness envelop as the women gathered to eat their lunch. A woman comes to me and asks 'So, seen enough? They bring people in all the time to show us like animals caged in a zoo.' I feel a pang of guilt and self-deprecating anger at my presence there since morning. I sit there immobile, as if glued to the floor, and look at all the women that I spoke to in the morning. They were lively and animated in their conversations with me, but now their faces wore a grim sadness. Their exposure to relentless interrogation by authorities, police, medical officers, the court, social workers and researchers like me had made them clinical about themselves, and like actors who leave the stage after their role – they left me to eat their lunch. Like well-trained soldiers they sit down in a single row, under the trees and their faces wait with no interest for the two *rotis* thrown into their out-stretched hands. A lady from among the 'inmates' is a leader who carried a thick stick, a green branch of a tree that has just fallen to ground. She hits the ground as she walks around, ensuring they sit in a straight line. She hits one of the women and shouts, 'Aye *nakhrewali*, sit! Keep your *nakhras* outside!' In the morning, the women spoke to me with a sense of hope and they turned to me, for a job, help to get out of that place. But now their faces had seemed resigned to their fate as hopelessness clouded them and my own self. They all had one thing in common – a yearning to go home. What it meant to each of them was perhaps different, but one thing was sure – it certainly did not mean the beggars' home.

24 February 2011, Chembur

In the middle of the night, bright halogen lamps and headlights of fast vehicles light up the street. Police cars and vans make their rounds in silence, as they slow down to scrutinize the street corners. Dogs bark in the distance at people picking the garbage of urban waste. Watch dogs of our city? Is it not ironic that those that society discards as garbage are the ones who clean it up for the rest of us? At least 15 *sarees* hang long under the bridge, different colours and lengths. Babies and young children sleep in them; the perfect rocking cradle that vibrates with every speeding vehicle. A corner under the bridge has more *sarees* stretched on two bamboo poles – their 'private bath and toilet' gleaned a woman whose torn *saree* across the shoulder revealed the glistening dark skin under the diffused light of the street. More than 100 people live under the bridge, and they have been there for at least a decade, she said. 'We work, we eat, we sleep, just like everyone else. But they are going to evict us soon, they are just waiting for the elections to end.' I inform them about the census enumeration that was to happen a week later, and they ask, 'What good will come of it?' I feel struck for words, even as I lazily utter the importance of being counted and how it might be the basis for policy and programmes. Lines of the poem 'Unknown Citizen' by W.H. Auden haunt me: 'Was he free? Was he happy? The question is absurd: Had anything been wrong, we should certainly have heard'. And yet their pleas were unheard, drowned by the sounds of the vehicles and dogs in the dead of the night. I could not help but wonder what it means – to be a citizen, to be enumerated, to be human.

26 February 2011, Chembur

Sunitha sat on a pavement under a bridge in a dark corner. She was clutching her small cloth bundle and a torn bag. She seemed dazed, as though she had not slept for nights in a row. I reached my hand out and placed it on her arm, but she shuddered at that touch and curled her body closer to herself. I thought I also saw fear, distrust and anxiety. I tried speaking to her, but she refused to speak to me, and soon a passerby told me, 'She has been there for a week, she will be taken to the beggars' home again. She will sit there until then, this is her routine. She is *madrasi*, so she cannot understand you.' I then spoke to her in Tamil, 'my name is Ranjana, what is yours?' Sunitha. 'Family is there. They checked my body. Kids are there. And my bags. In-laws sent me. Officers sent me out. I live there. I have house. I have family. I have children. They feed me. They keep my things.' I did not try to comprehend the incoherence of her broken phrases and convinced myself that perhaps she just wants to speak, in her native tongue. She went on speaking and I asked if she would like to go somewhere else; but even as I asked her, I had no clue where. I knew that there were some shelters that might take her in temporarily, but not in the middle of the night. Alternatively, I thought I might take her to sleep among the group of families under the bridge not far away, but she shook her head vigourously and continued to look at the street, muttering more phrases in Tamil: 'No. No'. She waits on the street, at the same location, until the beggars' squad takes her back to the beggars' home, for months or a year.

Rationale and Methodology

The extent of 'homelessness' and its linkages to growing urban poverty is a disturbing trend. Its specific impact on women and women's experiences is the crux of my exploration. Research studies on the issue of homelessness of women are predominantly from the West. These studies have compared the varied needs of single homeless women, homeless women with children and women in the context of homeless families. They have also described several aspects such as the causes of homelessness, characteristics of the population of homeless individuals, their need for assistance, the presence of mental illness, depression and substance abuse, their utility of services and access to welfare programmes. However, there is little literature about the women's experiences of being homeless, about their interactions with society, systems and structures. There is an even greater paucity of literature in the Indian context. The articles and reports published are from non-government organizations and independent activists engaged with the issue of housing rights in India are mainly based in the city of New Delhi. There is no research in the urban Indian context approaching homelessness among women from a feminist perspective. The issues are either subsumed under the larger politics of housing, shelter and migration or the changing landscape of the city forging ahead in a globalized economy driven by neoliberal policies.

I was intrigued by the ubiquitous phenomenon of homelessness in the city of Mumbai and especially its impact on women. The primary objective of my engagement with women was to document their experiences through reflections about their stories and narratives; thus, a qualitative research methodology was adopted. The fieldwork for this research involved two years of deep engagement with Mumbai and homeless women in multiple unstable spaces: on the streets and pavements, in shelter spaces run by non-governmental organizations and in the beggars' home where most inmates happen to be destitute or homeless. During my fieldwork, I interacted with the women through group discussions and in-depth interviews. The broad themes that guided these interactions were: survival on the streets (food, water, shelter, toilets), identity, healthcare, employment, abuse experiences and challenges faced on the streets. Alongside my ethnography, I also engaged with groups fighting to get their ration cards, fieldwork with an agency that worked with homeless girls and young women, participant of a collective for the rights of homeless citizens in Mumbai and as a volunteer during the census exercise of enumerating the 'houseless' population in Mumbai. Over the course of two years, new themes and nuances emerged which form the crux of this paper – the layers of meanings and relentless questions.

What are the politics behind the words beggar, homeless, illegal, squatter, mental illness, public space?

Why is an institution under the criminal justice system (Beggars' Home) the best shelter option for homeless and destitute women?

Why is there silence when the state continues to commit acts of violence against its dispossessed people with such impunity?

Numbers and Words

I pored through a number of websites, reports and articles for data that would give me a picture, even if an approximation, about homeless people in India, and more specifically Mumbai. The numbers for India varied between 2 million, as stated in the Census of India (2001) and 78 million, an estimate of the non-governmental organization Action Aid (Action Aid International, 2003). In February 2011, I participated alongside other civil society organizations, volunteers and government agencies, in the census activity of enumerating the homeless population in Mumbai. The Government of India defines 'houseless' people as those not living in 'census houses', that is a structure with a roof, but live in the open or roadside, pavements, in hume pipes, under fly-overs and staircases or in the open in places of worship, *mandaps,* railway platforms, etc., (Office of the Registrar General and Census Commissioner, India, 2011). During the efforts to ensure that they are enumerated, to ensure that no one is missed by the officials, I could not help but ask myself the questions that the people asked me in the dead of the night – 'What will happen if we are counted? Will we get houses? Will we be allowed to sleep in peace? We get woken up tonight, to be counted, but other nights we get beaten up by police. Will that stop?'

I had, by now, grown weary of the many stories of extreme dispossession that I heard, saw and felt anguish for over the past two years. I started looking for numbers to speak the truth, because I found myself inadequate to speak the reality of their experiences through words. The estimates suggested 100,000 homeless people in the city alone. But the numbers only served to mystify and form an abstraction of the reality that we as a society, perhaps, lacked the capacity to look at in the eye, grasp or understand. What did the numbers mean? I realized how any question on the number of homeless people could be misleading. This brings us to face the complications of definitions and methodology. In some countries, such as the United States, enumeration happens on a given day or week (point-in-time). A second method of counting them over a given period of time (period prevalence) is also used. However, both have methodological issues that the former simply allows a snapshot picture and the latter cannot ensure that everyone gets counted, and such numbers are often criticized for misrepresenting the magnitude and nature of homelessness. A more important consideration is how homelessness is defined.

There is no universally accepted definition of homelessness and it derives its meaning from the meaning accorded to the concept of home. This understanding is based on related and often dichotomous ideas of public and private, the inside and outside (Mallett, 2004). In this dichotomy, the inside often denotes a safe and secure space, while the outside denotes a space more dangerous or threatening, and a space that is more diffuse, less defined. Any definition of home cannot be confined to the dichotomous binaries, and a more fluid understanding is necessary for the experiences that are often complex and shifting. Spaces generally understood as home may not be experienced as such. Thus, home has to be understood as a concept beyond the physical arrangement of space, to involve social meanings and identities. The many meanings of home are also possible precisely because it is not merely a physical space. Home is, thus, a multi-dimensional concept that embodies many ideas such as comfort, belonging, identity and security, translating into establishment of meaningful social relations with others or the individual agency to withdraw from them (Tipple and Speak, 2005).

Watson and Austerberry (1986) argue for a continuum approach: either a homelessness continuum or a home-to-homelessness continuum, between satisfactory and secure forms of housing on the one end to sleeping rough on the other end of the spectrum. The UN Special Rapporteur on adequate housing has reiterated that 'homelessness carries implications of belonging nowhere rather than simply having nowhere to sleep' (Chaudhry, Joseph and Singh, 2010: 1). The National Campaign for Housing Rights uses a broad, holistic, definition of home as a place where one is able to live with dignity in social, legal and environmental security and with adequate access to essential housing resources like land, building materials, water, fuel, fodder as well as civic services and finance (Tipple and Speak, 2005). Watson puts forth the difficulty in theorizing homelessness as defined by objective criteria and categories as opposed to subjective experiences (Watson, 1999). While it may be straightforward to determine who falls in and out of categories of need as defined by government, it is harder to explore this fluid terrain of meanings and discursive practices. What do these shifting meanings and definitions imply for feminist politics? What is the meaning of 'home' for a marginalized person in an urban, postcolonial and globalized space like Mumbai? And what does it mean for a woman who is a migrant or a victim of trafficking, or a woman who lives outside the 'private' realm of marriage, family or 'shelters'?

D.E. Smith (1992) argues that the standpoint of women situates inquiry in the actualities of people's living, beginning with their experience of living, and understands that inquiry and its product as in and of the same actuality. Through the various definitions and enumerations, what then ensues is a process of exclusion and objectification, whereby the subject is progressively marginalized by the discourse in question and 'written out' of the textual account. One can extend this argument and witness the role that institutionalized discourses play in the suppression and distortion of the gender component in everyday life. One of Smith's primary interests is how the phenomenon of mental illness is constructed in official discourses.[1] She argues that all formal institutions, whether private or state-sponsored, have developed various techniques and procedures for data accumulation and interpretation regarding the 'correct' versus 'aberrant' behaviour of individuals (Gardiner,

2000). It is in this context that one must consider not only the exclusion of the experiences of homeless women, but also the politics of labelling them as such – homeless, beggar, encroachers, mentally ill, etc. It serves to delegitimize their very existence and renders their experiences invisible, silenced.

Gender and Homelessness

'Home is the girl's prison and the woman's workhouse' (Shaw, *Women in the Home*).

The appearance of the metaphor 'home' in feminist critiques highlight the extent of oppression that women are confined to under the discourses of home, especially within families. It is an arduous task for me to reconcile the ambivalences in social policies and interventions around the concept 'home' that reinforce patriarchal codes; feminist critiques of 'home' by the likes of Simone de Beauvoir or Luce Irigaray; and a longing and desire for 'home' by the marginalized woman (Young, 2005).

Studies in the West have cited deindustrialization, unemployment, welfare cuts, limited low-cost housing, increasing poverty, deinstitutionalization and an increase in domestic violence, spouse battering and sexual abuse as factors contributing to homelessness among women (Stoner, 1983; Malloy, Christ and Hohloch, 1990; Hill, 1991; Wardhaugh, 1999). The different accounts of the women in Mumbai highlight not just their differing meanings of 'home', but the factors that caused their subjective experiences of 'homelessness'. The paths to homelessness are many and people often trace the roots of their homelessness to their experience of home. Some had made choices to be away from their 'homeless-at-home' situations, while some others were pushed out of their homes into homelessness. Their narratives point to a lack of affordable housing, slum demolitions, evictions on basis of suspicion and illegitimacy, eviction caused by construction and development projects, domestic violence, breakdown of family and partnership/marriage, inequitable planning and land use and inadequacy of the law.

All this point to several disjunctures: intimate and structural violence, politics of housing rights and the changing landscape of city spaces in a globalized neo-liberal economy.[2] Following Appadurai (2003), I saw Mumbai, the epitome of the modern global city, as an unstable space with layers of social existence and 'relations of disjuncture' that is beyond a spatially bounded economy, a site of contestation and negotiating boundaries. I saw how the statist and media discourses on homelessness often silenced the gendered subjectivity of a homeless woman. I saw many more layers of existence for a woman on the streets, and yet no consideration made about this in the politics of shelters or housing policy. Their experiences revealed the gendered meanings of home and homelessness, and the experiences of home-as-prison among many women, which are deeply entrenched in cultural and social mores that dictate a woman's life. She is pushed further into the fringes, where housing politics, economics of migration and cultural discourses of morality render her invisible.

Through my numerous interactions with the women, I realized that their experiences could only be understood dialectically, through simultaneous degradation and counter-hegemonic qualities of their strategies for resistance and survival. There were several points of collisions of the experiences of the women in the beggars' home, the women on the streets, and the notions of 'home' created by middle-class women through discourses of a threatening 'outside'.[3] The boundaries between home and homelessness blurred, as rhetoric of sexual codes, morality and family diffused into the textures of unintelligible realities of their lives. An unaccommodated woman then becomes the deviant 'other',[4] whose existence outside the social and spatial boundaries of home, family and domesticity undermines the construction of home as a source of identity and as a foundation of social order. It is Wardhaugh (1999) who further observes that an unaccommodated woman is actually an aberration and a contradiction because she represents the act of rejecting, or having been rejected by, traditional family and domestic structures. These women are the homeless, single mothers, battered and abused women, women working in the streets who have not been accepted or sometimes been refused their space in the world.

Phadke (2010) analyses the gendered usage of public spaces using the city of Mumbai as a case study, by examining the women's access to public space in relation to questions of citizenship, civic safety and sexual safety, risk and respectability. Her study lays out the broad terrain of conceptual categories and ideological context within which women's access to public space is located. The key concepts discussed are public space, gendered space, notion of private and public, safety and risk. These are relevant in understanding the experiences of homeless women, especially those living in open public spaces, and their negotiation or coping for their safety. Class is, thus, an important determinant not only of access to public space, but also of how notions of threat and ideas of risk are constructed in relation to public space, contextualized around unspoken boundaries that control these spaces.

Following Smith, I too attempted to move away from the epistemological debates of truth and adopted a method to locate the multiple layers of their existence through the lens of gender and class.[5] The ethnographic narratives point to several points of ruptures and questions: What does 'home' entail beyond housing, shelter and a bourgeois, commodity-based identity? How do women's experiences of 'homelessness' within the confines of 'home' or institutional spaces account for the possible variations in understanding the concept of homelessness? It is antithetical to view the gendered nature of their existence without considering the impact of globalization on urban poverty.

Globalization, Urban Poverty and Homelessness among Women

Cities support half the world population. By 2015, it is expected there will be 23 megacities, and all but four will be in developing countries. In India, during the past five decades, a phenomenal growth of urban population has witnessed the addition of about seven to eight million people every year. The level of urbanization was 11 to 12 per cent in first three decades of the 20th century but it surged noticeably from 17.3 per cent in 1951 to 25.7 per cent in 1991 (Devadas, 2002). Mumbai, which now has a population of 16.4 million in its metropolitan area according to the census data of 2001, will be the world's second largest city after Tokyo by 2015. The characteristic feature of India's urbanization is the concentration of population in few cities. In 1991, the slum population in Mumbai was 55.3 per cent of the total population. Estimates suggest that about 60 per cent of Mumbai lives in slums, and this does not include the estimated 100,000 homeless people.

The urban poor are especially vulnerable to the adverse effects of such unbridled urbanization. Cities are undergoing major transformation through many 'urban development' projects, which actively push out the poor from the domain of public space. Globalization or the version of neo-liberal economy, a ubiquitous reality today, has a significant impact on housing systems, housing law, policy and housing rights. While global economic integration is creating new wealth, the number of homeless or inadequately sheltered persons continues to grow globally.

The (UN) Special Rapporteur notes with grave concern that governments continue the practice of mass evictions in cities as a means of creating 'world-class cities,' lured by the prospect of international investment. Economic globalization has created competition amongst cities that is detrimental to the poor. The example of Mumbai, India, is very recent. Between December 2004 and January 2005, 80,000 homes were demolished rendering 300,000 people homeless. For the vast majority of those evicted, there was no advance notice, the evictions were violently carried out and the belongings, including identity cards, of many were damaged or burnt. Those evicted have not been offered alternative accommodation, clearly exacerbating the situation of homelessness in Mumbai. The Chief Minister explained these brutal demolitions as the only way to create a 'world-class' city in the future[6] (Kenna, 2008).

The growth of corporations involved in housing, the globalization of property rights and housing finance markets, globalized real estate investment in housing and the reordering of cities and slums are some of the most pressing challenges today. This has led to the shooting up of property prices in places like Mumbai, making cities more expensive and lucrative for property investment returns. In the process, the poor are driven out of their living areas. This coupled with a withdrawal of the state from providing basic necessities for the poor, such as shelter, transport, water and sanitation, makes cities a place of terror for the poor. Additionally, punitive laws such as the Bombay Prevention of Begging Act, 1959, destroy the relationship between the people and space (Banerjee-Guha, 2011). Conditions of the homeless is more precarious as compared to that of the slum dwellers, as they do not have any chance of access to state housing, thus increasing social inequality and making them more vulnerable. Appadurai (2001) evocatively refers to them as 'citizens without a city' because of multiple reasons.

Their lack of sanitary facilities increases their need for medical care to which they have poor access. Their inability to document their claims to housing translate into invisibility in the urban space, making it impossible for them to claim any related rights to rationed foods, health and education facilities, police protection and voting. Thus, the inability to secure claims to proper housing and other political handicaps reinforce one another.

'Housing – and its lack – are the stage for the most public drama of disenfranchisement in Mumbai. In fact, it can be argued that housing is the single most critical site of this city's politics of citizenship' (Appadurai, 2001: 28).

Of those who have had to bear the brunt of global deprivation and denial of human rights, the most are women and 70 per cent of the world's population living in absolute poverty are women. The process of globalization has led to polarization of social groups, intensification of poverty and an increase in female headed households,[7] thereby increasing poor women's risk of further deterioration of conditions. This is also reflected in the gender bias in housing policies and programmes, which are primarily concerned with home ownership and not on rental tenements. It is also well-established that the value of women's contribution, both within the household and economy, has received less recognition and as a result, women's needs are often forgotten both in times of crisis as also during crisis management, be it forced evictions, displacement due to development projects, relocation/resettlement and rehabilitation following dislocation of families or communities, armed conflict and riots, rehabilitation that follows such conflicts or riots at the time of any disaster management.

Speaking from a Marxist-feminist perspective, Watson and Austerberry (1981) were among the earliest researchers to look at the issue of housing from a feminist approach, suggesting that housing is located in the domestic sphere, the traditionally privatized area of life, but its role in moulding and reinforcing both patriarchal and capitalist structure of the family has been ignored. They attribute this weakness as one of the reasons explaining the failure to develop coherent socialist housing policies. This calls for a need to examine the many contradictions in the relationship of a woman to housing, through the concepts of household, financial dependence and sexual division of labour, which in turn impact government housing policy, housing tenure and the owner occupied sector. They further assert that women's homelessness is the result of a variety of social, material and emotional deficits – all tellingly stamped with women's specific family roles and relation to the home. They, like other authors, concluded that psychological or social factors affect women's access to housing, domestic violence, evictions, and the like can exacerbate or bring on mental problems. A capitalist society dominated by patriarchal social relations defines roles to such an extent that marginalized women even experience great guilt. It is this context that Mohanty (2003) argues for making anti-globalization a key factor for feminist theorizing and struggle and suggests the construction of anti-globalization pedagogies in women's studies and the recognition of the place of feminism within anti-globalization movements.

Homelessness and the State

Theorists of 'everyday life' have pointed out the fluid and permeable spheres of activity in pre-modern societies, and the consolidation of power with a structural differentiation of knowledge and the establishment of dualisms (mind vs. matter, nature vs. culture, private vs. public) with the transition to modernity. With the consolidation of modernity, the scope of the mechanisms of social control have broadened, encroaching upon more and more areas of life and, simultaneously, human powers are increasingly transferred to an anonymous, bureaucratic apparatus '(Gardiner, 2000).

It was not so long ago that in colonial Africa, women's right to urban housing was denied. Urban housing was tied to employment and, hence, available only for men as labourers of company plantations. Thus, the only means for women to access urban housing was through their relationships with men, often in exchange for sexual and domestic favours. Recently, the Government of Maharashtra submitted an affidavit to the Supreme Court on 24 August 2010, in compliance of its directions dated 5 May 2010 in a Writ Petition (C) No. 196 of 2001, about the state's plans for addressing the issue of the urban homeless and shelter needs. The government of Maharashtra clearly acknowledges that the homeless people are the poorest of the poor and they cannot even afford informal housing. Despite this, the affidavit only mentions about the schemes for slum dwellers as its measures to address the issue, which is clearly irrelevant to the issue of homelessness – those without access even to informal housing. It further classifies the inflow of poor people as:

(i) The poor who come to the city for livelihood on their own accord
(ii) The poor who are brought to cities by employers like developers, contractors, etc.

The affidavit has not submitted the actions to tackle the issues of those it categorizes as (i), and enumerates its assumption that workers on construction sites are all given temporary shelters by the employers or BMC. Not only is this contrary to the experiences of many workers who are not given any kind of shelter or are inadequately housed, but it also reinforces the gender gap in access to housing, as a woman's access to shelter is linked to her marital or family linkages to an employed man. Furthermore, the affidavit openly criminalizes the poor by stating and accepting that the government 'compels them to shift' to beggars' homes, as this can happen only through arrest under the Bombay Prevention of Begging Act, 1959.[8] In effect, the affidavit has equated the urban homeless to migrants either employed or unemployed, and those with employment are assumed to be adequately housed by the employers and those without employment are 'compelled to shift' to the already existing government shelter – the beggars homes!

In the present urban scenario, the narratives of the women make it clear how the state exacerbates homeless women's experiences of gender-based and economic oppression through laws that criminalize their existence, through systems that render them non-entities, through agents that violate their liberties and policies that do not consider their rights or requirements. The multifarious processes, with intersecting realities, also point to a consolidation of power with state and its institutions like the police, civil service, bureaucracy and the courts; thereby legitimizing its use of violence against the urban poor deemed as illegal citizens. The state agents render them anonymous without an identity and hunt them down for the lack of an identity that criminalizes their existence. Senior lawyer and human rights activist Rani Jethmalani opined as follows: 'The aggressive anti-beggar legislation is aimed at wiping the desperately poor off the city's radar so that society can continue to neglect them without pricking its collective conscience.'

Wacquant (2004: 1–2) analyses the penalization of poverty and its linkages to the rise of neo-liberalism: 'The regulation of the working classes by what Pierre Bourdieu (1998) calls 'the left hand' of the state, symbolized by education, public healthcare, social security and social housing (Bourdieu 1998) is being superseded – in the United States – or supplemented – in Western Europe – by regulation through its 'right hand', i.e., the police, courts and prison system, which are becoming increasingly active and intrusive in the lower regions of social space. This new 'government' of social insecurity – to speak like Michel Foucault – rests, on the one hand, on the disciplining of the deskilled and deregulated labour market and, on the other, on an intrusive and omnipresent penal apparatus.'

Conclusion

There are several forces that cause and sustain homelessness among women, and they can be looked at through two predominant structures that operate in the lives of homeless women: patriarchy and poverty. The women's narratives highlight an alternative way of viewing the issue of homelessness among women, as an interface of these structures, as an experience that begins at 'home'. This also provides us with new meanings, definitions and ways of looking at the issue, beyond economic factors, beyond its meaning as a commodity or a shelter. The experiences of women on the streets are deeply mired in poverty with struggles for daily survival and needs like sanitation, health and food, society's responses to them that render them invisible in public spaces and agoraphobia due to women being treated as sexual bodies. This is further exacerbated among homeless women with children, and those with mental illnesses or psychological distress.

As the homeless people lay sprawled over the busiest of streets in Mumbai, they do not go unnoticed, but continue to lead shadow lives of exclusion and deprivation. What is remarkable is their source of strength and ability to fight in a world that has been reduced to a marketplace, their bodies a sexual commodity, their identities a consumer or service user. While these may point to a moral decay of the social fabric of the times, it underscores the complete failure of society which has selectively and systematically thrived on the deprivation of the many for the benefit of a few and, perhaps, burgeoning number games of economics.

Notes

1. The central essay in this context is 'K is Mentally Ill: The Anatomy of a Factual Account', originally published in the late 1970s.
2. Appadurai (2001) expounds on the ideas of 'Globalization from the Below' in the context of housing rights in Mumbai. In 'Spectral Housing and Urban Cleansing', Appadurai (2000) argues that ethnic violence is a response to uncertainty and a way in which community is produced; the material substance of the city – spaces, infrastructure and legalities – was the site where it was played out.
3. Martin and Mohanty (1986).
4. Gambacorta (1989: 131) cogently summarizes, the 'sense of alienation that pervades this daily life experience (means that) daily gestures establish relationships not with 'others' but with 'the other' – that is, with the perennial degeneration of every activity into something objectified and divided, with what is perennially remote, inaccessible and a constant source of threat to one's integrity' (quoted in Gardiner, 2000).
5. In rejecting mainstream sociological approaches, whether functionalist or micro-oriented, an alternative is to embrace a postmodernist relativism, to accept the intrinsically pluralistic nature of all accounts of the social world and their epistemic equivalence. However, this is not a path that Smith (1987: 121) chooses to follow. She proposes to move the focus away from arcane and obstructive epistemological debates about what 'truth' really means, towards what she takes to be a more productive consideration of 'how our everyday worlds are organized and how they are shaped and determined by relations that extend beyond them' (quoted in Gardiner, 2000).
6. See also ECOSOC, Comm. on Human Rights (2005). *Economic, Social and Cultural Rights: Report of the Special Rapporteur on Adequate Housing as a Component of the Right to an Adequate Standard of Living*. 3 March, pp. 35–39, UN Doc. E/CN.4/2005/48.
7. Feminization of Poverty as elucidated by Stoner (1983).
8. Also see Ramanathan (2005, 2008) and Rao (1981).

Bibliography

Action Aid International (2003). Action Aid National Conclave: Towards a People's Alliance. Retrieved from: http://www.actionaidindia.org/on_the_issues_conclave.htm on 26 December 2009.

Appadurai, A. (2001). 'Deep Democracy: Urban Governmentality and the Horizon of Politics'. *Environment and Urbanization*, 13 (2): 23–43.

——. (2003). 'Illusion of Permanence: Interview with Arjun Appadurai by Perspecta 34'. *Perspecta*, 34: 44–52.

——. (2000). 'Spectral Housing and Urban Cleaning: Notes of Millennial Mumbai'. *Public Culture*, 12 (3): 627–51.

Banerjee-Guha, S. (2002). 'Critical Geographical Praxis: Globalization and Socio-Spatial Disorder'. *Economic and Political Weekly*, 37 (44/45): 4503–09.

——. (2011). *Homeless in Neoliberal Cities: View from Mumbai*. Mumbai: Tata Institute of Social Sciences Housing, pp. 62–75.

——. (2002). 'Shifting Cities: Urban Restructuring in Mumbai'. *Economic and Political Weekly*, 37 (2): 121–28.

Bapat, M. and S. Patel (1993). 'Shelter, Women and Development: Beating a Path towards Women's Participation'. *Economic and Political Weekly*, 28 (11): 465–72.

Centre for Development and Human Rights (2007). 'The Price of Being Poor: Urbanisation, Poverty and Destitution in India'. *Rights and Development Bulletin*, 1 (3): 21–24.

Chaudhry, S., A. Joseph and I.P. Singh (2010). *Homeless Women and Violence*. New Delhi, India: Centre for Equity and Inclusion (CEQUIN).

Devadas, P. (2002). *Government Programs for Slum Improvements in India: A Critical Review*. Spain: University of Valladolid. Retrieved from: http://www.ciudadderechos.org/eindex.html on 25 November 2009.

Dietrich, G. (1987). 'Women's Struggle for Housing Rights'. *Economic and Political Weekly*, 22 (42/43): 1793–94.

Gardiner, M.E. (2000). *Critiques of Everyday Life*. London: Routledge.

Hill, R.P. (1991). 'Homeless Women, Special Possessions and the Meaning of 'Home': An Ethnographic Case Study'. *Journal of Consumer Research*, 18 (3): 298–310.

Housing and Land Rights Network – Habitat International Coalition (2001). 'Women and Housing Rights: A Legal Overview'. Retrieved from: http://www.hicsarp.org/documents/hicwomen&rah.doc on 28 September 2010.

Kenna, P. (2008). 'Globalization and Housing Rights'. *Indiana Journal of Global Legal Studies*, 15 (2): 397–469.

Mallett, S. (2004). 'Understanding Home: A Critical Review of the Literature'. *The Sociological Review*, 52 (1): 62–89.

Malloy, C., M.A. Christ and F.J. Hohloch (1990). 'The Homeless: Social Isolates'. *Journal of Community Health Nursing*, 7 (1): 25–36.

Martin, B. and C.T. Mohanty (1986). 'Feminist Politics: What's Home Got to Do with it?'. In C.T. Mohanty (ed.), *Feminism without Borders: Decolonizing Theory, Practicing Solidarity*. Durham: Duke University Press, pp. 85–105.

Mohanty, C.T. (2003). *Feminism without Borders: Decolonizing Theory, Practicing Solidarity.* Durham: Duke University Press.

Neale, J. (1997). 'Theorising Homelessness: Contemporary Sociological and Feminist Perspectives'. In R. Burrows, N. Pleace and D. Quilgars (eds), *Homelessness and Social Policy*. London and New York: Routledge, pp. 35–49.

Office of the Registrar General and Census Commissioner, India (2011). *Instruction Manual for Houselisting and Housing Census.* New Delhi: Ministry of Home Affairs.

Phadke, S. (2010). *Gendered Usage of Public Spaces: A Case Study in Mumbai.* Mumbai: Centre for Equity and Inclusion. Retrieved from: http://cequinindia.org/pdf/special_reports/gendered_usage_of_public_spaces by Shilpa Phadke.pdf on 7 February 2011.

Ramanathan, U. (2005). *Demolition Drive.* Geneva: International Environmental Law Research Centre (IELRC). Retrieved from: http://www.ielrc.org/content/a0507.pdf on 24 January 2011.

——. (2008). 'Ostensible Poverty, Beggary and the Law'. *Economic and Political Weekly*, November: 33–44.

Rao, A. (1981). 'Poverty and Power: The Anti-Begging Act'. *Economic and Political Weekly*, 16 (8): 269–70.

Smith, D.E. (1992). 'Sociology from Women's Experience: A Reaffirmation'. *Sociological Theory*, 10 (1): 88–98.

Stoner, M.R. (1983). 'The Plight of Homeless Women'. *The Social Service Review*, 57 (4): 565–81.

Tipple, G. and S. Speak (2005). 'Definitions of Homelessness in Developing Countries'. *Habitat International*, 29: 337–52.

Wacquant, L. (2004). *The Penalisation of Poverty and the Rise of Neoliberalism.* Spain: University of Valladolid. Retrieved from: http://www.ciudad-derechos.org/eindex.html on 25 November 2009.

Wardhaugh, J. (1999). 'The Unaccommodated Woman: Home, Homelessness and Identity'. *The Sociological Review*, 47 (1): 91–109.

Watson, S. (1999). 'A Home is Where the Heart is: Engendering Notions of Homelessness'. In P. Kennett and A. Marsh (eds), *Homelessness: Exploring the New Terrain*. UK: The Policy Press, pp. 81–100.

Watson, S. and H. Austerberry (1981). 'A Woman's Place: A Feminist Approach to Housing in Britain'. *Feminist Review*, 8: 49–62.

——. (1986). *Housing and Homelessness: A Feminist Perspective.* London: Routledge.

Young, I.M. (2005). 'House and Home: Feminist Variations on a Theme'. In I.M. Young (ed.), *On Female Body Experience: 'Throwing Like a Girl' and Other Essays*. New York: Oxford University Press, pp. 123–54.

4 Economic Inequality in Maternal and Child Health in Urban India

Assessment from NFHS, 1992–2006

Abhishek Kumar

In the recent past, many developing countries, including India, have witnessed considerable improvement in maternal and child health, particularly in terms of under-five mortality. For instance, under-five deaths have declined from 13 million in 1990 to 9.2 million in 2007 (UNICEF, 2008). Similarly, maternal mortality has reduced from 480 per 100,000 live births in 1990 to 450 per 100,000 live births in 2007 (WHO, 2007). Apart from decreasing mortality, marked increase is also observed in utilization of maternal and child healthcare services in recent decades. Thus, the present scenario leads us to believe that developing countries are on the track to achieve the Millennium Development Goals (MDGs) related to maternal and child health within the target period.

Several factors ranging from rapid urbanization, economic development, improvements in healthcare systems, implementation of target oriented approach, etc., have been held responsible for such decline in child mortality and improvement in maternal and child health (MCH) in developing countries. Urbanization, particularly in developing countries, is perceived as an indicator of socio-economic development and associated with higher income level, better educational and employment opportunities, improved healthcare facilities and greater access to them (Ronsmans et al.,

2003; Say and Raine, 2007). As a result, in the past, most nations have experienced substantially better maternal and neonatal survival in urban areas than in rural areas (Bartlett et al., 2005; Ronsmans and Graham, 2006).

Contrary to this urban advantage, the other part of the urban story is quite unpleasant and miserable. A large majority of urban population in developing countries is contributed by large-scale rural-to-urban migration that, over the decades, has led to rapid growth of slums within these urban centres (Matthews et al., 2010). Slums are informal settlements characterized by overcrowding, polluted environment, poor water and sanitation facilities and hazardous living condition. The dwellers of these settlements are quite diverse than the rest of the urban dwellers in terms of socio-economic aspects. Moreover, it has also been noted that economic inequality is increasing in the urban centres resulting in growing marginalized and poor population (UN-HABITAT, 2006; UNFPA, 2006). The urban poor are characterized with underutilization of MCH services and higher rate of maternal and child mortality as compared to rest of urban dwellers (Hu et al., 2008; Shah et al., 2009; Zhao et al., 2009; Ziraba et al., 2009). In some countries, the utilization of healthcare service is comparatively lower and maternal, newborn and child mortality is higher among urban poor than the rural residents (APHRC, 2002; Fotso et al., 2007; Gupta et al., 2008; Madise et al., 2003; UN-HABITAT, 2006; de Poel et al., 2007).

In India, the proportion of urban population has increased from 17 per cent in 1951 to 32 per cent in 2011 (almost doubled in last 60 years), contributing 377 million to the total population of the country (Census of India, 2011). In future, urban population is likely to grow faster than the rural population – 2.5 per cent annually in urban India compared to less than 1 per cent in rural India (World Urbanization Prospects, 2006). Like other developing countries, urban population of India is largely contributed by natural increase and massive rural-urban migration. A large section of this population is living in slums which is characterized by overcrowding, pollution, lack of basic services, such as clean water and sanitation, and spread of infectious diseases. About 57 per cent of the urban population in Mumbai lives in slums (IIPS and Macro

International, 2007). The level of urban poverty is relatively high in the country and almost equal to the rural population – 26 per cent in urban and 28 per cent in rural India during 2004–05 (Planning Commission of India, 2007).

These marginalized sections of the population are largely contributed by the reproductive age group of women and children, which need a greater amount of healthcare services, particularly related to maternal and child health. But, like other developing countries, health and social services in urban areas have not kept pace with growth of urban population in India. For instance, studies documented that slum dwellers were at a disadvantage in terms of utilization of maternal healthcare services compared to households residing in non-slum areas (APHRC, 2006; Islam et al., 2006). Evidence from India also indicated poor utilization of maternal healthcare services in urban slums (Khan et al., 2008). Though there is a small body of literature that has compared the utilization of MCH services between slums and non-slums in particular cities in India, there is lack of evidence focused on unmasking the economic inequality in health status and healthcare utilization in urban population as a whole at national level. The present study, therefore, make an effort to assess the economic inequality in selected MCH services and child health indicators during 1992–2006 in urban India.

Data and Methods

This study used data from the first and third round of the National Family Health Survey (NFHS) conducted during 1992–93 and 2005–06, respectively. The NFHS is large-scale, multi-round survey which provides estimates of fertility, family planning, infant and childhood mortality, utilization of maternal and child healthcare services, nutritional status of children, at national and state levels, and across urban-rural residence. The survey adopted two-stage sampling design in most of the rural areas and three-stage sampling design in most of the urban areas and covers more than 99 per cent of the national population. The sample design remained similar over the period, thus, the subsequent rounds of the surveys are comparable (Ram and Roy, 2004). The NFHS-1 covered 88,562 households (28,822 from urban and 59,740 from rural areas) and 89,777 women (27,534 from urban and 62,243 from rural). The NFHS-3 covered 109,041 households (50,236 from urban and 58,805 from rural areas) and 124,385 women (56,961 from urban and 67,424 from rural areas). The details of the sampling procedure, sample size and the findings are available in national and state reports (IIPS and Macro International, 2007).

Identification of Urban Poor and Non-Poor in India

The first exercise in this study is to measure the urban poor using the NFHS, as NFHS does not provide direct information on income and expenditure. In the absence of data on monetary indicators in the NFHS, information on economic proxies such as (1) housing conditions, (2) sanitation facilities, (3) ownership of household consumer durables, and (4) possession of agricultural land and accessories are used increasingly to measure the household's economic status. This is the standard practice to measure economic status of the household in Demographic Health Surveys including NFHS (Filmer and Pritchett, 2001; Howe et al., 2009; Montgomery et al., 2000; O'Donnell et al., 2008; Rutstein, 2008; Vyas and Kumaranayake, 2006). Applying the Principal Component Analysis (PCA), these proxy indicators are used to generate a composite index called the standard of living index (SLI) or wealth index and largely used in order to assess the household economic status as well as health disparity across economic groups.

However, the wealth index suffers with certain limitations: *first,* it provides a single estimate at the national level and ignores rural-urban differentials in poverty level; *second,* it does not consider the rational of selection of indicators; and *third,* it does not provide true cut-off point for the poor (Mishra and Dilip, 2008). Owing the flaws of the wealth index, the present study computed a separate wealth index using selected consumer durables, household amenities, and housing qualities only for urban India for both the periods. The variables were selected based on a theoretical rationale and statistical significance. The theoretical rationale refers to the extent of sensitivity of the variables to the poor. For example, a variable like ownership of agricultural land is not included in the analysis because of its limited utility in urban areas. For statistical significance, a descriptive analysis has been carried out for all the available variables related to the economic aspect of the household (table not shown). Variables with higher frequencies and lower standard deviations (closer to zero) are not included in the analysis. A standard deviation with zero value indicates that all households own that particular variable or no households own the variable. After selecting the variables, the PCA is used to compute the wealth index. As a first step, all the selected variables are re-coded into binary form (0=no, 1=otherwise). In the second step, the PCA is used to derive the factor score and generate eigenvalue (variance). The derived factor score is used as weight for each selected variable in computing the wealth index. In the third step, a percentile (100% distribution) of wealth index is obtained for the country. The cut-off point to demarcate the urban poor and non-poor is equated with the officially accepted poverty estimates derived from consumption expenditure data by the Planning Commission, Government of India, closer to the survey period. For instance, according to official estimates, 32 per cent urban population was poor in 1993–94 and 26 per cent were in 2004–05 in the country (Planning Commission of India, 1994, 2007). These proportions are used for NFHS-1 (1992–93) and NFHS-3 (2005–06), respectively. Reliability of computed index is checked by Kronbach's alpha test and higher alpha-value is observed for both periods – 0.85 for 1992–93 and 0.87 for 2005–06.

Outcome Variables

Outcome variables included in the study are defined as follows:

MCH Services

Contraceptive use is defined as currently married women aged 15–49 using any methods of family planning at the time of the survey. We excluded all those women who were pregnant at the time of survey.

Four antenatal check-ups are considered as at least four visits of antenatal care during the last pregnancy. It is the gold standard definition recommended by the World Health Organization (WHO, 2009).

Complete/full antenatal care means a minimum of three antenatal visits with at least two injections of tetanus toxoid and consumption of iron folic tablets/syrup is defined as complete antenatal care. It is calculated for last pregnancy only.

Medical assistance at delivery is defined as any institutional or home delivery assisted by a doctor/nurse/or any health personnel. Last three births in last four years are considered in computation of medical assistance at delivery.

Full immunization is considered as surviving children who have received one dose of BCG, three doses of DPT, three doses of polio, and one dose of measles. Immunization is estimated for children age 12–23 months only, as per the WHO schedule of immunizations.

Child Health Indicators

Underweight is defined as children in the age group 0–47 months whose weight-for-age Z-score is minus two standard deviations below the median of the reference population.

Stunting is defined as children in the age group 0–47 months with a height-for-age Z-score minus two standard deviations below the median of the reference population.

Wasting: Children aged 0–47 months with a weight-for-height Z-score minus two standard deviations below the median of the reference population are considered wasted.

Infant Mortality Rate (IMR): The probability of dying before the first birthday and estimated from births in the last 10 years preceding the survey.

Under-five Mortality Rate (U5MR): The probability of dying before the fifth birthday and estimated from births in the last 10 years preceding the survey.

Different rounds of NFHS collected information on aforementioned MCH indicators with varying reference period and number of births. Thus, to make the estimate comparable over the period all samples were drawn from same reference period in both rounds of the survey. Nutritional status of children is estimated based on US NCHS reference population for all two rounds of NFHS due to the unavailability of the new WHO reference population (WHO, 2006) in NFHS-1 dataset. All outcome variables are compared between urban poor and non-poor in the country, as it is the prime focus of the study. However, rural population is also used for comparison purpose with urban poor.

Analysis

Descriptive statistics is carried out to examine the differentials in the selected outcome variables among urban poor, urban non-poor and rural residents in India. Non-poor/poor ratio, concentration indices, and concentration curve are used to measure the economic inequality in selected healthcare and health indicators in urban India. Concentration index is a measure of socio-economic inequality and is defined as twice the area between the concentration curve and the line of equality. It varies between –1 to +1, the closer the value to 1 the more unequal is the healthcare indicators and the closer to 0 more equal is the healthcare across the group. In case of health outcome, the closer the value to –1, the more unequal is the health outcome and closer the value to 0, the more equal the health outcome between the groups (O'Donnell et al., 2008). The descriptive analysis is followed by a multivariate analysis examining the significant influence of household poverty and residence on outcome variables after adjusting a number of pertinent covariates such as sex of child, parity, age of mother, education of mother, exposure of media and current working status of mother, religion, caste, etc. Binary logistic regression is used for all outcome variables (except infant and under-five mortality) as they are binary in nature (0 = no, 1=otherwise). Cox proportional hazard model is used for infant and under-five mortality rate to take care of censoring cases. Results of the binary logistic regression are presented in terms of predicted probability in order to make the interpretation easier. Finally, proportional decomposition analysis is used to understand the proportional contribution of poverty reduction in improvement in the outcome variables over the periods.

Result

Overview of Socio-economic and Demographic Characteristics in Urban India in Last Two Decades

Table 1 presents an overview of socio-economic and demographic characteristics in urban India for the last two decades. The information is gleaned from various sources. Table 1 shows a steady increase in proportion of urban population in the country in the last

10 years. Increased population density (people/km^2) shows that urban centres of the country are being crowded over the period. Demographic indicators have improved in urban India over the period. For instance, infant mortality and total fertility rate has reduced resulting in increased life expectancy over the period in urban India. On the other hand, female literacy rate has increased in urban India over the period.

Table 1 *Socio-economic and Demographic Profile of Urban India in Last Two Decades (contemporary to the survey periods), 1991–2001*

Urbanization Characteristics	*1991*	*2001*	*2011*
Population (in millions)[a]	217.2	285.3	377.1
Population (%)[a]	25.72	27.7	31.8
Decadal growth (%)[a]	36.5	31.1	31.8
Density of population (people/km2)	3,370	3,657	–
Sex ratio (females/1,000 males)[a]	868	900	926
Female literacy rate[a]	63.9	72.9	79.9
Crude birth rate (births/1,000 mid-year population)[b]	24.3	20.2	18.3
Crude death rate (deaths/1,000 mid-year population)[b]	7.1	6.3	5.8
Total fertility rate[b]	2.7	2.3	2
Infant mortality rate[b]	53	42	34
Life expectancy at birth (in years)[c]	63.4	67.3	68.8
Population below poverty line (%)[d]	32.4	25.7	–

Sources: [a] Census of India, 1991, 2001, 2011. Office of the Registrar General and Census Commissioner, New Delhi, India.

[b] Compendium of India's Fertility and Mortality Indicators 1971–2007, the Sample Registration System. Office of the Registrar General and Census Commissioner, India, Ministry of Home Affairs, New Delhi. Total Fertility Rate for 2011 is given for year 2007.

[c] Compendium of India's Fertility and Mortality Indicators 1971–2007, the Sample Registration System. Office of the Registrar General and Census Commissioner, India, Ministry of Home Affairs, New Delhi. Life expectancy for 1991 is given for 1986–90; for 2001 it is given for 1996–2000; and for 2011 it is given for years 2002–06.

[d] Planning Commission Estimates of Poverty, 1994, 2007.

Trends, Differentials and Changes in Maternal and Child Health Indicators Among Urban Poor, Urban Non-Poor and Rural Residents in India

Differentials in selected outcome variables are examined between urban poor and non-poor in the country between 1992–93 and 2005–06 (Table 2). Urban poor are also compared with rural residents. Result shows that all selected outcome variables (either healthcare services or child health) differed starkly between urban poor and non-poor in the country over the study period. In case of service utilization, difference between urban poor and non-poor is more profound for four antenatal check-ups. For instance, among urban poor little more than one-fourth of women (28%) compared to about three-fifths (59%) among the non-poor women have visited more than four times for antenatal check-ups during last pregnancy in 1992–93. Such differentials remained 36 per cent vs. 71 per cent during 2005–06. The utilization of full antenatal care also varied starkly between urban poor and non-poor women. The coverage of full antenatal care was 36 per cent among urban poor compared to 64 per cent among urban non-poor in 1992–93. The differential was 39 per cent versus 68 per cent in 2005–06. Similar differential is observed for medical assistance at delivery. Among the urban poor, 44 per cent mother delivered their birth under medical facilities compared to 74 per cent among urban non-poor during 1992–93. The differential was 48 per cent versus 83 per cent in 2005–06. Poor/non-poor differential was comparatively smaller for current contraceptive use (57% and 67% among urban poor and non-poor, respectively, in 2005–06) over the period. The gap remained similar over the period.

Likewise, the coverage of maternal healthcare services and childhood immunization also differed profoundly between urban poor and non-poor in the country. In 1992–93, the coverage of full immunization was only 32 per cent among urban poor compared to 59 per cent among non-poor in the country. Such differential was 37 per cent versus 64 per cent in 2005–06. Like MCH services, poor/non-poor differentials were also stark for child nutritional status and mortality. In 1992–93, proportion of underweight children was 60 per cent among urban poor compared to 40 per cent among urban non-poor; in 2005–06, the difference was 53 per cent versus 33 per cent among urban poor and non-poor, respectively. Similar result was observed for stunting – 57 per cent versus 40 per cent in 1992–93 and 48 per cent versus 30 per cent in 2005–06 among urban poor and non-poor, respectively. Such differential was minimal for wasting – 19 per cent versus 15 per cent in 1992–93 and 20 per cent versus 15 per cent in 2005–06 among poor and non-poor, respectively. Infant mortality and under-five mortality was considerably higher among urban poor as compared to urban non-poor in the country. In 2005–06, IMR was 64 per 1,000 live births among urban poor as compared to 39 per 1,000 live births among urban non-poor. Under-five mortality was about twice among urban poor (84 per 1,000 live births) than urban non-poor (46 per 1,000 live births) in 2005–06. Differentials remained similar over the periods.

A comparison of urban poor with rural residents shows an interesting picture. The utilization of maternal and child healthcare services was higher among urban poor than rural residents in the country. On the contrary, the nutritional status of children was worse among urban poor than rural residents, though the gap was small. For instance, proportion of underweight children was 53 per cent among urban poor compared to 51 per cent among rural residents in 2005–06. Similar pattern was observed for stunting (48% among urban poor as compared to 44% among urban non-poor) and wasting (20% among urban poor and 19% among urban non-poor) during 2005–06. The pattern remained similar over the years. The level of childhood mortality was similar among urban poor and rural residents in the country in 2005–06. For instance, IMR was 64 per 1,000 live births among urban poor compared to 65 per 1,000 live births among rural residents. Similarly, U5MR was 84 per 1,000 live births among both the urban poor and rural residents in the country.

Table 2 also shows percentage change in all selected dependent variables among urban poor, non-poor and rural residents in the last 14 years. It is observed that utilization of MCH services has increased among both urban poor and non-poor in the last 14 years. Increase is higher for current contraceptive use followed by four antenatal check-ups, medical assistance at delivery and full immunization coverage among urban poor as well as non-poor. Similarly, child nutritional indicators (except for wasting) and mortality has declined among urban poor and non-poor in the last 14 years. Rural residents have also witnessed considerable improvement in all selected outcome over the periods. Moreover, the improvement was higher in rural areas than that of urban poor for all the outcome indicators. In rural areas, percentage increase was the highest for medical assistance at delivery (74%) followed by coverage of full immunization (68%), current contraceptive use (44%) and four antenatal check-ups (29%).

Table 2 *Differentials in Selected Healthcare Services and Child Health Indicators between Urban Poor, Urban Non-poor and Rural Residents in India, 1992–2006*

	1992–93			*2005–06*			*% Change during 1992–2006*		
	Urban poor	*Urban non-poor*	*Rural total*	*Urban poor*	*Urban non-poor*	*Rural total*	*Urban poor*	*Urban non-poor*	*Rural total*
Contraceptive use	40.4	55.8	36.9	56.8	66.5	53.0	40.6	19.1	43.7
Four antenatal visits	27.5	58.6	21.7	36.1	71.2	27.9	31.5	21.5	28.7
Full antenatal care	36.1	64.4	28.7	38.5	67.6	34.3	6.6	5.1	19.7
Medical assistance at delivery	44.2	73.6	22.1	47.8	82.9	38.5	8.1	12.7	74.2
Full immunization	32.3	59.0	22.9	36.8	64.3	38.6	14.1	9.1	68.3
Underweight	60.3	39.7	56.8	52.8	33.4	50.9	–12.4	–15.8	–10.4
Stunting	57.2	39.7	54.2	47.5	28.9	43.9	–17.0	–27.2	–19.0
Wasting	18.7	14.9	18.1	20.4	14.8	18.9	9.0	–0.4	4.6
Infant mortality	84.1	45.7	87.4	64.3	39.2	64.6	–23.5	–14.2	–26.1
Under-five mortality	115.6	56.3	119.6	84.4	45.7	83.8	–27.0	–18.8	–29.9

Economic Inequality in Maternal and Child Health Indicators in Urban India

In order to measure economic inequalities in utilization of MCH services and child health outcomes, non-poor/poor ratio,[1] concentration index and concentration curve is employed (Table 3, Figure 1–2). For MCH services, the non-poor/poor gap was greatest for four antenatal check-ups (1.97), followed by full antenatal care (1.76), immunization coverage (1.75) and medical assistance at delivery (1.73), while it was minimal for current use of contraceptive (1.17) during 2005–06. In case of childhood nutritional indicators, the non-poor/poor gap was greatest for stunting (0.61), followed by underweight (0.63) and wasting (0.71). The non-poor/gap was 0.61 for IMR and 0.54 for U5MR during 2005–06. In general, the non-poor/poor gap remained higher in urban India over the periods.

Table 3 *Non-poor/Poor Ratio and Concentration Index for Selected Healthcare Services and Child Health Indicators in Urban India, 1992–2006*

	Non-poor/Poor Ratio		*1992–1993*		*2005–2006*	
	1992–93	*2005–06*	*C.I.*	*Standard Error*	*C.I.*	*Standard Error*
Contraceptive Use	1.38	1.17	0.09	0.003	0.04	0.002
Four Antenatal Check-ups	2.13	1.97	0.20	0.005	0.16	0.004
Full Antenatal Care	1.78	1.76	0.16	0.005	0.14	0.004
Medical Assistance at Delivery	1.66	1.73	0.15	0.004	0.13	0.003
Full Immunization	1.83	1.75	0.17	0.010	0.14	0.008
Underweight	0.66	0.63	–0.15	0.006	–0.16	0.006
Stunting	0.69	0.61	–0.13	0.007	–0.19	0.007
Wasting	0.79	0.73	–0.09	0.015	–0.09	0.012
Infant Mortality	0.54	0.61	–0.19	0.012	–0.18	0.012
Under-five Mortality	0.49	0.54	–0.22	0.010	–0.19	0.011

C.I. Concentration Index

Result of concentration index showed pro-rich condition for healthcare services and pro-poor for child health indicators in urban India. However, degree of the concentration varied across the services. In 2005–06, the value of concentration index was the highest (in case of service indicators) for four antenatal check-ups (0.20) followed by full immunization (0.17), complete antenatal care (0.15) and medical assistance at delivery (0.13) in 2005–06.

Figure 1 *Concentration Curves Showing Inequalities in MCH Services in (Current Contraceptive Use, Four Antenatal Check-ups, Complete Antenatal Care, and Full Immunization) by Economic Status in Urban India, 1992–2006*

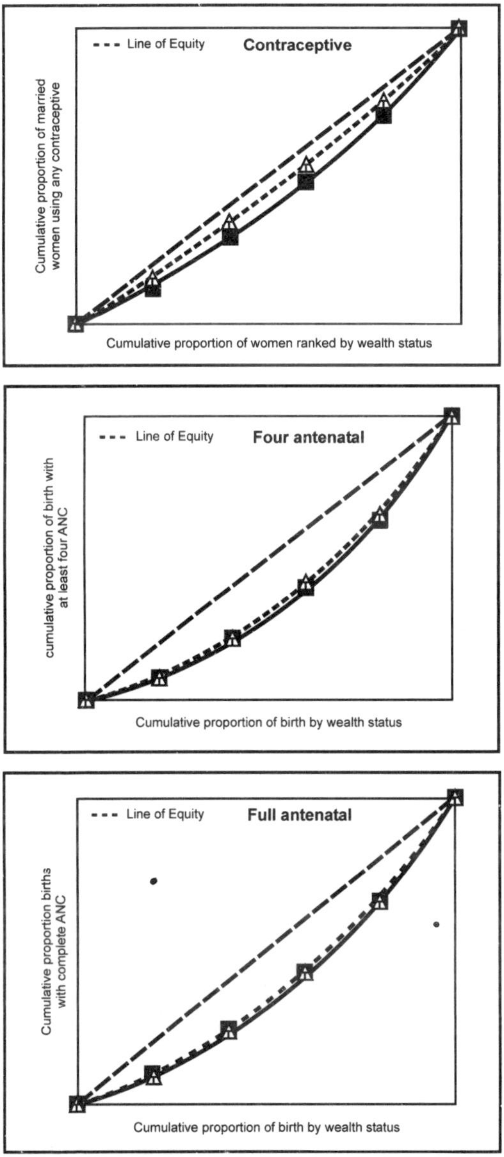

Cont'd...

...Cont'd

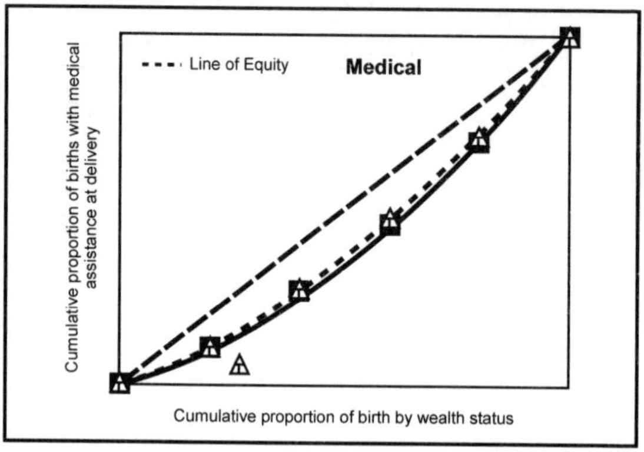

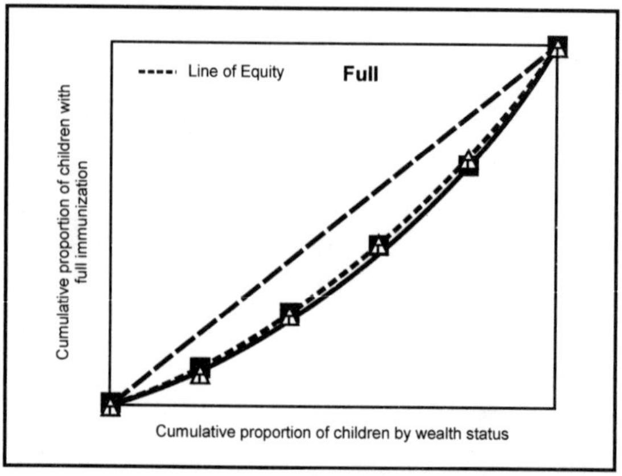

While, for child health indicators, the value of concentration index was the greatest for stunting and under-five mortality (–0.19 for both) followed by infant mortality (–0.18) and underweight (–0.16). The value of concentration index has reduced for all the healthcare indicators while it has either increased or stagnated for child health indicators over the periods.

Figure 2 *Concentration Curves Showing Inequalities in Child Health Indicators (Underweight, Stunting, Wasting, Infant Mortality, and Under-five Mortality) by Economic Status in Urban India, 1992–2006*

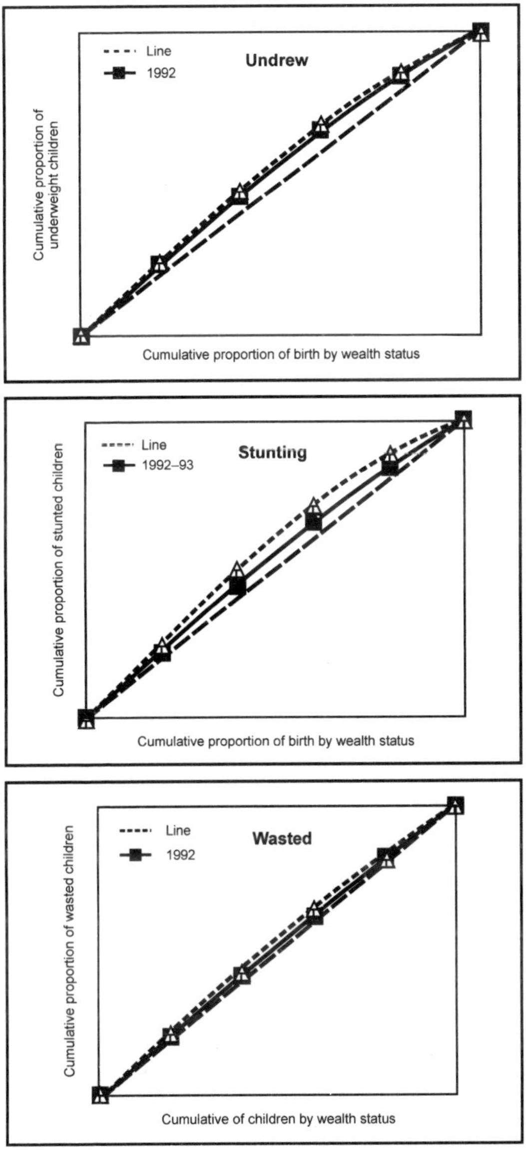

Cont'd...

...Cont'd

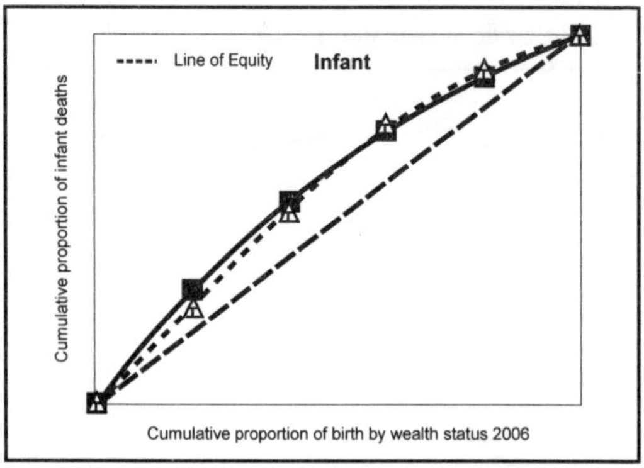

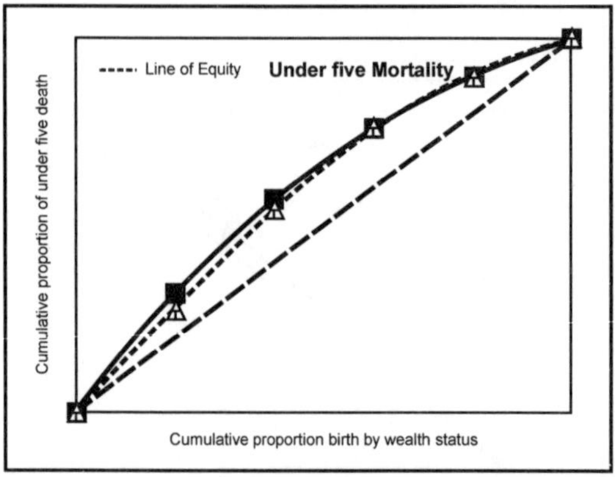

Multivariate Analysis

Multivariate analysis is used to understand the significant influence of household's poverty status on selected outcome indicators after adjusting other confounders. Binary logistic regression and Cox proportional hazard model (for IMR and U5MR) is used for the purpose. Several confounders such as sex of child, number of living children, birth order, age of mother, educational status of mother, exposure to mass media, current working status of mother, religion and caste are adjusted in the analysis. However, result is only presented for household poverty status (urban poor and non-poor) and residents. The obtained odds ratio from binary logistic regression is converted into predicted probability to make the interpretation easier (Table 4).

Table 4 *Predicted Probabilities (95% Confidence Intervals) for Healthcare Services & Child Nutritional Indicators and Hazard Risk (95% Confidence Intervals) for Infant and Under-five Mortality Across Urban Poverty and Residence in India, 1992–2006*

	1992–93			*2005–06*		
	Urban Poor	*Urban Non-poor*	*Rural Total*	*Urban Poor*	*Urban Non-poor*	*Rural Total*
	Predicted Probabilities					
Contraceptive Use	0.37 (0.35, 0.40)	0.55 (0.53, 0.56)	0.34 (0.33, 0.35)	0.61 (0.60, 0.62)	0.74 (0.74, 0.75)	0.59 (0.59, 0.60)
Four Antenatal Check-ups	0.25 (0.23, 0.28)	0.57 (0.55, 0.60)	0.19 (0.18, 0.20)	0.34 (0.33, 0.36)	0.75 (0.74, 0.76)	0.29 (0.28, 0.29)
Full Antenatal Care	0.30 (0.28, 0.33)	0.60 (0.58, 0.33)	0.25 (0.24, 0.26)	0.37 (0.35, 0.39)	0.70 (0.69, 0.70)	0.34 (0.34, 0.35)
Medical Assistance at Delivery	0.37 (0.34, 0.41)	0.74 (0.72, 0.76)	0.22 (0.21, 0.23)	0.49 (0.46, 0.51)	0.89 (0.88, 0.90)	0.41 (0.40, 0.41)
Full Immunization	0.20 (0.15, 0.25)	0.49 (0.44, 0.53)	0.17 (0.15, 0.19)	0.31 (0.27, 0.35)	0.65 (0.63, 0.67)	0.36 (0.34, 0.37)
Underweight	0.49 (0.46, 0.53)	0.36 (0.34, 0.38)	0.49 (0.48, 0.50)	0.51 (0.49, 0.53)	0.30 (0.29, 0.31)	0.47 (0.47, 0.48)
Stunting	0.53 (0.49, 0.56)	0.36 (0.34, 0.39)	0.48 (0.47, 0.50)	0.47 (0.45, 0.49)	0.27 (0.26, 0.28)	0.41 (0.41, 0.42)
Wasting	0.13 (0.11, 0.16)	0.12 (0.11, 0.14)	0.15 (0.14, 0.16)	0.19 (0.17, 0.20)	0.14 (0.13, 0.15)	0.18 (0.17, 0.18)
	Hazard Risk					
Infant Mortality	Ref.	0.67 (0.61, 0.73)	1.04 (0.97, 1.11)	Ref.	0.78 (0.70, 0.86)	1.06 (0.98, 1.16)
Under-five Mortality	Ref.	0.65 (0.60, 0.71)	1.03 (0.97, 1.09)	Ref.	0.75 (0.68, 0.82)	1.05 (0.97, 1.14)

Note: Multivariate (either Binary logistic regression or Cox proportional Hazard model) analysis is adjusted for a set of socio-economic and demographic variables such as sex of child, number of living children parity, age of mother, maternal education, exposure to mass media, working status, religion and caste.

Number given in parenthesis are 95 per cent of confidence interval.

Ref.: Reference category. In the table urban poor is served as reference category.

In case of utilization of MCH services, predicted probability was higher among urban non-poor than among urban poor. For instance, probability of contraceptive use was higher among urban non-poor (0.74) than among urban poor (0.61) in 2005–06. Similarly, for four antenatal check-ups, the predicted probability was 0.75 among urban non-poor compared to 0.34 among urban poor. For full antenatal care, the predicted probability was 0.70 among urban non-poor compared to 0.37 among urban poor. Probability of medical assistance at delivery was 0.89 among urban non-poor compared to 0.49 among urban poor. On the other hand, the predicted probability for childhood nutritional status was lower among urban non-poor than among urban poor in the country. For instance, probability of being underweight was 0.30 among urban non-poor compared to 0.51 among urban poor. Similarly, for stunting, the predicted probability was 0.27 among urban non-poor and 0.47 among urban poor in the country. Result of Cox proportional hazard model (lower panel of the table) shows that hazard risk of infant and under-five mortality was significantly lower among urban non-poor in the country. The pattern remained similar over the period.

A comparison of rural residents with urban poor shows that the probability for utilization of MCH services was lower among rural residents than among urban poor in the country. However, probability of nutritional status – being underweight, stunting and wasting – was lower among urban poor than that of rural residents in India. In case of mortality, risk of IMR and U5MR was higher among rural residents but the result was not significant. The pattern remained similar over the period. In conclusion, results of multivariate analysis support the result obtained in the descriptive analysis.

Decomposition Analysis

An effort is made to understand the contribution of poverty reduction in improvement in service utilization or health status between 1992–93 and 2005–06 by using proportional decomposition analysis. One of the simple methods used in demography for assessing the effects of changes in the levels of one or more contributing factors on a dependent variable over time is the method of decomposition of the changes in the dependent variable attributable to changes in the various contributing factors by the method of standardization (Srinivasan and Mohanty, 2008). In principle, this method assumes that there is no change in the distribution of a particular factor over time, allowing others to vary, and estimates the effect of the changes on the dependent variables. This study deployed same technique where changes in dependent variables were substantial during 1992–2006, and estimated the effects of changes in the poverty level during the same period in urban India. Wasting is excluded from the analysis as it has shown increasing trends in urban India in the last 14 years. Result of the decomposition analysis is presented in Table 5. It was found that for most of the indicators (either healthcare or health outcome) more than 10 per cent improvement was contributed by of reduction of poverty level in urban India during last 14 years. The maximum contribution was observed for full antenatal care (33%), followed by full immunization coverage (24%), medical assistance at delivery (22%), underweight (15%), and four antenatal check-ups (15%).

Table 5 *Result of Decomposition Analysis Showing Percentage Contribution of Poverty Reduction in Improvement of Selected MCH Services and Child Health Indicators in Urban India, 1992–2006*

	Per cent Contribution
Contraceptive Use	4.5
Stunting	10.1
Proportion of Under-five Death	13.2
Proportion of Infant Death	14.2
Frequency of Antenatal Care	15.0
Underweight	15.4
Medical Assistance at Delivery	21.5
Full Immunization	24.3
Full Antenatal Care	33.0

Discussion and Conclusion

The present study provides an overview on economic inequality in utilization of selected MCH services and child health indicators in urban India using the data of the National Family Health Survey conducted during 1992–2006. Urban poor and non-poor are defined based on selected economic proxies using Principal Component Analysis for both the periods. To demarcate the urban poor, official estimates of Government of India is used as cut-off point.

The findings demonstrate that all selected outcome variables (either MCH services or child health indicators) differed profoundly between urban poor and non-poor in the country. However, the differences are more pronounced for four antenatal check-ups, full antenatal care and medical assistance at delivery. Utilization of these services was about twice higher among urban non-poor than among urban poor. The findings are in similar direction with other studies which have shown the marked gap in utilization of healthcare services between the economic groups (Chattopadhyay and Roy, 2005; Ladusingh and Singh, 2007; Mohanty and Pathak, 2008; Pathak and Mohanty, 2010). Like the utilization of MCH services, child health indicators differed starkly between urban poor and non-poor in the country cutting across the time.

A key finding of the study is that the urban poor are better in utilization of healthcare services than rural residents are but nutritional status of children is better among rural residents than urban poor. The advantageous position of urban poor in healthcare utilization may be because of well-functioning health infrastructure and its physical accessibility within the urban areas. The finding that urban poor are in abysmal condition in child nutritional status than rural residents is supported by previous studies which have shown that proportion of underweight and stunting is higher among urban poor than rural residents (Brockerhoff and Brennan, 1998; de Poel et al., 2007; Tim and Lush, 1995). This suggests that urban poor are living in a worse condition than rural residents that may have impact on child health. Moreover, poverty may also limit the advantage that poor can reap from the better food supply in urban areas, while the rural residents can benefit from their own food production and support networks (de Poel et al., 2007).

Non-poor/poor gap in MCH services, child nutritional indicators and mortality is considerably higher in urban India over the period. Moreover, the gap has increased in case of medical assistance at delivery and childhood nutritional status. Result of concentration indices showed pro-rich condition in utilization of healthcare services and pro-poor condition in child health indicators and the pattern remained similar over the period. It indicates that the poor and marginalized segments of society suffer from poor accessibility to healthcare services as well as abysmal health status, as shown by previous studies (Houweling et al., 2007; Zere et al., 2007; Yazbeck, 2009).

In addition to the poverty status of household, concerned outcome variables may be influenced by other socio-economic factors. However, the results obtained from descriptive analysis are corroborated by the results of multivariate analysis. The predicted probability (adjusted for other socio-economic and demographic variables) is considerably higher for utilization of healthcare services and lower for child malnourishment and mortality among urban non-poor. In comparison with rural residents, the predicted probability of utilization of healthcare services is higher among urban poor than that of rural residents. However, the probability of being underweight and stunting is lower among rural residents compared to urban poor. The findings obtained from multivariate analysis are similar to that of other studies conducted in the past that have established a link between socio-economic status and poor health outcomes (Fotso et al., 2008; Kunst and Houweling, 2001; Mohanty, 2009; Monica, 2004; Monica et al., 2003; Montgomery and Hewett, 2005; Wagstaff and Watanabe, 2000; Zere and McIntyre, 2003). Result of decomposition analysis shows that poverty reduction has a considerable contribution in improvement of MCH services and child health status in urban India.

In conclusion, the salient findings of the study bring out substantive economic divide in utilization of MCH services and child health over the past decades in urban India. The country has witnessed rapid economic growth in the last decades with the introduction of New Economic Policy in early 1990s. Moreover, the Government of India has accorded high priority to improve the maternal and child health status by implementing several health programmes such as Child Survival and Safe-motherhood Programme (CSSM, 1992), Reproductive and Child Health Programme (RCH, 1997), National Rural Health Mission (NRHM, 2005–12) over past decades. However, the interplay of economic boom and public health intervention is not successfully reflected in urban India either for utilization of MCH services or for child health, as the study showed marked gap between urban poor and non-poor in all the selected outcome variables. The gap remained stagnant over the period and even increased in case of child nutritional status. It suggests that the more affluent socio-economic groups benefitted first with existing economic and health policies and then it goes to less affluent groups leading to greater disparities within the group at early stages.

Findings show that substantive proportion of urban population in the country is out of reach from utilization of MCH services particularly prenatal care and delivery care and a considerable proportion of children were malnourished in urban India. The proportion is even higher than that of rural residents. These two crucial findings explain the vulnerability of urban poor in the country in terms of utilization of MCH services and child health indicators of the MDGs. In the second most populous country, where a large (one-fourth) proportion of urban population lives under poor economic and very deleterious health conditions, it seems very difficult to achieve the MDGs within the given period while ignoring them. Though the condition of rural residents is worse than that of urban poor, they are improving rapidly over the period. One of the reasons behind such improvements could be the formulation of special programmes for rural areas like National Rural Health Mission (NRHM), while no such programmes exist for urban areas despite the fact that urban poor is more or less similar to their rural counterparts in terms of health status and healthcare utilization. Therefore, this study argues that in order to improve the reproductive and child health condition in the country, the attention should also be given to the urban poor. Programmatic interventions similar to NRHM could be one of the ways out.

Note

1. Non-poor/poor ratio is calculated by dividing the urban non-poor with urban poor, thus in case of healthcare services (either maternal or child) value greater than 1 indicates higher gaps, while in case of health indicators (child nutrition and mortality), value lesser than 1 indicates higher gaps.

References

APHRC (2002). *Health and Livelihood Needs of Residents of Informal Settlements in Nairobi City*. Nairobi: African Population and Health Research Centre.

——. (2006). Averting Preventable Maternal Mortality: Delays and Barriers to the Utilization of Emergency Obstetric Care in Nairobi's Informal Settlements. Unpublished Report of the World Bank-funded Maternal Health Survey.

Bartlett, L., S. Mawji, S. Whitehead, C. Crouse, S. Dalil, D. Ionete and P. Salama (2005). 'Where Giving Birth is a Forecast of Death: Maternal Mortality in Four Districts of Afghanistan, 1999–2002'. *The Lancet*, 365: 864–87.

Brockerhoff, M. and E. Brennan (1998). 'The Poverty of Cities in Developing Countries'. *Population and Development Review*, 24 (1): 75–114.

Census of India (1991, 2001, 2011). *Provisional Population Totals*. New Delhi, India: The Office of Registrar General and Census Commissioner.

Chattopadhyay, A. and T. Roy (2005). 'Are Urban Poor Doing Better than their Rural Counterpart in India? A Study of Fertility, Family Planning, and Health'. *Demography India*, 34 (2): 299–312.

Compendium of India's Fertility and Mortality Indicators (1971–2007). The Sample Registration System. Office of the Registrar General and Census Commissioner, Ministry of Home Affairs, New Delhi, India.

de Poel, Ellen van, Owen O'Donnell and Eddy van Doorslaer (2007). 'Are Urban Children Really Healthier? Evidences from 47 Developing Countries'. *Social Science and Medicine*, 65: 1986–2003.

Filmer, D. and H. Pritchett (2001). 'Estimating Wealth Effects without Expenditure Data-or Tears: An Application to Educational Enrollments in States of India'. *Demography*, 38: 115–32.

Fotso, J.C., A. Ezeh and R. Oronje (2008). 'Provision and Use of Maternal Health Services among Urban Poor Women in Kenya: What Do We Know and What Can We Do?'. *Journal of Urban Health*, 85 (3): 428–42.

Fotso, J.C., A. Ezeh, N. Madise and J. Ciera (2007). 'Progress towards the Child Mortality Millennium Development Goal in Urban Sub-Saharan Africa: The Dynamics of Population Growth, Immunization, and Access to Clean Water'. *BMC Public Health*, 7: 218.

Gupta, M., J. Thakur and R. Kumar (2008). 'Reproductive and Child Health Inequities in Chandigarh Union Territory of India'. *Journal of Urban Health*, 85: 291–99.

Houweling, T., C. Ronsmans, O. Campbell and A. Kunst (2007). 'Huge Poor-rich Inequalities in Maternity Care: An International Comparative Study of Maternity and Child Care in Developing Countries'. *Bulletin of the World Health Organization*, 85 (10): 745–54.

Howe, L., J.R. Hargreaves, S. Gabrysch and S. Huttly (2009). 'Is the Wealth Index a Proxy for Consumption Expenditure? A Systematic Review'. *Journal of Epidemiology and Community Health*, 63: 871–77.

Hu, X., S. Cook and M. Salazar (2008). 'Internal Migration and Health in China'. *The Lancet*, 372: 1717–19.

IIPS and Macro International (2007). 'Health and Living Conditions in Eight Indian Cities'. *National Family Health Survey (NFHS-3), 2005–06, India*, Vol. 1, Mumbai: International Institute for Population Sciences.

Islam, M., M. Montgomery and S. Taneja (2006). *Urban Health and Care-Seeking Behavior: A Case Study of Slums in India and the Philippines*. Final Report, Bethesda, MD: The Partners for Health Reform plus Project and Abt Associates Inc.

Khan, Z., S. Mehnaz, N. Khalique, M. Ansari and A. Siddiqui (2008). 'Poor Perinatal Care Practices in Urban Slums: Possible Role of Social Mobilization Networks'. *Indian Journal of Community and Medicine*, 34 (2): 102–07.

Kunst, A. and E. Houweling (2001). 'A Global Picture of Poor-rich Differences in the Utilization of Delivery Care'. *Studies in Health Service Organisation and Policy*, 17: 297–315.

Ladusingh, L. and H. Singh (2007). 'Rich-poor Gap in Maternal Care: The Case of Northeast India'. *Asian Population Studies*, 3 (1): 79–94.

Madise, N., E. Banda and K. Benaya (2003). 'Infant Mortality in Zambia: Socio-economic and Demo-graphic Determinants'. *Social Biology*, 50: 148–66.

Matthews, Z., A. Channon, S. Neal, D. Osrin, N. Madise and W. Stones (2010). 'Examining the 'Urban Advantage' in Maternal Healthcare in Developing Countries'. *PLoS Medicine*, 7 (9): e1000327. doi: 10.1371/journal.pmed.1000327.

Mishra, U. and T. Dilip (2008). 'Reflections on Wealth Quintile Distribution and Health Outcomes'. *Economic and Political Weekly*, 43 (48): 77–82.

Mohanty, S.K. (2009). 'Alternative Wealth Indices and Health Estimates in India'. *Genus*, LXV (2): 113–37.

Mohanty, S.K. and P. Pathak (2008). 'Rich-poor Gap in Utilization of Reproductive and Child Health Services in India'. *Journal of Biosocial Science*, 41 (3): 381–98.

Monica, M. (2004). 'Maternal and Child Health among the Urban Poor in Nairobi, Kenya'. *African Population Studies*, 19 (2): 179–98.

Monica, M., E. Zulu and M. Brockerhoff (2003). 'The Inequality of Maternal Health Care in Urban Sub-Saharan Africa in the 1990s'. *Population Studies*, 57 (3): 347–66.

Montgomery, M. and P. Hewett (2005). 'Urban Poverty and Health in Developing Countries: Household and Neighborhood Effects'. *Demography*, 42 (3): 397–425.

Montgomery, M., M. Gragnolati, K. Burke and E. Paredes (2000). 'Measuring Living Standards with Proxy Variables'. *Demography*, 37: 1556–74.

More, N., U. Bapat, S. Das, S. Barnett, A. Costello, A. Fernandez and D. Osrin (2009). 'Inequalities in Maternity Care and Newborn Outcomes: One-year Surveillance of Births in Vulnerable Slum Communities in Mumbai'. *International Journal of Equity in Health*, 8: 21.

O'Donnell, O., E. Doorslaer, A. Wagstaff and M. Lindelow (2008). *Analyzing Health Equity Using Household Survey Data: A Guide to Techniques and their Implementation*. World Bank Institute Learning Resource Series, Washington, DC: The World Bank.

Pathak, P. and S.K. Mohanty (2010). 'Does the Safe-motherhood Program Reach the Poor in Uttar Pradesh, India?'. *Asian Population Studies*, 6 (2): 173–91.

Planning Commission of India (2007). Poverty Estimates for 2004–05. Planning Commission, Government of India. http://planning commission.nic.in/news/pramar07/pdf

Ram, F. and T. Roy (2004). 'Comparability Issues in Large Sample Surveys: Some Observations'. In T.K. Roy, M. Guruswamy and P. Arokiaswamy (eds), *Population, Health and Development in India: Changing Perspectives*. Mumbai: International Institute for Population Sciences and Jaipur: Rawat Publications, pp. 40–56.

Ronsmans, C. and W. Graham (2006). 'Maternal Mortality: Who, When, Where and Why?'. *The Lancet*, 368: 1189–200.

Ronsmans, C., J. Etard, G. Walraven, L. Hoj, A. Dumont, L. de Bernis and B. Kodio (2003). 'Maternal Mortality and Access to Obstetric Services in West Africa'. *Tropical Medicine International Health*, 8: 940–48.

Rutstein, S. (2008). 'The DHS Wealth Index: Approaches to Rural and Urban Areas'. DHS Working Paper No. 60, Calverton, MD: Macro International Inc, USA.

Say, L. and R. Raine (2007). 'A Systematic Review of Inequalities in the Use of Maternal Health Care in Developing Countries: Examining the Scale of the Problem and the Importance of Context'. *Bulletin of World Health Organization*, 85: 812–19.

Srinivasan, K. and S.K. Mohanty (2008). 'Household Deprivation and its Linkages with Reproductive and Child Health Care and Health Outcome'. *Economic and Political Weekly*, 43 (48): 67–76.

Tim, I. and L. Lush (1995). 'Intra-urban Differentials in Child Health'. *Health Transition Review*, 5: 163–90.

UN-HABITAT (2006). *The State of the World's Cities Report 2006/7: The Millennium Development Goals and Urban Sustainability*. London: Earthscan.

UNFPA (2006). *The State of the World Population 1996: Changing Places: Population, Development and the Urban Poor*. New York: UNFPA.

UNICEF (2008). *The State of the World's Children 2009: Maternal and Newborn Health*. New York: UNICEF.

Vyas, S. and L. Kumaranayake (2006). 'Constructing Socio-economic Status Indices: How to Use Principal Component Analysis'. *Health Policy and Planning*, 21: 459–68.

Wagstaff, A. and N. Watanabe (2000). 'Socio-economic Inequalities in Child Malnutrition in the Developing World'. Policy Research Working Paper No. 2434.

World Health Organization (2006). Provision of Effective Antenatal Care: Integrated Management of Pregnancy and Child Birth (IMPAC). Geneva, Switzerland: Standards for Maternal and Neonatal Care (1.6), Department of Making Pregnancy Safer.

——. (2007). United Nations Children's Fund, United Nations Population Fund and the World Bank, Maternal Mortality in 2005: Estimates developed by WHO, UNICEF, UNFPA and the World Bank, WHO, Geneva, p. 35.

World Urbanization Prospects (2007). *The 2006 Revision Population Database and World Population Prospects*.

Yazbeck, A. (2009). *Attacking Inequality in the Health Sector: A Synthesis and Evidence of Tools*. Washington, DC: The World Bank.

Zere, E., M. Moeti, J. Kirigia, T. Mwase and E. Kataika (2007). 'Equity in Health and Healthcare in Malawi: Analysis of Trends'. *BMC Public Health*, 15 (7): 78.

Zhao, Q., A. Kulane, Y. Gao and B. Xu (2009). 'Knowledge and Attitude on Maternal Health Care among Rural-to-urban Migrant Women in Shanghai, China'. *BMC Women's Health*, 9: 5.

Ziraba, A., N. Madise, S. Mills, C. Kyobutungi and A. Ezeh (2009). 'Maternal Mortality in the Informal Settlements of Nairobi City: What Do We Know?'. *Reproductive Health*, 6: 6.

5 Contraceptive Use Behaviours Among Slum and Non-Slum Dwellers in Mumbai City

Raj Narayan and Rajiva Prasad

India has the unique distinction of sponsoring the first national family planning programme in the developing world. Since the state-sponsored programmes were initiated in 1952, India's demographic and health profile has changed radically. As a result of continuing efforts made by national/international/voluntary organizations, considerable progress has been made in reducing the birth rate during the last few decades. During the same period, the infant mortality rate has also reduced substantially (Health Information of India, 1999). Today, knowledge of family planning is almost universal and nearly half of the couple is using some means of contraception. However, the government-supported family planning programme is dominated by voluntary sterilization, especially female sterilization, which account for 75 per cent of all contraceptive use (NFHS, 2000). However, it is widely acknowledged that over-riding emphasis on single method is unlikely to meet the clients' need. Traditionally, the National Family Welfare Programme in India sought to promote responsible and planned parenthood through voluntary and free choice of family planning methods best suited to individual acceptors (Government of India, 2000).

Contraceptive use is considered as an intervention aimed at changing the risk of pregnancy. Any purposeful practice of a method undertaken by sexually active women or men to reduce the risk of conception is considered as contraception. Contraception refers only to the control of fertility through the use of various fertility regulation technologies by individual or a couple with the ultimate aim of limiting family size and subsequently reducing the population growth. Birth control measure suggests that among the different factors of fertility determinants, none has a direct effect on the individual than the use of contraception methods (Ross, 1983). However, the influential factors that affect the use of method include age at marriage, education, ideal number of living children, spacing between successive births, employment, poverty, health and status of women. These factors in turn increase contraceptive use among the couples when structural changes such as socio-economic development or modernization take place (Coale, 1997). Such transformation brings cognitive change among couples to limit their number of children through adoption of contraception.

One of the principal objectives of any family planning programme, as endorsed by Programme of Action adopted at Cairo in the 1994 during International Conference on Population and Development (ICPD), is to enable couples to decide the timing and spacing of the future births, to ensure that they make informed choices and to make use of a full range of available safe and effective methods of contraception. Among different methods, however, sterilization (mainly female sterilization) is the most commonly used methods in India (IIPS, 2000). When couples achieve their desired family size, the majority chooses to undergo sterilization, which is considered as the most effective and safest method to stop childbearing in India and people often equate the term family planning with sterilization (Bose, 1990). India is currently undergoing a fertility transition and an important feature of this transition is the fact that contraceptive use has spread to even uneducated women (McNay et al., 2003). The advantage with the rising prevalence of contraceptive usage is the fact that abortion incidence has declined (Marston and Cleland, 2003). National Population Policy (2000) envisages universal access to various methods of contraception and fertility regulation.

The current level of contraceptive use defined as the percentage of currently married women aged from 15 to 49 years who are currently using a contraceptive method or whose husbands are using a contraceptive method. It is the most widely used measure of level of family planning and is one of the most useful indicators in family planning policy. The contraceptive prevalence can also be considered a measure of the final stage in the process of contraceptive innovation. Although, the contraceptive usage has increased over a period of time, there exists a gap in knowledge, attitude and practices regarding contraception (Ashoke et al., 2000). With the above facts taken into consideration, we aim to find out prevalence of contraceptive usage amongst eligible currently married women in selected cities of India in this paper. The spread of contraceptive use within a society can be viewed as a diffusion process. The stage is to become aware of and informed about contraceptive methods. In a population with family planning policies designed to increase contraceptive use, measuring the level of awareness of contraception also provides a useful measure of the success of information, education and communication activities and may help to identify the programme areas that need to be strengthened.

Studies of fertility behaviour in the Third World have relied heavily on two variables, income and education, to explain variations in fertility rates. The socio-economic variables traditionally employed to account for differences in infertility rates are invariant. On the basis of data from 180 slum households in Calcutta (India), Shaw (1988) examined the fertility and child spacing among the urban poor. His research indicates that in a situation where material and social conditions are comparable, cultural and demographic variables play a major role in influencing reproductive behaviour. Kayembe et al. (2003) studied the prevalence and determinants of the use of modern contraceptive methods in Kinshasa, Democratic Republic of Congo. Five hundred females in age group of 15–49 years were selected through a stratified sampling procedure. The result showed condoms appear to be the most widely known modern contraceptive method. The pill was cited by only 28 per cent, a noticeable proportion reported unwanted pregnancies.

Thang and Anh (2002) studied accessibility and use of contraceptives in Vietnam. Accessibility of contraceptives was an important factor in use of family planning because contraceptive access in Vietnam varies sizably by region and only one method (the IUD) predominates in Vietnam's contraceptive method mix. Reddy (1984) examines the differential contraceptive use among the slum and non-slum dwellers in Hyderabad. A two-stage simple random sampling technique was used in this study designed to examine the differentials in contraceptive practice between the slum and the non-slum dwellers of Hyderabad, and the effect of a few selected variables namely age, marriage duration and number of living sons, and socioeconomic status on contraceptive behaviour. A total sample of 480 couples, consisting of 240 slum and 240 non-slum dwellers, were selected at random. Contraceptive use was significantly higher among the non-slum dwellers than the slum dwellers.

Need for the Study

A number of studies have been conducted in India on contraceptive behaviour. These studies mainly focus on the variation between the rural-urban differential in contraceptive prevalence and method use. However, there is a dearth of literature on contraceptive use pattern among urban slum dwellers. Studies conducted on contraceptive behaviour of women living in urban slum are mostly conducted in local setting and they are based on primary sample surveys. These surveys provide local estimates which do not provide an overall picture of contraceptive behaviour in Indian slums. A study conducted in Bangladesh during 1994 shows that the contraceptive prevalence rate (CPR) among currently married women in slums was only 40 per cent compared to the national average of 54 per cent (Barkat et al., 1995). Such type of difference in CPR among currently married women of slum and non-slum areas are also expected in India. Very little is known about reproductive behaviour and family planning utilization in the urban slums in India. To achieve the goal of achieving the replacement level of fertility by 2010, it is imperative to understand the determinants of family planning practice for the people who are living in a slum. The third round of National Family Health Survey (NFHS-3) has collected data from statistically representative slums of eight mega cities of India for the first time, so it would be very interesting to have a comparative study of contraceptive use among currently married women living in slum and non-slum in cities in India.

Objective

The aim of this study is to examine the differential and determinant of contraceptive use with demographic as well as health consequences among slum and non-slum dwellers in Mumbai city.

Data Sources

This study utilizes the data obtained from National Family Health Survey-3, which was conducted in 2005–06, covering 29 states in India, comprised about 99 per cent of India's population. The NFHS-3 survey is suitably designed to provide estimates of important indicator on the family welfare, nuptiality, fertility, mortality, child health and nutrition. It also provides information about reproductive health, tuberculosis and malaria. For the first time in 2005–06, NFHS collected data for slum and non-slum population of eight mega cities, namely, Delhi (3,106), Mumbai (2,159), Kolkata (2,471), Chennai (2,060), Meerut (2,713), Indore (2,280), Hyderabad (3,140), and Nagpur (2,979) on health-related issues and population estimates, which provide us ample opportunities to look at the demographic and socio-economic determinant of contraceptive use and effect of accessibility of contraceptive use among slum and non-slum dwellers of selected cities in India. The present study has utilized data on married women belonging to the age group of 15 to 49 years living in only Mumbai city.

Method

The study uses bivariate and multivariate techniques to understand the contraceptive behaviour among currently married women living in slums and non-slums in Mumbai. Multinomial logistic regression has been applied to examine the association of socio-demographic variables with contraceptive use.

Contraceptive Prevalence

Contraceptive prevalence is one of the principal determinates of fertility. The contraceptive prevalence rate is defined as the percentage of currently married women in the age group of 15–49 years, who are currently using a contraceptive method or whose husbands are using a contraceptive method.

Contraceptive use, as a dependent variable, has been classified into three categories, i.e., modern method, traditional method and not using any method and *independent variables* are age group, education level, caste, religion, occupation, number of living children, standard of living index, mass media exposure and family planning message.

Multinomial Logistic Regression Analysis

Multinomial logistic regression is the most appropriate technique in a situation where the dependent variable is categorical but has more than two outcomes (Choe, 1985). The model permits the study of the effect of a unit change in the independent variable on the dependent variable considering the simultaneous effects of several variables. A multinomial logistic regression model is the generalization of the binary (or logistic) regression model. In the binary model, a binary outcome (0 or 1) of events is modelled. If p is the probability of outcome being one, then the model specifies where b_k represents the coefficients of each of the predictor variables included in the model, while e_k is an error term. In [p/(1–p)] represents the natural logarithm of the odds of the outcome. We have estimated the adjusted percentage for the multinomial logit model by using an excel sheet. The most convenient way to represent the effects of the predictor variable on p is in the form of an MCA table. To measure of goodness of fit pseudo R square is used in multinomial logit regression.

$$In\frac{p}{1-p}=\Sigma b_k x_k + e_k$$

Results and Discussion

Level of Contraceptive Use in Mumbai

Table 1 shows that the prevalence of contraceptive method is higher in non-slum dwellers compared to slum dwellers in Mumbai city. The analysis shows that huge differentials exist in terms of the prevalence of modern and traditional contraceptive methods among slum and non-slum dwellers. The prevalence of modern methods, like IUD, condom and female sterilization, are higher in non-slum area. However, in slums traditional methods as periodic abstinence is higher in among slum dwellers.

Table1 *Level of Contraceptive Methods Use Among Slum and Non-slum Dwellers in Mumbai*

Contraceptive Methods	*Mumbai*	
	Slum	*Non-slum*
Not Using	45.3	36.1
Modern Methods		
Pill	2.8	1.8
IUD	3.6	7.7
Condom	6.6	11
Female Sterilization	38.1	40.4
Traditional Methods		
Periodic Abstinence	2.3	1.5
Withdrawal	0.9	1.3

Differentials of Contraceptive Methods in Mumbai

Table 2 presents the contraceptive prevalence of modern and traditional methods among currently married women living in slum and non-slum areas in Mumbai. The prevalence of modern method is higher among late adult women while middle adulthood women of slum have higher contraceptive prevalence of traditional method followed by slum and non-slum women. Primary educated women among slum and non-slum areas have the highest contraceptive prevalence of modern method. Likewise, Scheduled Caste (SC)/Scheduled Tribe (ST) women have higher prevalence of modern method compared to Other Backward Class (OBC) and other women, while traditional method prevalence among other category women was the highest. Contraceptive prevalence of modern method was found higher among Hindu women compared to women belonging to other religions. However, this similar picture is not seen in case of the traditional method. The proportion of working women using contraceptive methods was considerably higher compared to non-working women for both types of methods. The women having two children have the highest use of modern methods, while the traditional method used among women with one child was large in slum as well as non-slum areas. For the women belonging to high SLI category, the uses of modern methods were high in both areas. Among the women having partial exposure to mass media, and those having no exposure to family planning messages, the use of modern method was prevalent.

Table 2 *Contraceptive Prevalence Among Slum and Non-Slum Dwellers in Mumbai According to Background Characteristics*

Background Characteristics	*Contraceptive Methods*			
	Modern Method		*Traditional Method*	
	Slum	*Non-Slum*	*Slum*	*Non-Slum*
Age Group				
Early Adulthood	40.5	45.2	1.8	2.2
Middle	63.0	68.8	4.6	3.5
Late Adulthood	66.4	70.4	2.2	2.6
Education				
No Education	58.0	72.9	1.3	0.0
Primary	63.9	73.7	0.0	0.0
Secondary & Above	53.4	57.6	3.9	3.6
Caste				
Others	55.3	61.0	2.7	1.7
SC/ST	58.8	67.4	1.0	2.2
OBC	55.4	57.9	5.4	8.8
Religion				
Hindu	58.8	62.8	2.6	2.4
Muslim	44.2	55.6	2.7	0.0
Others	50.9	58.8	5.6	5.9
Occupation				
Not Working	52.5	58.4	2.3	1.9
Working	63.0	66.7	4.9	4.9
Number of Living Children				
No Child	5.1	11.8	1.7	0.0
1 Child	49.5	62.7	4.3	4.2
2 Children	73.8	82.6	1.9	1.1
3+ Children	40.0	75.0	3.3	0.0
Standard of Living Index				
Low	25.0	0.0	0.0	0.0
Middle	55.7	0.0	3.0	0.0
High	55.6	61.4	2.9	2.8
Mass Media Exposure				
No Exposure	19.4	25.0	2.8	0.0
Partial Exposure	59.9	65.3	3.5	4.0
Full Exposure	53.5	58.4	2.5	1.9
Exposure to Family Planning Message				
No Exposure	56.3	36.2	3.0	4.3
Any Exposure	52.3	36.0	3.1	2.6

Determinant of Contraceptive Use in Mumbai

To understand the correlates of contraceptive use of currently married women, a multinomial logistic regression model has been used considering that dependent variable is categorical having more than two categories. The dependent variable has been categorized into three categories, namely, not using method, modern methods and gravitational methods.

Table 3 *MCA Shows Adjusting Percentage for Contraceptive Use of Currently Married Women of Age Group 15–49, 2005–06*

Background Characteristics	*Contraceptive Method*					
	Not Using Method		*Modern Method*		*Traditional Method*	
	Adjusted %		*Adjusted %*		*Adjusted %*	
	Slum	*Non-Slum*	*Slum*	*Non-Slum*	*Slum*	*Non-Slum*
Age Group						
Early Adulthood®	53.9	56.8	39.9	31.8	6.2	11.4
Middle	66.7	67.7	28.9***	18.5***	4.5***	13.8***
Late Adulthood	59.4	52.4	35.1	39.5***	5.4	8.1***
Education						
No Education®	58.7	60.6	35.8	30.3	5.5	9.1
Primary	63.1	64.0	31.9	25.8	4.9**	10.2
Secondary & Above	73.8	60.1	22.7	27.8	3.5	12.1
Caste						
Others®	59.8	62.4	34.8	28.9	5.4	8.6
SC/ST	64.3	61.5	30.9	28.6	4.8	9.9
OBC	60.8	56.3	33.9	30.2	5.2	13.5
Religion						
Hindu®	64.1	62.4	31.1	26.0	4.8	11.6
Muslim	46.6	53.3	46.2***	38.6***	7.2***	8.1***
Others	57.5	55.0	36.8	29.0	5.7	16.0
Occupation						
Not Working®	57.8	56.8	36.5	30.1	5.6	13.1
Working	68.8	68.7	27.0***	23.3***	4.2*	8.0***
Number of Living Children						
No Child®	6.0	11.4	81.4	85.2	12.6	3.4
1 Child	59.1	60.5	35.4***	25.2***	5.5***	14.3***

Cont'd...

...Cont'd

2 Children	81.6	76.9	15.9***	15.6***	2.5***	7.5***
3+ Children	68.8	63.4	27.0***	27.2***	4.2***	9.4***
Wealth Index						
Low®	45.8	65.0	47.0	28.5	7.3	6.5
Medium	57.2	62.3	37.1**	28.5	5.7**	9.2
High	64.2	60.1	31.0***	27.9	4.8***	11.9
Mass Media Exposure						
No Exposure®	46.2	44.4	46.6	45.3	7.2	10.3
Partial Exposure	61.1	60.3	33.7***	28.4***	5.2**	11.3
Full Exposure	61.8	62.1	33.1***	26.4***	5.1*	11.5
Exposure to Family Planning Message						
No Exposure®	60.6	59.4	34.2	30.8	5.3	9.8
Any Exposure	61.1	60.7	33.7	27.7	5.2	11.6

Level of significance: *** Significant at $p<0.01$, ** significant at $p<0.05$, * significant at $p<0.1$, ® = Reference category

Table 3 presents the results of multinomial logistic regression in terms of adjusted percentage showing the effect of various demographic and socio-economic variables on the likelihood of using contraceptives methods. However, the major emphasis is laid on the adjusted percentage for modern methods as the prime endeavour here is to understand the correlates which influence modern methods. It is clear that most of the variables included in the model (adjusted percentage of modern methods) have statistically significant effect in explaining the likelihood of using modern methods in the slum as well as in the non-slum areas. The predictors which significantly affect the prevalence of modern methods after controlling others variables include age group of currently married women, education, caste, religion, occupation, number of living children, standard of living index, mass media exposure and exposure to family planning messages. The results of the multinomial analysis for slum and non-slum as a whole reinforce the importance of age group of women, religion, occupation, number of living children and mass media exposure as the most important determinant of modern methods of contraception.

Results indicate that the women belonging to middle and late adulthood age groups in non-slum areas are more likely to use modern methods. The likelihood of using modern methods by the religion, as reported by Muslim compared to Hindu was significantly high in both areas. An interesting finding that has emerged from the analysis is that the prevalence of modern methods among non-working women is higher compared to working women in the slum as well as non-slum areas but in these slums, the prevalence is higher compared to non-slum areas. The likelihood of using modern methods is higher among women having no children compared to those who have one, two, and three and more children in both areas. The prevalence of modern contraceptive use is higher among those who belong to the high standard of living index only in the slums. The use of modern family planning methods is lower among those having partial and full exposure to mass media compare to no exposure to mass media.

Conclusion

The findings show that there is a wide difference in prevalence of modern contraceptive method and traditional contraceptive method among slum and non-slum dwellers in the city of Mumbai. It also indicates that as the age of the women increases, the prevalence of modern method in slum and non-slum rises. Working women living in slum areas are found to have better knowledge about contraceptive methods compared to non-working women. The use of contraceptive is higher among women having two children in the non-slum areas compared to slum areas.

The results of the multinomial logistic regression model in terms of adjusted percentage have shown the effect of age group of women, religion, occupation, number of living children, standard of living index and mass media exposure have statistically significant effect on the likelihood of use of contraceptive methods after controlling for the confounding variables. The slum/non-slum difference in contraceptive prevalence is small in Mumbai. However, middle age women are more likely to use modern contraceptive methods in both slum and non-slum areas. It is interesting to know that women in the slum areas are more likely to use modern contraceptive methods than their counterparts. Another important finding is, contrary to popular belief, women belonging to the Muslim religion, irrespective of their place of residence, are more likely to use modern contraceptive methods. The number of living children has a significant impact on the use of contraceptive. Women belonging to middle and high categories of the standard of living index in slum areas are more likely to use modern contraceptives than their non-slum counterparts.

Policy Implications

- To make it effective, programmes must include counselling and education to help women. Separate fact from invention regarding health concern and side effects of methods.
- Efforts to promote societal acceptance of contraceptive use can help women overcome the cultural and societal barriers to use contraceptive and achieve their desired family size.
- Policy and programme efforts should encourage women to have fewer children and support to use modern and effective family planning methods.

Limitations of the Study

- The study could not analyse the trends of contraceptive use because data is only available for one point of time.
- Sample size was very small in some of the categories in independent variables.

References

Ashoke, S., S. John and M. Jayanti (2000). 'The KAP-Gap in Nepal: Reasons for Non-use of Contraception among Couples with an Unmet Need for Family Planning'. *Asia-Pacific Population Journal*, 6 (1): 25–38.

Census (2001). *Provisional Population Totals: Series 1*. New Delhi: Government of India.

Coale, N. (1997). 'The Demographic Transition: A Summary, Some Lesson and Some Observation'. In J. Lee and K. Kazumasa (eds), *Fertility Transition of the East Asian Populations*. Honolulu: The University Press of Hawaii.

Government of India (2000). *Social Marketing Police*. New Delhi: Ministry of Health and Family Welfare.

IIPS (2000). *Reproductive and Child Health Project: Rapid Household Survey*. Phases I & II. Mumbai: International Institute for Population Sciences.

Kayembe, P. et al. (2003). 'Prevalence and Determinants of the Use of Modern Contraceptive Methods in Kinshasa'. *Contraception*, 74: 400–06.

Marston, C. and J. Cleland (2003). 'Relationships between Contraception and Abortion'. *International Family Planning Perspectives*, 29 (1): 6–13.

McNay, K., P. Arokiasamy and R. Cassen (2003). 'Why are Uneducated Women in India Using Contraception? A Multilevel Analysis'. *Population Studies*, 57 (1): 21–40.

NFHS (2000). *Final Reports of the National Family Health Survey 1998–99*. Mumbai, India: International Institute for Population Sciences.

Nguyen, M. et al. (2002). 'Accessibility and Use of Contraceptives in Vietnam'. *International Family Planning Perspectives*, 28 (4): 214–19.

Reddy, P. (1984). 'Differential Contraceptive Use among the Slum and Non-slum Dwellers: A Study of Hyderabad City'. *Health and Population Perspectives and Issues*, 7 (2): 115–28.

Ross, J., K. Hardee, E. Momfold and S. Eid (2000). 'Contraceptive Method Choice in Developing Countries'. *International Family Planning Perspectives*, 28 (1): 32–40.

Shaw, A. (1988). 'Fertility and Child Spacing among the Urban Poor in a Third World City: The Case of Calcutta, India'. *Human Ecology*, 16: 329–42.

6 Economic Impact of Illness on the Nepalese Community in Mumbai

Anisha Thomas

> 'I will remember that I do not treat a fever chart, a cancerous growth, but a sick human being, whose illness may affect the person's family and economic stability. My responsibility includes these related problems, if I am to care adequately for the sick.'
>
> —Louis Lasagna in 'A Modern Hippocratic Oath', 2005

Impoverishment is said to have occurred when asset depletion and income loss together lead to the fall of consumption levels below the minimum needed. Ill-health is one of the major causes of impoverishment of a population, as increased spending on treatment and related expenditures and decreasing wage earning capacity take their toll on households. Further, it is recognized that differences in health status exist between different social groups and it has been shown that the vulnerable and disadvantaged bear heavier burden as compared to the wealthy (Whitehead, Dahlgren and Evans, 2001). It has also been documented that one of the most advantaged groups in the cities are the migrants. Migrants usually not only struggle to adapt to newer conditions but also sometimes face discrimination. This discrimination is not only reflected in the way they are treated in the labour market or in social space but also in terms of access to different kinds of essential services such as healthcare. They must also overcome barriers such as lack of awareness, language, culture and exclusion and unfamiliarity with the health system in the receiving country. Most importantly the financing of expenditures on health acts as a deterrent from seeking medical attention. This exacerbates the problem as households delay seeking medical attention in the hope of avoiding expenditure and in doing so increasing costs which could have been avoided had treatment been sought earlier.

The vicious cycle of poverty and ill health has been the focus of many studies in the past (World Bank, 2000; Wagstaff et al., 2001; Wagstaff, 2002) and has led to the growing consensus that this is an iniquitous state of affairs. Wagstaff and Van Doorslaer argue that expenditures on health are involuntary and outside of the control of the household and, therefore, must be borne by communities as a whole in order to limit the crippling effects and widening of inequality. Similarly, in the case of migrant communities, there arises the question of how healthcare of the people is to be financed as local population themselves struggle with limited resources.

A study of the economic impact of illness on the Nepalese community in Mumbai was undertaken as it was felt that the needs of international migrant communities in India are largely ignored. We make a distinction here between migrants from developed countries and migrants from other developing nations and restrict ourselves here to the latter, which form a much larger but weaker group.

This paper is divided into four parts – the first is a short introduction to the history of the Nepalese diaspora in India; the second is the methodology, assumptions and limitations of the study; and the third part is a presentation and discussion of the results followed by the conclusion.

Nepalese Diaspora in India

International relations in the South Asian subcontinent have usually been tense and occasionally interspersed without bursts of violence. The relationship between India and Nepal is remarkable in its degree of openness and stability. This can be attributed to the similarities in cultures, religions and languages as well as shared history. This has contributed to the easy movement of people between the two countries. It was further formalized by the signing of the Treaty of Peace and Friendship between India and Nepal in 1950.

It is noted that the migration of Nepalese people to India in pursuit of employment is not a new phenomenon and is a trend that has been beneficial to both countries. For example, the Ghurkha regiment which primarily comprises members of the Ghurkha tribe from Nepal has a long and distinguished record of service in the Indian Army. Conversely, remittances from migrants mainly to India have contributed significantly to the economy of Nepal (Lokshin et al., 2007; Thieme, 2003).

There are many factors which trigger migration of population. Using Marion Weiner's framework of international migration, Subedi (1991) suggests four variables that are mainly responsible for high rates of migration into India. These are – differential variables, affinity variables, spatial variables and access variables. The differential variables are the differences in wage and employment rates, affinity variables are the similarities in religion, culture and language as previously mentioned. Spatial variables include distance and cost of transportation, lastly access variables refer to the relative ease of entering and exiting the country (ibid.). Recently there has been a sharp increase in the rates of migration which has largely been attributed to the recent violence and political instability in Nepal (Williams and Pradhan, 2009).

Nepalese migrants have settled across India; however, cities such as Delhi and Mumbai are usually more favoured as final destinations and as a result have large communities with strong social networks. Documentation of the flow of migrants to India in general and Mumbai in particular has been made difficult by the existence of the open border policy. Estimation of the number of Nepalese in Mumbai is further complicated by the invisibility of the community in part due to the informality of employment that is usually undertaken, the apprehensions of the community in engaging with the authorities due to negative perceptions, as well as the existence of illegal and inhumane trafficking of Nepalese women.

Methodology, Assumptions and Limitations of the Study

The major focus of the study was to examine the economic impact of illness and for this data on both expenses and financing was collected. The data required for the completion of the study could broadly be classified into three types. First, data regarding the monetary impact of illness, that is out of pocket expenditures on treatment, transport, loss of wages, etc. Secondly, data regarding the use of healthcare facilities and the rationale for the use of the same as opposed to others. Thirdly, data regarding the financing of expenditures on healthcare and how households met the need for increased funds in case of large expenditures. In order to compliment the focus areas of the study, it was also decided to collect data regarding the willingness to pay for insurance, the public health programmes available and registered medical practitioners frequented.

Altogether, 80 household heads were interviewed. In some cases, where the head of the household was not available, an adult family member was interviewed. Open ended group discussions and informal personal discussions were also conducted. The recall period was set as one year prior to the survey. Five study sites were identified for the purpose of data collection – Airoli, Mankhurd Rabale, Sewri and Thane. Table 1 shows the number of households covered in each area by the sex of the household.

Table 1 *Area, Number of Households and Gender*

Area	*Households*	*Males*	*Females*	*Total*
Thane	12	29	18	47
Sewri	5	11	11	22
Mankhurd	31	82	70	152
Airoli	8	22	19	41
Rable	24	64	57	121
Total	80	208	175	383

In Thane, Mankhurd, Rabale and Sewri households were settled in close proximity. This was attributed to the migration pattern where a migrant first settles in a particular area and then assists relatives and friends who migrate later to find accommodation in the same area. This provides a measure of social security which becomes important as in many cases it is the only form of support. In Airoli, however, households were situated at a much greater distance from each other and there were no ties between the households.

Since the study largely focuses on the economic impact of illness, it takes into account costs alone and, therefore, is limited by the fact that it is not sensitive to quantity and quality of medical attention sought, that is it cannot differentiate between high cost combined with low use or low costs combined with high use. The other limitation of the study is its small sample size which can have some implications for inferences.

Results and Discussions

The male population was slightly more in number than females. It is not surprising given the pattern of migration where initially young men between the ages of 18 and 35 years migrate in search of employment, followed by their spouses after a short gap. This pattern also results in an uneven distribution dominated by youth and those in the working age groups with older people constituting a small percentage of the total population.

On the whole, the economic condition of the community is extremely depressed. One hundred thirty seven people belonging to 25 families had an income of less than ₹ 1,000 per month. In other words, they actually lived on less than ₹ 33 a day. Eighteen families with 101 members in total can be classified as Below Poverty Line (BPL) families given the official poverty line of the Indian Planning Commission of ₹ 965 expenditure per month for urban areas, which itself has been criticized as being a measure of 'destitution' and not 'poverty' (Patnaik, 2011; Agarwal, 2011). There is also an observed positive correlation between degree of poverty and size of family. Average household size in the study of population is 4.8 people per household. The average size of the family is found to be largest (5.9 people) where average income per person was the least (less that ₹ 1,000 per person) and is the smallest (4.4 people) where average income per person was the greatest (less than ₹ 4,000 per person).

Table 2 *Average Income and Expenditure Per Person Per Month*

Area	*Average Income Per Person/month*	*Average Pre-payment Expenditure/person*
Mankhurd	1,523	1,332
Rabale	1,315	1,016
Sewri	2,090	1,886
Thane	1,425	1,234
Airoli	1,902	1,573

Utilization of Healthcare Providers

Mumbai's healthcare needs are met by a combination of public and private providers as well as some health facilities run by non-governmental organizations (NGOs). The Brihanmumbai Municipal Corporation (Greater Mumbai Corporation – BMC) is the main provider for public healthcare services and has three Teaching Hospitals, 14 Municipal General Hospitals, 26 Maternity Homes, 185 Municipal Dispensaries and 176 Health Posts. The state government too has one medical college hospital, three general hospitals and two health units in the city (BMC, 2000; Government of Maharashtra, 2001). The respondents were aware about presence of private practitioners in the surrounding areas. Awareness of public healthcare providers was not as high as awareness of private practitioners. Respondents identified and reported visiting only a handful of the large public hospitals. In all areas except Thane, it was reported that a major deterrent to seeking healthcare services from public hospitals was the distance and travelling time involved. Respondents did not report discrimination when accessing these services but, at the same time, were careful not to reveal their nationality when seeking treatment.

Table 3 *Area-Wise Distribution of Choice of Healthcare Providers*

Area	*Private*	*%*	*Public*	*%*	*Combination*	*%*	*Total*
Airoli	5	63	0	0	3	38	8
Mankhurd	22	81	3	11	2	7	27
Rabale	23	72	9	28	0	0	32
Sewri	5	83	1	17	0	0	6
Thane	9	69	4	31	0	0	13
Total	64	74	17	20	5	6	86

The largest proportion of respondents using public hospitals among these areas was from Thane. It could be attributed to several factors. First, people in Thane are more aware about the public health facilities. It was the oldest settlement of the five areas sampled and, therefore, it is not surprising that the community might have become familiar with the public health services available in Thane. The distance from the nearest public hospital, in this case the Thane Municipal Hospital, was also the least distance from a site to a public hospital. This made it relatively easy to access the public health care services.

Respondents in Airoli either use private health services entirely or a combination of private and public but there were no instances of only public providers being used. This indicates that in Airoli, the first point of contact, when illness occurred, was a private practitioner and approached the public healthcare system when the private was inadequate or proving too expensive. This trend was brought up during the group discussions in all the areas. There was consensus among respondents across sample areas that in case of tertiary care or in case where respondents were aware that the treatment was going to be long drawn and expensive, there tended to use services provided by the public health system.

A related question included in the group discussion was why respondents spent such large amounts on healthcare to pay for private practitioners when the healthcare in public health system was cheaper. A respondent explained that the first time a member of the family fell ill, the closest source of treatment was a private practitioner. Due to the distance of the sites from government hospitals, these were approached only if it was felt that the cost of treatment or quality of care outweighed the advantages of seeking treatment closer.

Respondents from Mankhurd area showed the highest preference for private services with correspondingly low preference for public or a combination of public and private healthcare services. A review of the primary data shows that there were large expenditures on recurring or chronic illnesses such as malaria, pneumonia and fever. This is similar to the trend in Airoli with lack of information about the eventual cost of medical treatment. In such cases, the members of the household make small but frequent payments unaware of the fact that there are many more payments to be made. This situation hinders a household's ability to make rational decisions.

Thus, it can be seen that the decision-making about where to obtain treatment from was made difficult by the inability of the household members to judge at the onset of the illness. They were not sure if the treatment was going to be expensive. This hypothesis is reaffirmed in light of the evidence regarding the choice of health providers for pregnancies. There were three pregnancies reported in the entire survey – one from Airoli and two from Rabale. Despite being the two areas farthest from the public hospitals, it is seen that two only went to public hospitals and the third used a combination of both public and private hospitals. Pregnancy is one of the few medical conditions where it is possible to say without doubt that considerable expenditures will be incurred thus prompting the use of public hospital. More interesting still is the fact that the two households where the pregnancies were treated by public hospitals alone did not take any loans to pay off their expenditures. The household with third pregnancy which partially used private services needed to take a certain amount of loans to cover the expenditures incurred. It is possible to make an inference here that when an expense is predictable households cope by trying to self-insure as well as seeking public health services which are cheaper.

Table 4 *Income Range and Choice of Providers*

Monthly Income Per Person	*Private*	*Public*	*Combination*	*Total Incidences*	*Total Population*
Below 1,000	26	4	0	30	137
1,000–2,000	21	9	4	34	169
2,000–3,000	14	3	0	17	47
3,000–4,000	3	1	1	5	31

This leads us to the question of the nature of payments in health. Respondents revealed that very often the health services sought were emergency services – due in part to the delay in seeking treatment in the hope that illnesses would run their course without having to seek medical attention. Healthcare emergencies also carry with them the added burden of higher than normal costs of treatment as well as the sudden cash crunch. Respondents also opined that private practitioners often resorted to tactics such as prolonging treatment unnecessarily to justify high costs of treatment. In an interview with a private practitioner, under the condition of anonymity, stated that it was not a baseless allegation and that unethical practices were rife.

It was interesting to see that how households with different average per person incomes chose healthcare providers. It would be logical to assume that poorer households would show a marked preference for public healthcare services over private practitioners. The actual preferences shown were contrary to this. The households with the lowest per person income per month showed the most preference for private practitioners.

Financing Expenditures

As has emerged from the discussion above, the ability to pay plays a major role in determining if medical attention can be sought as well as the choice of health care providers. There also arises the question not only of direct costs associated with illness but also indirect costs such as loss of wages travelling expenses so on and so forth.

In Table 5, we see the minimum expenditure, the maximum expenditure and average expenditure on health incurred by a household. The calculation of maximum expenditure was at a household level and, therefore, included the health expenditures of all the members of the family. The average costs were calculated by dividing the sum of expenses on health care incurred in an area by the number of households who incurred such payments.

Table 5 *Consolidated Area-Wise Distribution of Health Expenditures Per Person*

Area	*Minimum Expenditure Per Year*	*Maximum Expenditure Per Year*	*Average Expenditure Per Year*
Airoli	1,000	25,000	10,625
Mankhurd	150	25,000	8,085
Rabale	200	26,000	4,812
Sewri	300	12,000	6,450
Thane	200	7,000	1,961

The average expenditure per household is largest in Airoli which, as was seen in Table 3, was the only area which utilized only private provisioning or a combination of private and public but never public provisioning alone. It also has the highest minimum expenditure. The lowest average expenditure was in Thane which, as has been seen before, due to the many advantages both geographical as well as social that it has over the other areas.

Coping Mechanisms

This section examines the data regarding the coping mechanisms adopted by the households when faced with expenditures on health. Table 6 gives an area-wise breakdown of the sources of funds to pay for expenditures. Respondents reported that they made payments using savings or by taking loans. The term loan was loosely used by respondents to mean either loan from formal institutions such as banks, borrowings from employers as well as borrowings from a moneylender. Borrowing from money lenders usually entailed keeping assets as collateral. During the group discussions and informal interviews, it emerged that borrowings from formal institutions was almost never undertaken due to the red tape and documents required. Borrowings from employers was a preferred strategy as a part of the loan was cut out of the future monthly income at source and interest was minimal, if charged at all. The drawback of this strategy was that it was possible only if a family member was regularly employed and had a good relationship with the employer.

Borrowings from moneylenders were charged at extremely high interest rates and further, in case of non-payment at any stage, the collateral was lost and this resulted in the loss of the asset as well as any instalments paid. This made it an extremely undesirable means of raising funds however, when no other options were available or in case of cash crunch due to emergencies where ready cash was required, this method was resorted to. Respondents also reported using the savings of the household to pay for expenditures. They also included borrowings from extended family members or neighbours under this category as it did not entail any interest. This was acceptable when paying for small medical expenditures; however, it was not a viable means of funding extremely large expenditures which were paid from using savings and thereby depleted the household's ability to absorb future health shocks and left them in a more vulnerable state than before.

Table 6 shows that Thane followed by Rabale had the lowest percentage of health expenses financed by loan-taking which is in line with its indicators in other tables. Airoli which had the highest average expenditure per year has the second highest percentage of expenditures financed by loan taking. Mankhurd had the highest percentage of expenditures on health financed by loan taking. This indicates that Mankhurd and Airoli have sacrificed future consumption in order to pay off expenditures in the present. Households in Sewri, on an average, financed expenditures on health equally from loans as well as savings.

Table 6 *Area-wise Coping Mechanism*

Area	*Loan*	*Savings*	*Total*	*% Loan*	*% Savings*	*Total*
Airoli	5	3	8	63	38	100
Mankhurd	19	8	27	70	30	100
Rabale	11	21	32	34	66	100
Sewri	3	3	6	50	50	100
Thane	2	11	13	15	85	100
Total	40	46	86	47	53	100

In Table 7, average loan was calculated by dividing the total loan taken in an area by number of households taking loans. The maximum loan indicates the highest total loan taken by a household in an area. This is important to underline since some households have taken more than one loan to finance expenditures arising at different times in the year or arising out of the expenditures in treating more than one member of the household.

Table 7 *Area-wise Distribution of Size of Loan*

Area	*Minimum Loan*	*Maximum Loan*	*Average Loan*
Airoli	1,000	28,000	13,250
Mankhurd	2,000	35,000	11,200
Rabale	1,000	31,000	10,444
Sewri	1,000	12,000	10,667
Thane	7,000	7,000	7,000
Total	1,000	35,000	10,939

The minimum loan is ₹ 1,000 in both Airoli and Sewri indicating that some households in these areas were unable to raise even low amounts from savings or borrowings and reflects very poor financial condition. The lowest average loan was in Thane where only two loans were taken by two households and both for ₹ 7,000 which is why the minimum, maximum and average loan were the same amount. The highest average loan is in Airoli which is not surprising as it was also the area with the highest average expenses.

Catastrophic Expenditure

A catastrophic threshold is said to be a pre-defined percentage of pre-payment income (PPI) or ability to pay above which expenditures on health care should not cross. This is an ethical and value laden parameter which is necessarily arbitrary. When an expenditure made by a household crosses this threshold it is said to have been a catastrophic expenditure.

Calculating on the basis of PPI has the drawback of not being able to show if the expenditure was catastrophic alone or if it was impoverishing as well. This problem can be seen in the following example. Given that the catastrophic threshold is set at 10 per cent of PPI. If a household with two members and a total income of ₹ 2,00,000 per month incurs ₹ 20,000 as health expenditure such an expenditure would be considered catastrophic but it would not be impoverishing as the post payment income is still well above the poverty line and therefore, most studies use the ability to pay where difference between income and essential expenditures is used. It was reported that in almost all the households, all prepayment expenditures are essential and non-negotiable. Therefore, the calculations were completed using PPI. This was done at a household level as when a family member fell sick, the expenditures were incurred by the household and the impoverishing effects were also felt by the household unit as a whole.

Expenditures on health were taken to be catastrophic if they exceed 10 per cent of households PPI which has been used by most studies in the past (Wagstaff and Van Doorslaer, 2003; Ranson, 2002; Pradhan and Prescott, 2002; O'Donnell and Van Doorslaer, 2005). While the threshold for what constituted a catastrophic payment was fixed at 10 per cent, the calculation was also carried forward to 15 per cent, 20 per cent and 40 per cent to see how many households overshot the threshold and by how much.

Large parts of the communities in the study are extremely vulnerable to health shocks. Data confirm to the trends that have slowly emerged from the data as it was analysed. Thane, as seen throughout the analysis, had the best indicators and it can be inferred that even in terms of catastrophic payments only one household crossed the threshold (15% of total capacity to pay). Sewri too had only one household which crossed the threshold (10% of total capacity to pay). Rabale showed the highest number of households (8) who crossed the catastrophic threshold; however, none crossed the 40 per cent threshold which as was the case in both Mankhurd and Airoli. The fact that any households crossed the 10 per cent threshold is itself a worrying trend and crossing of the 40 per cent threshold is much more alarming. The closet point of reference to compare the results obtained is to the national averages is Van Doorslaer's et al. (2006) study on Asian countries which calculated that on an average, in India, 10 per cent of the population made out-of-pocket payments equal to or greater than 10 per cent of total household expenditure. In this study, 29 per cent of the population surveyed spent equal to or greater than 10 per cent of total household income. The intensity of the expenditures was also greater as about 2 per cent of the population made OOP payments equal to or greater than 25 per cent of their pre-payment expenditures whereas in the study, it was shown that 16 per cent of the community made payments equal or greater than 20 per cent of their income. Given that the difference in income and expenditures was marginal, it is still possible to see that the Nepalese community was much worse off than the national average.

Conclusion

There were several points which were thrown into high relief over and over again during the study. It is possible to learn what is effective in reducing the number of households which face catastrophic expenses as well as reducing the debit that households take on to finance such debit. The reasons why one particular area of migrants was better off than the other areas, in this case why households in Thane did not bear as heavy a burden as the remaining areas when it came to expenditures on health, should be studied in order to be replicated in other areas in order to improve the standard of living of the vulnerable in those areas as well. It must also be acknowledged that certain parameters cannot be replicated for example the social capital of a community is very difficult to create in another community. But some, such as community insurance, awareness of the public services available, better access to hospitals, etc., make a huge difference.

Expenditures on health, as we have seen in the discussion, are not normal expenditures. They are unpredictable and seem non-discretionary and this makes them difficult to factor into a household budget. Expenditures on health eat into other consumption and restrict a household not only from improving its economic standing but, if anything, reduce its stability. Any serious effort to address the problems of urban poverty cannot ignore the damaging effects of ill health. Short-term knee-jerk approaches are no replacement for sustained long-term planning and investment in public services without which progress is unforeseeable.

References

Agarwal, S. (2011). 'Theory of Inhumanism'. *The Sunday Times*, 5 June. Retrieved from: http://www.thesundayindian.com/article_print.php?article_id=15501 on 15 January 2012.

Asfaw, A. and J. von Braun (2004). 'Is Consumption Insured against Illness? Evidence on Vulnerability of Households to Health Shocks in Rural Ethiopia'. *Economic Development and Cultural Change*, 53 (1): 115–29.

Benach, J., C. Muntaner, H. Chung and F. Benavides (2010). 'Immigration, Employment Relations and Health: Developing a Research Agenda'. *American Journal of Industrial Medicine*, 53 (4): 338–43.

Braveman, P. and S. Gruskin (2003). 'Poverty, Equity, Human Rights and Health'. *Bulletin of the World Health Organization*, 81 (7): 539–45.

Brihanmumbai Municipal Corporation (2000). BMC Health Care Services: A Cost Analysis. Unpublished document prepared as a part of Women and Health Project, BMC, Mumbai: CEHAT.

Chowdhury, S. (2011). 'Financial Burden of Transient Morbidity: A Case Study of Slums in Delhi'. *Economic and Political Weekly*, XLVI (33), August 13.

Claeson, M. et al. (2001). *Health, Nutrition and Population: Poverty Reduction Strategy Sourcebook*. Washington, DC: The World Bank.

Corbett, E. et al. (2003). 'The Growing Burden of Tuberculosis: Global Trends and Interactions with the HIV Epidemic'. *Arch Intern Med*, 163 (9), 12 May.

Dilip, T. and R. Duggal (2003). *Demand for Public Health Services in Mumbai*. Mumbai: Centre for Enquiry into Health and Allied Themes.

Fewtrell, L. et al. (2007). *Water, Sanitation and Hygiene: Quantifying the Health Impact at National and Local Levels in Countries with Incomplete Water Supply and Sanitation Coverage*. Environmental Burden of Disease Series No. 15, Geneva: World Health Organization.

Gertler, P. and J. Gruber (1997). 'Insuring Consumption against Illness'. National Bureau of Economic Research, Working Paper Series No. 6035.

Gottret, P. and G. Schieber (2006). *Health Financing Revisited: A Practitioner's Guide*. Washington, DC: The World Bank.

Government of Maharashtra (2001). *Performance Budget 2001–2003*. Medical Education and Drugs Department, Aurangabad, India.

Lasagna, L. (2005). 'A Modern Hippocratic Oath'. Retrieved from: www.aapsonline.org on 7 February 2012.

Lokshin, M., M. Bontch-Osmolovski and E. Gliskaya (2007). 'Work-related Migration and Poverty Reduction in Nepal'. Policy Research Working Paper, WPS 4231, The World Bank.

Marmot, M. (2005). 'Social Determinants of Health Inequalities'. *Lancet*, 365: 1099–104.

O'Donnell, O. et al. (2005). 'Who Pays for Health Care in Asia?'. EQUITAP Working Paper # 1, Erasmus University, Rotterdam and IPS, Colombo.

——. (2007). 'The Incidence of Public Spending on Health Care: Comparative Evidence from Asia'. *World Bank Economic Review*, 21 (1): 93–123.

O'Donnell, O. and E. Van Doorslaer (2005). 'Explaining the Incidence of Catastrophic Expenditures on Health Care: Comparative Evidence from Asia'. EQUITAP Working Paper # 5, Erasmus University, Rotterdam and IPS, Colombo.

Patnaik, U. (2011). 'How Little Can a Person Live on?'. *The Hindu*, 30 September. Retrieved from: http://www.thehindu.com/opinion/lead/article2497773.ece on 15 January 2012.

Peters, D. et al. (2001). *Better Health Systems for India's Poor*. Washington, DC: The World Bank.

Pradhan, M. and N. Prescott (2002). 'Social Risk Management Options for Medical Care in Indonesia'. *Health Economics*, 11: 431–46.

Ranson, M. (2002). 'Reduction of Catastrophic Health Care Expenditures by a Community-based Health Insurance Scheme in Gujarat, India: Current Experiences and Challenges'. *Bulletin of the World Health Organization*, 80 (8): 613–21.

Regional Plan for Mumbai Metropolitan Region 1996–2011 (1999). *Government Gazette*. Konkan Division, Maharashtra.

Roberts, A. (1965). 'Public Health Service Activities in Chronic Respiratory Diseases'. *Public Health Reports*, 80 (4): 336.

Russell, S. (2004). 'The Economic Burden of Illness for Households in Developing Countries: A Review of Studies Focusing on Malaria, Tuberculosis, and Human Immunode?ciency Virus/Acquired Immunode?ciency Syndrome'. *American Journal of Tropical Medicine and Hygiene*, 71 (2): 147–55.

Segall, M. et al. (2000). *Health Care Seeking by the Poor in Transitional Economies: The Case of Vietnam.* Brighton: Institute of Development Studies, University of Sussex.

Subedi, B. (1991). 'International Migration in Nepal: Towards an Analytical Framework'. *Nepalese Studies*, 18 (1): 83–102.

Szucs, T. (1999). 'The Socioeconomic Burden of Influenza'. *Journal of Antimicrobial Chemotherapy*, 44 (1): 11–15.

Singh, D.P. (2007). 'Migration in Mumbai: A Review of 50 Years'. *Demography India*, 36: 315–27.

Thieme, S. (2003). *Savings and Credit Associations and Remittances: The Case of Far West Nepalese Labor Migrants in Delhi, India*. Geneva: International Labor Office.

Upreti, B. (2002). *The Marginal Migrants: A Study of Nepali Emigrants in India*. Delhi: Kalinga Publications.

United Nations (2009). *International Migration 2009*. United Nations: Department of Economic and Social Affairs, Population Division.

Van Doorslaer, E. et al. (2006). 'Effect of Health Payments on Poverty Estimates in 11 Countries in Asia: An Analysis of Household Survey Data'. *The Lancet*, 368 (14): 1357–64.

Wagstaff, A. and E. Van Doorslaer (2003). 'Catastrophe and Impoverishment in Paying for Health Care: With Applications to Vietnam 1993–1998'. *Health Economics*, 12: 921–34.

Wagstaff, A. (2002). 'Poverty and Health Sector Inequalities'. *Bulletin of the World Health Organization*, 80 (2).

Williams, N. and M. Pradhan (2009). 'Political Conflict and Migration: How has Violence and Political Instability Affected Migration Patterns in Nepal?'. PSC Research Report No. 09–677, May.

Whitehead, M., G. Dahlgren and T. Evans (2001). 'Equity and Health Sector Reforms: Can Low-income Countries Escape the Medical Poverty Trap?'. *The Lancet*, 358 (9284): 833–36.

Weiss, J. and J. Montgomery (2004). 'Great Expectations: Microfinance and Poverty Reduction in Asia and Latin America'. ADB Institute Discussion Paper No. 14, The Asian Development Bank Institute.

World Bank (2004). *The Millennium Development Goals for Health: Rising to the Challenges.* Washington, DC: The World Bank.

——. (2000). *World Development Report 2000–2001: Attacking Poverty.* Oxford: Oxford University Press.

World Health Organization (2003). 'International Migration, Health and Human Rights'. *Health and Human Rights Publication*, 4 December.

——. (2010). *Health of Migrants – The Way Forward: Report of a Global Consultation*. Madrid, Spain, 3–5 March.

Xu, K. et al. (2003). 'Household Catastrophic Health Expenditure: A Multicountry Analysis'. *Lancet*, 362 (9378): 111–17.

7 Lifestyle and Decision-making Among Youth in Selected Mumbai Slums

Mahesh Nath Singh and Aditya Singh

Around the world, the term 'youth' generally refers to a time of life that is neither childhood nor adulthood, but rather somewhere in between. Youth is also identified with a particular mindset or attitude. Youth is an individual aged between 15 and 24 years. They constituted slightly more than 20 per cent of the Indian population in 2001. Not only does this cohort represent India's future in the socio-economic and political realms, but also its experiences are going to determine India's achievement of its goal of population stabilization to a large extent and the extent to which the nation will be able to harness its demographic dividend. While today's youth are healthier, more urbanized and better educated than earlier generations, social and economic vulnerabilities persist. They are often vulnerable to substance, physical and sexual abuse. In their transition to adulthood, they generally face several other risks apart from substance, physical and sexual abuse.

Many studies in the past have looked into substance abuse in India. However, most of them have looked at men in general. Among males aged 15–24 years, unmarried males are highly mobile and difficult to be contacted. Despite the fact that youth are more prone to substance abuse, very few studies examining this issue have been conducted across India. Research and data regarding these issues for unmarried males in Mumbai slums is almost absent. Most of the studies on single males have been conducted either in observation homes or via surveys. Looking at the dearth of research and data available on this issue, we interviewed the youth (15–24 years) living in three slums of Mumbai, namely, Mankhurd, Mahim and Andheri in 2009. Our basic objective was to learn about their access to assess substance, physical and sexual abuse and analyse factors associated with them. However, this paper explores the patterns, characteristics and attitude towards substance abuse among unmarried males of Mumbai slums. It also looks at the role of youth in the decision-making within the families in slums of Mumbai. Thus, the present study is concerned about protecting and improving the lives of the unmarried males of Mumbai slums.

Definitions of Slum

The word 'slum' is thought to have originated from the Irish phrase '*S lom é* (pron. s'lum ae) meaning 'it is a bleak or destitute place'. An 1812 English dictionary defined slum to mean 'a room' (Cassidy, 2007). In legislation, slums are defined as areas that are *'environmentally and structurally deficient'* (GoI, 1988). The 1981 Census of India, in the light of Slum Area Act 1956, defines slums as 'areas where buildings are unfit for human habitation for reasons such as dilapidation, overcrowding, faulty arrangement of streets, and lack of ventilation, light or sanitary facilities'. In other words, slums are a group of buildings, or areas characterized by over-crowding, deterioration, unhygienic condition or absence of facilities or amenities which because of these conditions or any of them endangers the health, safety or morals of its inhabitants or the community (Census of India, 2001). The *Britannica Encyclopedia* (1978) further defines a slum as a congested urban or suburban residential district characterized by deterioration and unsanitary housing, boarding and social disorganization. According to Ford Foundation, a slum is a residential area in which the housing is so deteriorated and substandard or as unwholesome as to be a menace to the health, safety, morality or welfare of the occupants (Rathor, 2003). Thus, it can be seen that there is not one agreed definition of 'slums' around the world. However, it is not very difficult to reach a consensus as to what characterizes a slum.

Data and Methodology

The Study Area

This study is carried out in Greater Mumbai (Municipal Corporation), the capital of Maharashtra state. This densely populated and highly industrialized urban location is situated at the west coast of India. Greater Mumbai (Municipal Corporation) constitutes a geographical area of 43,777 square kilometres (Rama Rao, 2005). According to Census 2001, 11.9 million persons – 6.6 million male (55.2%) and 5.3 million females (44.8%) – reside in Greater Mumbai. The sex ratio is 811 females per thousand males and the population density is about 272 persons per square kilometre. The city, which is also the capital of Maharashtra, holds 12 per cent of total population of the state and about 1 per cent of the country's population (Census of India, 2001).

Design of the Study

Roughly half of Mumbai's population lives in urban slums which are spread throughout the city. Some slum localities are very densely populated. Multi-stage sampling design has been adopted for this research work. Primary data has been collected from slums that are representative of the city's slum population and cover different segments of the slum population. The Brihanmumbai Municipal Corporation has administratively divided the city into six zones. Each zone is further divided into a few wards and the wards are then divided into sections. We have selected three zones, namely, Zone 2, Zone 3, Zone 5, randomly. In the second stage of sampling, one ward with a slum settlement is randomly selected. The wards selected from different zones are: Zone 2 (Ward G/North), Zone 3 (Ward K/East), and Zone 5 (Ward M/East). The next stage of sampling consists of selection of sections wherein one section is randomly picked-out from each of the chosen wards. The sections selected from above-mentioned wards are – Ward G/North – Mahim, Ward K/East – Andheri, Ward M/East – Mankhurd. Since it was proposed to collect information from 688 households located in the selected slums for the study, the total number of households selected from each slum is 229 (688/3 = 229 approximately). The households in each slum were listed clockwise starting from the north-east corner. Slums, with more than 300 households, were segmented. After listing is done, households are selected by systematic random sampling procedure. Out of 676 households, about two per cent resulted in non-response. The respondent for this study is the head of the household or a responsible member of the family aged 18 years and above.

We found 676 unmarried males from 676 households selected for the study. Since households had more than one youth person, using KISH table only 427 people aged 15–24 years were interviewed to know about their lifestyles and other aspects. The rationale behind selecting only male members is the high prevalence of substance use (tobacco and alcohol use was 41 and 33 per cent, respectively, among Mumbai male and females (IIPS and Macro International, 2005–06). This study is a part of 427 youth selected from 676 households from Mumbai slums. The information was collected from three slums of Mumbai, viz. Mankhurd, Andheri and Mahim, during December 2008 and February 2009.

Simple bivariate analysis has been used to understand the distribution of youth by background characteristics and binary logistic regression analysis has been conducted to examine the association of different socio-economic characteristics with the dependent variables (substance abuse and decision-making). The results of regression have been presented using odds ratios.

Results

Socio-demographic Characteristics of Youth in Mumbai Slums

Table 1 presents the distribution of the youth by selected socio-economic and demographic characteristics in Mumbai slums. The youths who belong to 15–19 year age group are more in slums compared to 20–24 year age group, and their percentage is highest in Ward M-East. On an average, 61 per cent individuals in Mumbai slums have higher education. However, in some wards like in ward K-East, it is as high as 90 per cent. Although there are not many differentials among OBC and other castes in the slums of Mumbai as a whole, there exists a wide gap in case of ward G-North and ward M-East. A large number of Hindu youths live in G-North and K-East wards. In contrast, M-East ward presents a peculiar picture where the proportion of Muslims is four times that of Hindus. The proportion of students in these slums is high compared to people belonging to other occupational categories. The proportion of working youth varies from 27 per cent and 38 per cent, the highest being in K-East ward and the lowest in M-East ward. The percentage of youth who are working up to 8 hours and 9–11 hours, respectively, are almost similar in the slums of Mumbai. However, the ward-wise differential is higher in M-East ward. It is only in M-East ward that around 16 per cent of youth are working for 12 hours or more. About 44 per cent of youth earn between ₹ 3,001 to ₹ 5,000. This percentage is relatively higher in M-East ward (59%) compared to other Wards.

Table 1 *Percentage Distribution of the Youth by Selected Socio-economic and Demographic Characteristics in Mumbai Slums, 2009*

Background Characteristics	*Name of the Wards*			*Total*	
	Ward G-North	*Ward K-East*	*Ward M-East*	*Mumbai Slums*	*Number*
Age					
15–19	65.4	47.8	80.9	65.7	281
20–24	34.6	52.2	19.1	34.3	146
Level of Education					
Illiterate	1.3	—	1.6	0.9	4
Up to Primary	15.0	4.4	28.2	16.9	72
Above Primary–Up to Secondary	30.0	5.7	31.4	21.5	92
Higher	53.8	89.9	38.8	60.7	259
Caste					
SC/ST	40.0	15.7	7.0	16.4	70
OBC	52.2	40.9	39.0	42.3	180
Others	7.5	43.4	54.0	41.3	176
Religion					
Hindu	83.5	83.6	19.1	55.2	235
Muslim	13.9	14.5	80.9	43.7	186
Other	2.5	1.9	—	1.2	5
Occupation					
Non-working	23.5	3.8	26.5	17.5	75
Working	33.3	37.7	27.0	32.2	138
Domestic Help	3.7	6.3	1.6	3.7	16
Student	39.5	52.2	45.0	46.6	200

Cont'd...

...Cont'd

Working Hours					
Up to 8 Hours	42.3	63.3	33.3	48.2	66
9 to 12 Hours	57.7	36.7	51.0	46.0	63
More than 12 Hours	—	—	15.7	5.8	8
Monthly Income (in Rupees)					
Up to 3,000	4.9	0.6	11.6	6.3	27
3,001–5,000	39.5	28.9	59.3	44.3	190
5,001–10,000	39.5	38.4	26.5	33.3	143
10,001 and above	16.0	32.1	2.6	16.1	69
Wealth Index					
Poorest	11.4	—	44.7	21.9	93
Poorer	19	0.6	34.6	19.1	81
Middle	48.1	1.9	14.9	16.2	69
Richer	19.0	29.1	5.9	16.9	72
Richest	2.5	68.4	—	25.9	110
Number of Youth	80	159	188	100	427

Involvement of single males in decision-making is the lowest (14%) among the Scheduled Castes (SCs)/Scheduled Tribes (STs) and highest (36%) for others. Large differentials exist among different religious groups with regards to involvement of unmarried males in decision-making. More than one-third of Hindu unmarried males aged 15–24 years are involved in decision-making. One-third of the youth living in the Mumbai slums are involved in decision-making pertaining to the different type of family/household activities. Less than 3 per cent of one-third unmarried males belonging to other categories are involved in decision-making. In case of decision-making by occupation, it is found that around one-third students are involved in decisions-making. The highest percentage (39%) of involvement in decision-making is found among unmarried males (15–24 years) who are working. The economic status as measured by wealth index is another important factor that determines the involvement of unmarried males in decision-making. The involvement of unmarried males in decision-making fluctuates with the increase in one's economic status. Involvement in decision-making is the least (6%) among unmarried youth belonging to 'richer' quintile of wealth index.

Huge differentials are observed in the proportion of single males getting pocket money according to age. The proportion of unmarried males in the age group 15–19 years, getting pocket money is twice as much as those aged 20–24 years. About 57 per cent of highly educated unmarried males (15–24 years) get pocket money compared to only 25 per cent of those unmarried males who studied up to secondary level. The proportion of unmarried males (15–24 years) getting pocket money belonging to Other Backward Classes (OBCs) and others does not vary. However, the differential is glaring when we compare SC/ST with two other caste categories above mentioned. Only 11 per cent of the unmarried SC/ST males get pocket money as against 43 per cent of OBC males. About 53 per cent of unmarried Muslim males (15–24 years) get pocket money followed by Hindu males (46%). About two-thirds of all unmarried males (15–24 years) who are students get pocket money. There is a progressive decrease in the proportion of youth getting pocket money with an increase in the household economic status. For instance, among unmarried males (15–24 years) from the poorest wealth quintile, the proportion of youth getting pocket money is as high as 29 per cent, while in the highest wealth quintile; only 19 per cent youth get pocket money.

Table 2 *Percentage of Unmarried Males (15–24 years) According to Decision-making and Receiving Pocket Money by Background Characteristics in Mumbai Slums, 2009*

Background Characteristics	*Decision-making*		*Pocket Money*	
	Per cent	*Number*	*Per cent*	*Number*
Age				
15–19	61.0	86	82.5	198
20–24	39.0	55	17.5	42
Level of Education				
Illiterate	2.1	3	0.8	3
Up to Primary	16.9	24	16.7	40
Above Primary–Up to Secondary	26.1	36	25.1	60
Higher	54.9	78	57.3	137
Caste				
SC/ST	14.1	20	10.8	26

Cont'd...

...Cont'd

OBC	41.5	58	45.8	110
Others	44.4	63	43.3	104
Religion				
Hindu	39.0	55	46.4	108
Muslim	58.2	82	52.7	126
Other	2.8	4	0.8	2
Occupation				
Non-working	23.2	33	19.2	46
Working	39.4	56	17.1	41
Domestic Help	4.9	8	1.3	3
Student	32.4	46	62.5	150
Wealth Index				
Poorest	23.4	33	28.9	69
Poorer	25.5	36	22.2	53
Middle	22.0	31	16.3	38
Richer	6.4	9	13.4	32
Richest	22.7	32	19.2	46
Number of Youth	100.0	141	100.0	240

Socio-economic Differentials in Consumption of Intoxicating Substances

To have a better understanding of the lifestyle, it is necessary to have an insight into the behaviour of unmarried male slum dwellers with respect to usage or consumption of intoxicating substances. Socio-economic differentials are stark in many cases. It was found that 26 per cent of youth consume tobacco. However, the proportion of youth consuming tobacco rises to 60 per cent among young unmarried males. An increase in the level of education brings a decline in the proportion of males consuming 'intoxicating substances'. For instance, one-fourth of all primary educated unmarried males aged 15–24 years reported to consume intoxicating substance, while the same proportion was only 17 per cent among those who have higher education. About 13 per cent of SC/ST youth consume intoxicating substances. This proportion is considerably lower than OBCs (28%) and others (29%). As far religious groups, about 42 per cent of youth belonging to Muslim community use intoxicating substances while same proportion is considerably lower among Hindu youth (14%).

The proportion of youth consuming intoxicating substances varied according to the occupation of respondents. The consumption of intoxicants is lowest (15%) among students and highest (38%) among non-workers. A similar pattern can be seen in terms of alcohol consumption. The consumption of alcohol among students and those involved in household activity is less as compared to those who are either working or not working. Economic status of the respondent has an important bearing on the consumption habit related to intoxicating substances. As economic status improves, there is a decline in the consumption of intoxicating substances. The consumption of intoxicating substances is found to be the highest (48%) among the youth belonging to the poorest wealth quintile, whereas it is only 6 per cent among the richest wealth quintile.

Table 3 *Percentage of Unmarried Males (15–24 years) According to Consumption of Tobacco by Background Characteristics in Mumbai Slums, 2009*

Background Characteristics	*Tobacco Consumption*	*Number*
Age		
15–19	65.8	73
20–24	34.2	38
Level of Education		
Illiterate	1.8	2
Up to Primary	27.9	31
Above Primary–Up to Secondary	30.6	34
Higher	39.6	44
Caste		
SCs/STs	8.1	9
OBCs	45.9	51
Others	45.9	51
Religion		
Hindu	29.7	33
Muslim	70.3	78
Others	0.0	—

Cont'd...

...Cont'd

Occupation		
Non-working	25.5	28
Working	45.5	51
Domestic Help	2.7	3
Student	26.4	29
Wealth Index		
Poorest	40.0	45
Poorer	22.7	25
Middle	17.3	19
Richer	13.6	15
Richest	6.4	7
Number of Youth	100.0	111

Decision Taken by Youth and Parental Expectation

Involvement in Decision-making

Table 4 provides an idea about decision-making of young unmarried males in the slums of Mumbai. The crux of the analysis is that young single men residing in the slums of Mumbai are not much involved in decision-making. To be precise, around two-third of the youth are not involved in decision-making. Only 31 per cent of young unmarried males make their own decisions. Involvement of unmarried males aged 20–24 years in taking decisions related to family matters is 6 per cent higher (around 37%) as compared to the unmarried males aged less than 20 years. The involvement of illiterate unmarried males in decision-making is more than twice as much than those with some levels of education. Three-fourth of the illiterate unmarried males in the Mumbai slums participate in taking decisions regarding family matters. Unmarried males having secondary-level education are not extensively involved in decision-making.

Table 4 focuses on the involvement of young unmarried males in the participation of various decision-making processes and also the expectation levels of their parents from them as reported by the respondents. The youth participation in decision-making in family matters is quite low. Only one-third of young unmarried males are actively involved in decision-making. In terms of types of decision made, it is found that around three-fourth (72%) of young unmarried males are involved in taking decisions about financial matters followed by decisions related to medical treatment (12%). Involvement of respondents in all other types of decisions considered in the analysis is very meagre. The father is the most important decision-maker in the family which is evident from the fact that as high as 83 per cent of the respondents admit that decisions in all family matters are taken by their father, while only 9 per cent of mothers do so. Decisions taken by parents related to marriage are disliked by most of the respondents. Around 48 per cent of the respondents do not like their parents to take decisions on matters related to their marriage. Good jobs, marriage, education, care for parents, sharing expenditure and constructing their own homes are some of the expectations of the parents from the youth aged 15–24 years. A whooping majority (97%) of the parents of young unmarried males in the slums of Mumbai expect their children to get a good job.

Table 4 *Distribution of Young Unmarried Males by Involvement in Decision-making and Expectation of Parents in Mumbai Slums, 2009*

Characteristics	*Percentage*	*Number*
Participation in Decision-making		
Yes	33.1	141
No	66.9	286
Number	100	427
Type of Decision		
Visit to Certain Place	7	10
Medical Treatment	11.9	17
Study of Siblings	5.8	8
Financial Matters	72.1	102
Purchase of Articles	3.2	4
Important Decision-maker in the Family		
Father	83	355
Mother	8.7	37
Self	1.6	7
Parents	2.6	11
Others	4.1	17
Decision Taken by Parents Not Liked by Youth		
Education	15.2	65
Job	16.1	69

Cont'd...

...Cont'd

Marriage	48.3	206
Others	20.5	88
Expectations of Parents from Youth		
Get a Good Job	97.1	414
Marriage	94.2	401
Complete Study	89.3	381
Parent Care	92.5	394
Expenditure Sharing	92.5	394
Making Own House	90.1	384
Get Out From the Slum	61.3	262
Leave Bad Company	19.7	84
Leave Bad Habits	2.7	11
Others	0.2	1
Number of Youth	141	

Matters Discussed and Parents Discussion

Most of the respondents (58%) discuss about jobs with their friends too. About one-sixth of the adolescents (below 19 years of age) opined that they discuss about girlfriends with their friends. Similarly, one out of every ten adolescents discussed studies and films with their friends. An effort has also been made to know parents' reaction on certain matters. It is found, as illustrated in Table 6, that on certain matters, when parents get annoyed with their sons, they threaten them to leave the house and scold them. Approximately, 30 per cent to 70 per cent of the unmarried males report that their parents ask them to get out of their homes and scold them when they come to know about their discussions with friends on certain matters.

Table 5 *Distribution of Unmarried Males Aged 15–24 Years by Discussion of Certain Matters with Their Friends and Parents in Mumbai Slums, 2009*

Characteristics	*Percentage*	*Number*
Discussed Matters with Friends		
Study	10.5	45
Girls	16.3	70
Film	10.3	44
Sports	5.3	23
Jobs	57.7	245

Cont'd...

...Cont'd

Parents' Reaction on Certain Matters		
Scold	32.6	139
Beat	1.3	5
Get Out From Home	65.9	282
Others	0.2	1
Number	100.0	427
Discussed Matters with Friends		
Study	10.5	45
Girls	16.3	70
Film	10.3	44
Sports	5.3	23
Jobs	57.7	245
Parents' Reaction on Certain Matters		
Scold	32.6	139
Beat	1.3	5
Get Out From Home	65.9	282
Others	0.2	1
Number	100.0	427

Important Decision-makers

Some idea about the important decision-maker in a family and also the chosen mode of entertainment as reported by unmarried males aged 15–24 years is presented in Table 6. About 87 per cent of the unmarried male youth report that it is the father who takes all the important decisions in the family, while 76 per cent of respondents in the age group of 20–24 years report that someone else other than the father is involved in making important decisions related to family matters. The highest percentage of respondents (86%) having education levels ranging from the fifth to the eighth standard report that father is the main decision-maker on important family issues. The other 50 per cent that is illiterate report that other members besides the father also make important decisions in the family.

A large majority of respondents belonging to the OBC category of castes reports that the father is the most important decision-maker in the family; whereas, a majority of SC/ST respondents report that others take important decisions in family.

Father is the most important decision-maker in most of the Hindu and Muslim families. For a huge majority (93%) of respondents who are students, father is involved in making important decision in family followed by those who are working (70%). Those involved in household activities report that someone else other than father is the decision-maker in their family. Majority of the respondents in the poorest wealth quintile also report as the father being the most important decision-maker in the family.

Table 6 *Distribution of Young Unmarried Males About Important Decision Taker by Their Background Characteristics in Mumbai Slums, 2009*

Background Characteristics	*Important Decisions Taken by*		*Number*
	Father	*Others*	
Age			
15–19	86.8	13.2	280
20–24	75.5	24.5	147
Level of Education			
Illiterate	50.0	50.0	4
Up to Primary	84.7	15.3	72
Above Primary–Up to Secondary	86.0	14.0	92
Higher	81.9	18.1	259
Caste			
SC/ST	84.3	15.7	70
OBC	85.0	15.0	180
General	80.2	19.8	177
Religion			
Hindu	83.5	16.5	236
Muslim	83.4	16.6	186
Other	40.0	60.0	5
Occupation			
Non-working	83.8	16.2	74
Working	70.3	29.7	138
Domestic Help	70.6	29.4	16
Student	92.5	7.5	199
Wealth Index			
Poorest	92.4	7.6	92
Poorer	82.9	17.1	82
Middle	88.6	11.4	70
Richer	80.8	19.2	73
Richest	73.9	26.1	110
Numbers of Youth		427	

Youth Entertainment

Table 7 illustrates that irrespective of age, playing games emerges out to be the most important mode of entertainment among the unmarried males in the slums of Mumbai. Comparatively lesser percentage of respondents in the specified ages prefer going outside as a mode of entertainment, which is apparent from the fact that only 86 per cent and 82 per cent of the respondents in age groups 14–19 and 20–24 years, respectively, report outdoor visits as a mode of entertainment.

Going out as a mode of entertainment is universal among illiterate respondents. Apart from those who are illiterate, the majority of those belonging to all other educational categories consider playing as an important mode of entertainment. As the level of education increases, 'outdoor visits' as a mode of entertainment becomes more unpopular. The opposite trend can be seen in different educational categories other than 'illiterate' in case of playing as the mode of entertainment.

Huge differentials exist with regard to the mode of entertainment among respondents of different castes and religious groups. 'Play' is the most common mode of entertainment among respondents in different categories of religion and caste. Less than 50 per cent respondents in different caste groups report 'visiting outdoors' as their mode of entertainment compared to 'play'. 'Play' as the mode of entertainment is universal among respondents other than Hindus and Muslims. Further, 'play' as a mode of entertainment emerges out to be of utmost importance when we take a look at the mode of entertainment as reported by respondents in different occupational categories. Every nine out of ten students report that they entertain themselves by playing various games. Again, the existing differential between the uses of the two modes of entertainment among respondents in each occupation category is very small.

Irrespective of the economic status, a considerable proportion of respondents in each wealth quintile consider playing as their common mode of entertainment as compared to outdoor visits. Many differentials exists in the use of two modes of entertainment among the respondents in the richest wealth quintile. In the richest wealth quintile the respondents who consider play to be their common mode of entertainment is nearly four times more as compared to outdoor visits.

Table 7 *Distribution of Unmarried Males Aged 15–24 Years About Type of Entertainment by Their Background Characteristics in the Mumbai Slums, 2009*

Background Characteristics	*Type of Entertainment*		
	Play games	*Outings*	*Number*
Age			
15–19	66.8	72.3	280
20–24	33.2	27.7	147
Level of Education			
Illiterate	0.8	2.1	4
Up to Primary	14.1	20.6	72
Primary to Secondary	21.3	27.0	92
Higher	63.7	50.3	259
Caste			
SC/ST	16.6	15.4	70
OBC	41.2	41.0	180
General	43.2	43.6	177
Religion			
Hindu	56.0	40.7	236
Muslim	42.4	59.3	186
Other	1.7	—	5
Occupation			
Non-working	15.5	22.9	74
Working	30.7	26.6	138
Domestic Help	3.9	3.2	16
Student	50.0	47.3	199
Wealth Index			
Poorest	22.4	30.9	92
Poorer	16.3	26.5	82
Middle	16.9	16.0	70
Richer	17.2	13.3	73
Richest	27.1	13.3	110
Number of Youth		427	

Factors Associated with Decision-making

The considered dependent variable is whether unmarried males aged 15–24 years participated in household decision-making (visits to certain place, medical treatment, study of siblings, financial matters and purchase of articles) or not. Selected independent variables included in the analysis are: wealth quintile (poorest/poorer/middle/richer/richest); level of education (illiterate/up to primary/above primary–up to secondary/higher secondary); caste (SC/ST/OBC/others); religion (Hindu/ Muslims/others); occupation (not working/working/ domestic help/student); and get pocket money (yes/no). The first category of each independent variable is considered as the reference category.

Table 8 *Odds Ratio for the Participation in Household Decision-making Among Unmarried Males Aged 15–24 Years of Mumbai Slums, 2009*

Characteristics	*Categories*	*Exp (B)*
Wealth Quintile	Poorest	1.00
	Poorer	0.55
	Middle	0.41*
	Richer	0.38*
	Richest	2.57*
Level of Education	Illiterate	1.00
	Up to Primary	0.48
	Above Primary–Up to Secondary	2.83*
	Higher	1.09
Caste of the Respondents	SC/ST	1.00
	OBC	1.19
	General	0.96
Religion	Hindu	1.00
	Muslim	9.99*
	Others	3.71
Occupation	Non-working	1.00
	Working	0.39**
	Domestic Help	0.51*
	Student	0.36
Get Pocket Money	Yes	1.00
	No	2.72**

**Significant at $p<0.01$; * at $p<0.05$; ® Reference category

Respondents who belong to the richest households have a significantly higher chance of involvement in decision-making as compared to poorest households (OR=2.57, $p<0.05$). Respondents from middle and richer households have fewer chances of decision-making as opposed to the poorest households (OR=0.41, 0.38, $p<0.05$). Respondents with a secondary level of education are more likely to get involved in the decision-making compared to their illiterate counterparts. The results are found to be insignificant in the context of castes of the respondents. Muslims have higher chance of decision-making at 5 per cent level significance as compared to Hindus. Respondents who are working or are domestic workers are found to be less likely to be involved in the decision-making process as compared to non-working respondents ($p<0.05$). Respondents who were not getting pocket money have higher participation in household decision-making as compared to their counterparts who do not get pocket money.

Factors Associated with Consumption of Tobacco among Youth

The considered dependent variable was whether youth consumed tobacco or not. The variables are: wealth quintile (poorest/poorer/middle/richer/richest); level of education (illiterate/up to primary/above primary–up to secondary/higher secondary); caste (SC/ST/OBC/others); religion (Hindu/Muslims/others); occupation (not working/working/ domestic help/student); participation in decision-making (yes/no); and get pocket money (yes/no). The first category of each independent variable is considered as the reference category.

Respondents who belong to poorer households have significantly fewer chances of consuming tobacco as compared to those respondents who belong to poorest households. Respondents from poorer, richer and richest households also have fewer chances of consuming tobacco in comparison to members of poorest households. The results are found to be significant at 5 per cent level of significance. However, there is no association with the level of education, caste and religion of the respondents. Respondents who are working or are domestic workers have fewer chances of consuming tobacco as compared to those who are not working ($p<0.05$). The other variables like participation in decision-making and get pocket money are not found to be significant with the consumption of tobacco among youth in Mumbai.

Table 9 *Odds Ratio Showing the Association Between Tobacco Consumption and Socio-economic Characteristics of Youth in Mumbai Slums, 2009*

Characteristics	*Categories*	*Exp (B)*
Wealth Quintile	Poorest	1.00
	Poorer	0.10**
	Middle	0.21**
	Richer	0.21**
	Richest	0.21**
Level of Education	Illiterate	1.00
	Up to Primary	0.83
	Above Primary–Up to Secondary	0.99
	Higher	0.73
Caste	SC/ST	1.00
	OBC	2.10
	General	0.92
Religion	Hindu	1.00
	Muslim	0.00
	Others	0.00
Occupation	Non-working	1.00
	Working	0.36**
	Domestic Help	0.20**
	Student	0.39
Participation in Decision-making	Yes	1.00
	No	1.24
Get Pocket Money	Yes	1.00
	No	1.23

**Significant at $p<0.01$; * at $p<0.05$; ® Reference category

Factors Affecting Habit of Intoxicating Substance Use

The dependent variable for the analysis is whether the respondent consumed intoxicating items. The independent variables include wealth quintiles (poorest/poorer/middle/richer/richest); level of education (illiterate/up to primary/above primary–up to secondary/higher secondary); caste (SC/ST/OBC/others); religion (Hindu/Muslims/others); and occupation (not working/

working/domestic help/student). The first category of each independent variable is considered as a reference category. Table 10 shows the odds ratios for consuming any intoxicating items among unmarried males of 15–24 years in age in Mumbai slums. The wealth index, caste, level of education and occupation are the significant predictors of the consumption of intoxicating items. Among respondents who belong to poorer, middle, richer and richest wealth quintiles are 94 per cent, 88 per cent, 84 per cent and 88 per cent less likely to consume intoxicating items, respectively, compared to those who belong to the poorest quintile. Youth with eight or more years of education are 37 per cent less likely to consume any intoxicating items compared to illiterate youth. Those who worked or indulged in some household activity were 55 per cent and 77 per cent less likely to consume intoxicating items as compared to those who did not work.

Table 10 *Odds Ratio of Consuming any Intoxicating Items Among Youth in Mumbai Slums, 2009*

Characteristics	*Categories*	*Exp (B)*
Wealth Quintile	Poorest®	1.00
	Poorer	0.06***
	Middle	0.12***
	Richer	0.16***
	Richest	0.12***
Level of Education	Illiterate®	1.00
	Up to Fifth	0.75
	Sixth to Eight	0.81
	Eight & Above	0.63*
Caste	SC/ST®	1.00
	OBC	2.98***
	General	0.95
Religion	Hindu®	1.00
	Muslim	0.00
	Others	0.00
Occupation	Did Not Work®	1.00
	Working	0.45***
	Household Activity	0.23***
	Student	0.43

**Significant at $p<0.01$; * at $p<0.05$; ® Reference category

Conclusion

In recognition of the importance of investing in young people, several national policies and programmes formulated since 2000, including the National Population Policy 2000, the National Youth Policy 2003, the Tenth and Eleventh Five-Year Plans, the National Adolescent Reproductive and Sexual Health Strategy and the National Rural Health Mission, have underscored a commitment to addressing the multiple needs of this group in India. Effective implementation of policies and programmes has been difficult in India and there has been a lack of comprehensive evidence on the situation and needs of youth. This study is a contribution to the growing body of literature and evidence regarding these issues in urban India.

Using primary data from slums of Mumbai, this study reveals many aspects of life-style and decision-making among youth. Findings indicate that a substantial proportion of young unmarried men living in these slums are involved in substance use. However, it is the disadvantaged and marginalized groups, such as poor, uneducated and non-working (unemployed), who are more involved in such activities. Consumption of such intoxicating items could be harmful to their health which ultimately could affect their work capacity. For example, evidence suggests that the use of alcohol and drugs among youth is associated with physical fights, risky sexual activity, depression and suicide as well as irregular school or work attendance and other negative outcomes (DiClemente, 1992; Ellickson, Saner and McGuigan, 1997; Gruber et al., 1996; Lowry et al., 1994; Mohan, Sankara Sarma and Thankappan, 2005; Singh and Saini, 2007). It could be argued that promoting employment and providing educational opportunities could reduce the substance abuse among youth in Mumbai slum (IIPS and Population Council, 2010). Slums being congested spaces do not have enough playgrounds and that is reflected in the fact that most of the youth go for outing rather than playing in the fields or streets.

Results also indicate that many young men were also not able to exercise agency in their everyday lives. A little less than one third of unmarried males aged 15–19 years take their own decision. Similarly, less than one-fourth of Hindu unmarried males aged

15–24 years are involved in decision-making. While on the other hand, about three-fourth of the illiterate unmarried males in Mumbai slums participate in decision-making in family matters. The most important among decision-makers is the father of the respondent which indicates that traditional male supremacy in the household decision-making still exists in urban slums of Mumbai.

Government should develop and implement programmes to provide educational and employment opportunities and promote meaningful participation in society. Programmes must recognize the heterogeneity of the youth in slums, and interventions and delivery mechanisms for different groups should be appropriately tailored to meet their special needs, including the particular obstacles youth face in making a safe transition to adulthood. Evidence presented in this study may provide guide for the future planning regarding needs of youth in slum of Mumbai.

References

Cassidy, D. (2007). *How the Irish Invented Slang*. London: Counter Punch Press.

Census of India (2001). *Slum Population: Series 1*. New Delhi: Office of the Registrar General of India.

DiClemente, R. (1992). *Adolescents and AIDS: A Generation in Jeopardy*. London: Sage.

Ellickson, P., H. Saner and K. McGuigan (1997). 'Profiles of Violent Youth: Substance Use and Other Concurrent Problems'. *American Journal of Public Health*, 87: 985–91.

Gruber, E. et al. (1996). 'Early Drinking Onset and its Association with Alcohol Use and Problem Behaviour in Late Adolescence'. *Preventive Medicine*, 25 (3): 293–300.

International Institute for Population Sciences (IIPS) and Population Council (2010). *Youth in India: Situation and Needs Study 2006–2007*. Mumbai: IIPS.

Kumar, A. and V. Tiwari (2003). 'Knowledge, Attitude and Behaviour towards Pre-marital Sex: A Study among Youths from Two City-slums in India'. *Health and Population: Perspectives and Issues*, 26 (4): 126–34.

Lowry, R. et al. (1994). 'Substance Use and HIV-related Sexual Behaviours among US High School Students: Are they Related?'. *American Journal of Public Health*, 84: 1116–20.

Mohan, S., P. Sankara Sarma and K. Thankappan (2005). 'Access to Pocket Money and Low Educational Performance Predict Tobacco

Use among Adolescent Boys in Kerala, India'. *Preventive Medicine*, 41 (2): 685–92.

Ram, F. et al. (2010). 'Youth in India: Situation and Needs Study'. Policy Brief No. 26.

Rathor, A. (2003). *Slum Dwellers: Curse on Development*. New Delhi: Sarup and Sons.

Rhule-Louie, D. et al. (2008). 'Substance Use and Health and Safety among Homeless Youth'. *Journal of Child and Family Studies*, 17: 306–19.

Singh, S. and S. Saini (2007). 'HIV Risk Perception in Relation to Peer Pressure and Drug Abuse Behaviour among Adolescents'. *Indian Journal of Sexually Transmitted Diseases*, 28: 53–54.

8 Employment Patterns Among Informal Sector Workers in Mumbai City

Sanjay Rode

The processes of informalization of jobs observed during the past decades have affected both high and low-income countries (Beneria, 2001). India is not an exception to such changes as far as employment pattern is concerned. Some cities have either restructured employment or developed new trends in employment pattern. Mumbai is the financial capital of India. Apart from corporate headquarters of number of Indian companies and multinational companies (MNCs), most of the financial institutions such as stock exchange and central bank are located in the city. The growth of service sector, which includes finance, information technology (IT), telecom, tourism, entertainment, advertising and communication, is higher than any other sector. Due to its vast potential to provide enormous employment opportunities to people, it lures people from rural areas to the city. Therefore, it is not surprising that very few skilled and unskilled migrants remain unemployed in the region. They are easily consumed in the vast labour market in the city. Educational qualifications and skills of the workers are the two pre-requisites to get higher income. Highly educated workers play an important role in the production process. A highly trained worker will always work for innovation oriented and skilled jobs. Similarly, more educated workers do better in acquiring skills compared to the less-educated ones (Chakravarty, 2004). In the city, the segments of services that have grown faster in recent past and provided employment with relatively higher levels of earning, have high human capital requirements and have, therefore, mainly benefited the skilled workers. At the same time, the employment structure in the service sector is sharply polarized between a few high-end jobs in large corporations and a mass of low paid jobs in small and informal units. The industrial sector, on the other hand, has thrown up the demand for a wider spectrum of skills. Thus, it benefits workers with different skill levels and from all sections of society (Topala, 2009).

A large proportion of the workforce in Mumbai is still in the informal sector. These workers are engaged in economic activities with lower productivity and production, and it results in minor income. They are also engaged in activities with fewer stable employment contracts (including self-employed) and fewer social security benefits. While the wages and salaries of the formal sector workers are revised periodically to counter inflation, no such benefits accrue to the large proportion of workers in the informal sector (Unni, 2002).

However, due to lack of formal employment, these workers are doing various economic activities and live in the various slums across the city. Many workers are involved in furniture-making and polishing, carpentry, etc. The city has also witnessed rapid developments in real estate sector. There is a high demand of furniture in newly established malls, residential flats, shops, hospitals, etc. Some workers are engaged in the textile industry. The *city* boasts a great history of being the centre of big textile mills. Although the textile industry shifted to other cities, leftover workers still carry out weaving, dyeing, twisting, sari-cutting, spinning *jari,* gilding, etc., in small textile units. Self-employment, most of the time, is seasonal and sometimes workers do not find work at all. Self-employed male and female are engaged in the variety of jobs in the city. Most of the self-employed workers are less educated and are engaged in driving auto-rickshaw, transportation of goods, etc., to earn their livelihood. These people can be found living in suburbs and small dwellings near railway lines and stations. Some self-employed people work in roadside food stalls and small restaurants, while others are hawkers and vendors. There are many who move across several adjacent slums and sell various products or small articles such as cloths, toys, pots or even exchange garlic for pots. Some of self-employed people could be found running *paan-bidi* shops (small shops selling cigarettes, betel leaf, etc.), vending milk, selling fruits and vegetables on footpath, etc. Although people regularly purchase goods and services from such self-employed people, having a bad day at hawking or vending can massively impact their daily income generation.

New and old construction activities provide a number of informal sector jobs to different kinds of workers, both male and female. The male workers are involved in different construction activities. The women workers also work as causal labourers. They cart materials to and from building sites. They usually wake up early in the morning and prepare food for the family. If drinking water facilities are not available near the house, then it is a labourious activity to carry water from long distances. In such circumstances, women and children usually carry water from extended distances in the slums. The number of trips to carry enough water depends on the family size, the distance to the source of water, the price of water, the hygiene of family, the availability of time, etc. For each household, the water requirement and use is different. Generally, the households engaged in causal labour have fewer skills and work only in nearby areas around their house. Most of the women usually walk to their workplace. Competition is considerably high for the unskilled jobs in the city because of availability of workers through large-scale migration into this region. If workers fall sick and have to visit a health centre, the facilities are usually overcrowded and visiting them consumes a lot of precious time which they otherwise could utilize for their work. Women workers are required to go early and stand in a long queue in order to take their prescriptions from the doctor. The direct and indirect cost of visiting health facility, including travelling and medicines is often to forego their daily wages. Regular check-ups may raise the economic burden caused by medical care even further. In order to avoid getting sacked and in hope of regular income, the workers might opt for private health facilities and medical treatment. However, visiting private health facilities is costly because of high consultancy fees and medicine charges. Most of the time, poor people borrow money for medical treatment from their relatives, friends, contractors, etc. To avoid such debts and save money, many workers also try to find solutions to their health problems with home remedies.

The rising population in the city is putting added pressure on existing civic amenities in Mumbai and its Municipal Corporation. Inadequate civic amenities, such as water supply, housing, transportation, healthcare, solid waste and sanitation, affect the quality of life inversely. Most of the slums are neglected in terms of provision of infrastructural facilities. They are either declared as illegal settlements or referred to as new settlements. Most of the basic services such as water supply, electricity, housing and sanitation are beyond the reach of the poor living in slums. Poor people living in these slums have no choice but to purchase such services from the private providers who charge exorbitant prices. There are a few studies which are conducted on workers of slums in Mumbai city. This study is unique because we have conducted primary survey of the workers living in *kutcha* slums and involved in different sectors in Mumbai.

In the light of the above discussion, this paper looks at the employment patterns of workers in the urban slums of Mumbai. The first part of the paper explains the data and methodology used in the course of the study. Second section describes the employment patterns within the city in the context of income, educational attainment and body mass index of construction workers, self-employed and regular workers. Third section examines the association of type of employment with socio-economic characteristics of respondents using multinomial logit regression. Finally, the concluding section explores the policy implications of the study.

Data and Econometric Model

Data for this study was collected from the *kutcha* slums in Mumbai city. We had chosen stratified random sampling for collecting primary data for this study. The *kutcha* slum houses are of plastic sheet and they are without piped water supply, electricity and sanitation facilities. In Mumbai city, there are different pockets of *kutcha* slums. After selecting particular household, we have interviewed household head and took weight and height of each member. The sample was undertaken in May–June 2011. We administered detail questionnaire and collected data of 1,050 households in Mumbai city. The details of the survey and households covered in it are explained in the appendix. Workers information is collected in detail about income, education, health and measured weight and height. Such data has been collected from the eastern and western suburbs of 15 slum settlements. We categorized workers as self-employed, construction and domestic workers and regular workers in the city. The primary data has been analysed in Stata12 software. We used multinomial logit regression to examine the socio-economic characteristics of each type of workers in Mumbai city. Such regression helps to find the co-relation between different kinds of workers. Based on nature of dependent variable, an econometric model gets used for study. There are different types of regressions but it is the best fit regression for this study. We have compared the workers of regular jobs with self employment, construction and domestic workers.

The multi-nominal logit model is defined as follows:

$$\Pr(y_i = j) = \frac{\text{Exp}\,(X_i B_j)}{1 + \Sigma_j^J \exp\,(X_i B_j)} \quad (1)$$

and,

$$\Pr(y_i = 0) = \frac{1}{1 + \Sigma_j^J \exp\,(X_i B_j)'} \quad (2)$$

Where, for the ith worker, y_i is the observed outcome and X_j is a vector of explanatory variable. The parameters B_j are estimated by maximum likelihood. The positive and negative parameters are compared with the reference category workers of regular jobs (Greene, 2003). The results are presented in the Table 1.

Methodology

In order to calculate the total workforce in the city, we have assumed that there are manufacturing and service sectors. We cannot study the entire population and employment pattern of city.

But for model building, we are assuming the total workforce which is fixed for particular time period. We assumed that there is no worker involved in agriculture-related activities since agriculture within the city is a rare possibility. Therefore, in terms of equation it is represented as:

$$\sum_{t=1}^{i} wf = \sum_{t=1}^{i} m \sum_{t=1}^{i} s \qquad (3)$$

Where, *wf* is work force in the city in time *t* and i^{th} number of workers. We can further write as $t=1 \ldots n$ and $i=1 \ldots n$ work force. In above equation, summation *m* represents the work force involved in manufacturing sector. Similarly, summation *s* represents the work force involved in the services sector with time *t* and i^{th} workforce. Both *t* and *i* again noted from *1 to n* in the above equation.

$$\sum_{t=1}^{i} m = \sum_{t=1}^{i} f \sum_{t=1}^{i} if \qquad (4)$$

The workers in manufacturing sector in city are further classified as the workers in the formal and informal sector at time *t* and i^{th} number of worker. In city, the number of workers in the manufacturing formal sector is very less. Therefore, we assume that $\sum_{t=1}^{i} f = 0$ for analysis.

$$\sum_{t=1}^{i} s = \sum_{t=1}^{i} f + \sum_{t=1}^{i} if \qquad (5)$$

For services sector in city, the workers in the formal and informal sector at time *t* and i^{th} number of workers are explained in the above equation. Here, we again assumed that workers of formal services sector are $\sum_{t=1}^{i} f = 0$. Therefore, workforce in the informal sector in city comprises as follows:

$$\sum_{t=1}^{i} if = \sum_{t=1}^{i} m + \sum_{t=1}^{i} s \qquad (6)$$

The number of workers of the informal sector consists of workers of manufacturing and services sector. They are at time *t* and $i=1 to\ n$. We have further classified the workers of the informal sector as follows:

$$\sum_{t=1}^{i} if = \sum_{t=1}^{i} c + \sum_{t=1}^{i} se + \sum_{t=1}^{i} re \tag{7}$$

We have categorized the informal sector workers as workers of construction and domestic work (c), self-employment (se) and regular workers (re). All three categories of workers are considered for time t and $i=1\ to\ n$ workers.

The workers of the three informal sectors maximize their income subject to following constrains:

$$\sum_{t=1}^{i} Y = TE + (H_t^i + E_t^i + T_t^i + G^i \tag{8}$$

Total income in the t period for ($i=1\ to\ n$) worker depends on the type of employment (TE), health status (H), educational achievement (E), time spend (T) in informal sector labour market and gender (G). All of the above variables decide the income for the ith worker in time t. Construction sector, self-employment and regular job workers have three different functions for income maximization.

Results

Patterns of Employment in the Informal Sector of Mumbai City

The workers in Mumbai city are engaged in a variety of economic activities. For analysis, we have categorized the workers into three categories. The major categories are self-employed workers, construction labourers and other occupations. A large number of the work force of the urban slums is engaged in construction sector and providing domestic help. Workers engaged in the construction sector are working as *kadias, mistrys* (mason) and labourers carting materials at building sites, window fitters, painters, earth workers and layers of gutter lines. Women are also involved in the construction sector and they work as casual labourers carting materials to and from building sites. Other than this, women hold jobs in the informal sector where they work as domestic helps, petty traders, etc.

The self-employed workers are involved in sales, production, processing, repairs and services. They mainly work as drivers, including rickshaw drivers, transporters of goods in handcarts, cooks or bearers in wayside hotels and smaller restaurants. People engaged in sales frequently pursue jobs such as hawking and vending, running *paan-bidi* shops, which might also sell small items in retail. These items are generally purchased either outside the slum or in the wholesale market. Self-employed in processing activities comprises carpenters, tailors and blacksmiths. Some workers are engaged in work of small-scale textile industry. They are engaged in activities like weaving, dyeing, twisting, sari cutting, spinning *jari*, gilding, etc. These groups of the self-employed comprise those who are trying to respond to the market by adjusting themselves and their trade to changing demand patterns in the city of Mumbai. The workers engaged in sales are generally never able to depend on one area or type of product. There are large variations in earnings by different household groups. It also indicates similar variations in returns from specific occupation, types and jobs. Most of the jobs in the informal and especially in the self-employed sector provide low returns because of the irregularity of employment and a lower profit margin. There is no job security and even contractual jobs are scarce. They are involved in a lower category of less paid and casual jobs.

During the interview, it was repeatedly found that working members tend to report uncertain and lower income. This is particularly because most of the people are self-employed or casual labour, and their income varies from time to time and there being no income at all at certain times. In Mumbai, informal workers and entrepreneurs are entitled to seven essential securities, which are often denied to them: labour market security, employment security (protection against arbitrary dismissal regulation on hiring and firing, employment stability, compatible with economic dynamism), job security (career opportunity to develop a sense of occupation), work security (protection against accidents and illness at work through safety and health regulations, limits on working hours and so on), skills reproduction security (to gain, retain skills through innovative means, employment training), income security (provision of adequate income) and representative security (protection of collective voice in the labour market through independent trade unions and employers organizations and social dialogue institutions) (ILO, 2002).

Type of Labour Force by Slums

We have categorized workers into three categories – construction/domestic work, self-employment, regular job. A little more than 75 per cent of women from Mumbai slums are engaged in construction and domestic work. However, this proportion varies considerably from one slum to another. For instance, 20 per cent of all female workers engaged in this sector come from Mazgaon where only 1 per cent comes from Dahisar. About 20 per cent male workers from Mumbai slums are engaged in construction/domestic work.

Table 1 *Place and Type of Labour Force in City (%)*

Place	*Construction/ Domestic Work*		*Self-employment*		*Regular Job*	
	Male	*Female*	*Male*	*Female*	*Male*	*Female*
Jogeshwari	0.48	1.46	0.81	0.32	1.94	0.16
Malad	0.48	1.46	0.48	0.00	1.05	0.16
Chembur	1.86	3.08	1.29	0.32	2.67	0.65
Mankhurd	1.86	6.65	2.58	0.49	1.29	0.32
Kurla	1.13	2.59	3.47	0.00	3.63	1.62
Lower Parel	0.97	6.97	4.52	0.97	0.00	0.00
Dadar	2.02	4.38	2.75	0.32	5.41	3.73
Matunga	0.81	4.21	1.86	0.32	3.55	1.62
Bandra	2.26	3.89	2.10	0.49	1.13	1.62
Goregaon	1.78	6.97	1.37	0.16	2.26	0.65
Mazgaon	2.34	19.45	7.84	0.65	0.48	0.16
Govandi	0.89	9.56	5.82	0.97	0.00	0.00
Dahisar	0.16	1.30	0.97	0.00	11.07	5.35
Kandivali	1.78	3.24	3.72	0.00	5.82	1.94
Borivali	0.32	0.97	0.48	0.16	0.16	0.00
Total	19.14	76.18	40.06	5.19	40.47	17.99

Source: Compiled from data.

About 40 per cent male workers from slums are self-employed in Mumbai. About 6 per cent of them come from Govandi. Govandi area has many small shops preparing and selling different items. Everybody in slums is involved in different informal sector activity. The lowest percentages of self-employed workers are found in Borivali and Malad (0.48% each). The proportion of self-employed female workers is about 5 per cent in Mumbai city. They are 0.97 per cent in Lower Parel and Govandi. Male workers with regular job in the slums of city are 41 per cent. In Dahisar, workers who have regular jobs are 11 per cent. Such workers are absent in the slums of Lower Parel and Govandi. Approximately, about 18 per cent women from Mumbai slums have regular jobs. They are about 4 per cent in Dadar and 6 per cent in Dahisar. None of the female workers in Borivali, Govandi and Lower Parel was engaged in a regular job. With a lower educational attainment, it is difficult to find regular employment for women in the city. Most of the women are working at their homes and the number of women even surpasses that of men in informal employment. However, the gender bias in informal economy is probably underestimated. Apparel, leather and sports goods sectors, more number of women workers can be seen as they are deemed to be more skilful in working with different kinds of machines for cutting, sewing, stitching, etc. Apart from reasons based on grounds of efficiency, women workers are also preferred over their male counterparts because they are less prone to the formation of trade unions and related activities (Deb et al., 2009). Similarly, women labours are reluctant to unionize (Absar, 2002). Women are more likely than men to be in those informal activities that are under counted such as production for own consumption, paid domestic activities in private households and home work. The challenge is to determine how interventions can be devised that improves the livelihood of the poor while not removing incentives to formalization (Ruffer and Knight, 2007).

Age Pattern of Workers

It is important to understand the age pattern of the workers involved in construction, self-employment and regular job. Respondents aged 15 to 35 years have more chances of having a regular job in the city. The male workers in the age group of 35–45 years in construction/domestic work are about 5 per cent. Similarly, about 30 per cent of all female workers engaged in construction/domestic work were aged between 25 and 35 years. None of male workers in construction work were above 65 years of age. This is mainly because such tasks require more physical energy. It is also possible that at an older age energy for physical labour declines and they drop out of construction jobs. The female workers engaged in the same activities of 65 and above age group are almost negligible. They sometimes work as domestic helps. About 14 per cent of self-employed males belong to the age group of 35–45 years. However, only 3 per cent of all female workers belong to 25–35 years age group and are self-employed. It implies that female workers do not accept more self-employment jobs as compared to male workers. About 13 per cent males who have regular jobs belong to the age group of 15–25 years. The female workers in this age group are about 8 per cent of total female workforce.

Table 2 *Age Pattern of Workers (%)*

Age	*Construction/ Domestic Work*		*Self-employment*		*Regular Job*	
	Male	*Female*	*Male*	*Female*	*Male*	*Female*
Below 15	0.2	0.5	0.2	0.8	0.2	0.6
15–25	4.5	16.4	8.1	1.1	12.9	7.8
25–35	5.0	30.7	8.4	3.2	11.1	4.8
35–45	5.3	21.2	14.3	1.1	9.0	4.0
45–55	3.5	4.8	8.1	0.3	5.3	0.6
55–65	1.0	1.3	1.1	0.0	1.3	0.0
65–above	0.0	0.2	0.1	0.0	0.2	0.0
Total	19.4	75.0	40.2	6.5	40.0	17.8

Source: Compiled from data.

Educational Attainment Among Workers

Education is a resource and more educated workers can work with skilled jobs and earn more income. Educated workers can understand the new methods of production and work efficiently with modern machines or techniques. However, illiterate workers end up with less-skilled jobs and lower income.

Table 2 shows that about 41 per cent of all female workers are illiterate and engaged in construction/domestic works such as domestic work, carry material at construction sites, carting, etc., which do not require any special skill and education. Nearly 26 per cent women workers have education up to secondary level. As for male workers, 10 per cent of them have studied up till secondary level and work in construction work. Another 31 per cent who have an education up to the secondary level are self-employed. About 26 per cent of all male workers have secondary level education and a regular job, while among female workers, it is 9 per cent. Maximum number of workers from these slums involved in various jobs have mostly attended up till secondary level. The percentage of workers with graduation and post-graduation degrees are very less in the slums. Most of the less-educated workers are engaged in informal sector jobs.

Table 3 *Educational Attainment Among Workers (%)*

Education	*Construction/ Domestic Work*		*Self-employment*		*Regular Job*	
	Male	*Female*	*Male*	*Female*	*Male*	*Female*
Illiterate	6.7	41.4	5.1	2.9	4.2	3.5
Primary	1.8	6.2	2.2	0.2	1.8	1.4
Secondary	10.4	26.3	31.3	3.3	25.5	9.1
High School	0.5	1.1	1.5	0.2	6.9	2.9
Graduate	0.0	0.0	0.1	0.0	1.5	1.0
Postgraduate	0.1	0.0	0.0	0.0	0.1	0.0
Total	19.5	75.0	40.2	6.5	40.0	17.8

Source: Compiled from data.

Distribution of Workers by Income Level

Nearly 12 per cent of male workers are earning monthly income between ₹ 3,000–6,000 in construction work. About 54 per cent of all female workers earn between ₹ 1,000–3,000 by working in construction sector. Incomes in the construction sector are low and uncertain. During rainy season, when all construction work stops, construction workers remain unemployed. In such situations, some workers migrate to their native place. Most of the female workers work as domestic help. Since there is no specific law for the minimum wage for domestic work, incomes of such female workers are very low. Moreover, if the women worker is absent for a day even due to some inevitable circumstances, the wage is not paid to her. About 25 per cent of all male workers earn between ₹ 3,000–6,000 by engaging themselves in self-employment. A few of them also earn wages as low as ₹ 1,000–3,000. As far as regular job with ₹ 3,000–6,000 is concerned, about 20 per cent male and 7 per cent female workers fall in this category.

Table 4 *Income Generation Among Workers (%)*

Monthly Income (in ₹)	*Construction/ Domestic Work*		*Self-employment*		*Regular Job*	
	Male	*Female*	*Male*	*Female*	*Male*	*Female*
0–1,000	0.2	0.5	0.0	0.2	0.2	0.0
1,000–3,000	2.9	54.3	2.1	3.7	1.9	1.6
3,000–6,000	12.3	15.5	25.2	1.9	19.4	7.0
6,000–8,000	3.1	4.6	9.2	0.8	11.2	6.4
8,000–10,000	0.9	0.3	3.6	0.0	5.5	2.2
10,000–above	0.2	0.0	0.2	0.0	1.8	0.5
Total	19.4	75.2	40.2	6.5	40.0	17.7

Source: Compiled from data.

Body Mass Index and Income

Sometimes earnings are dependent on capacity to work and such work capacity is measured in terms of Body Mass Index (BMI). About 50 per cent of all workers who earn ₹ 0–1,000 per month have a BMI of 17–18.5 contrary to other income groups. It clearly indicates that low income is positively correlated with low BMI. However, this may not always be true. About 40 per cent of female workers who earn ₹ 1,000 or less have a normal BMI (18.5–25). In the ₹ 1,000–2,000 income category, nearly 38 per cent women workers have normal BMI. About 61 per cent male workers have a normal BMI in ₹ 2,000–3,000 income category, while about 82 per cent female workers who fall in ₹ 3,000–4,000 income category have normal BMI. It implies that as the income rises, the percentage of workers with normal body mass index increases.

Table 4 shows that in ₹ 5,000–6,000 income category, about 63 per cent male workers and 48 per cent female workers fall in normal BMI category. Similarly, in ₹ 6,000–7,000 income categories, about 63 per cent male workers and 68 per cent female workers are in normal BMI category. The same is true for income categories of ₹ 7,000–8,000 and ₹ 8,000–10,000. Overall, about 63 per cent male workers and 69 per cent female workers fall under normal BMI category. Nearly 22 per cent male workers and 8 per

Table 5 *Income and BMI Characteristics (%)*

BMI/Income	*<16*		*16–17*		*17–18.5*		*18.5–25*		*25–30*		*30–35*		*35–40*		*40>*	
	M	*F*	*M*	*F*	*M*	*F*	*M*	*F*	*M*	*F*	*M*	*F*	*M*	*F*	*M*	*F*
<1,000	0.0	0.0	0.0	0.0	50.0	40.0	25.0	40.0	25.0	20.0	0.0	0.0	0.0	0.0	0.0	0.0
1,000–2,000	0.0	0.0	0.0	0.0	0.0	12.5	0.0	37.5	33.3	25.0	33.3	25.0	33.3	0.0	0.0	0.0
2,000–3,000	5.6	1.1	0.0	1.7	11.1	5.1	61.1	82.3	11.1	6.9	11.1	1.7	0.0	0.0	0.0	1.1
3,000–4,000	5.7	1.4	2.9	1.8	11.4	4.1	67.1	71.1	10.0	13.3	1.4	4.6	1.4	2.8	0.0	0.9
4,000–5,000	7.9	2.5	4.8	4.9	9.5	7.4	62.7	48.2	11.1	24.7	2.4	11.1	0.0	0.0	1.6	1.2
5,000–6,000	3.6	2.2	6.3	0.0	14.4	6.5	61.7	58.7	6.3	26.1	5.4	6.5	1.8	0.0	0.5	0.0
6,000–7,000	2.6	0.0	2.9	0.0	16.8	1.6	63.3	67.7	8.4	19.4	3.7	8.1	2.1	1.6	0.3	1.6
7,000–8,000	2.2	8.3	2.2	0.0	13.8	16.7	66.7	50.0	8.7	16.7	4.4	0.0	0.7	0.0	1.5	8.3
8,000–10,000	2.3	0.0	4.1	0.0	11.6	0.0	67.6	56.3	9.8	37.5	1.2	0.0	3.5	6.3	0.0	0.0
>10,000	9.2	0.0	4.2	0.0	17.7	0.0	55.5	66.7	8.4	33.3	3.4	0.0	1.7	0.0	0.0	0.0
Total	4.1	1.4	3.8	1.8	14.4	5.3	63.1	68.5	8.8	15.5	3.6	5.1	1.8	1.3	0.5	1.1

Source: Compiled from data.

cent female workers are mild, moderate and severe malnourished in city. Around 23 per cent female workers and 15 per cent male workers are obese in city. Their BMI is above 25.

Higher level of education is normally associated with better income levels. Figure 1 shows the relationship between per capita income and educational attainment of workers. The educational attainment and monthly per capita income are positively correlated. As the level of education rises, it translates into more skills and capabilities which ultimately enable workers to get higher income. This is also possible in terms of self-employment. Self-employed educated workers work more efficiently and effectively to earn more income in the city. In *kutcha* slums, workers without education cannot earn income. Sometimes workers learn various skills at work and this leads to upward mobility in terms of job and income in the city. The city provides many vertical movement job opportunities as well. Yet, it depends on a worker's effort, job satisfaction, number of working hours, socio-economic background, etc. As for self-employment, such opportunities are unlimited. There are self-employed and uneducated workers who earn a monthly income of up to ten thousand rupees. In some cases, auto-rickshaw drivers, sellers of goods and carpenters work more than normal working hours and earn more income. However, the usual trends in Figure 1 show that as the education level of a worker

Figure 1 *The Relationship Between Monthly Income (in Rupees) and Educational Attainment of Workers (%)*

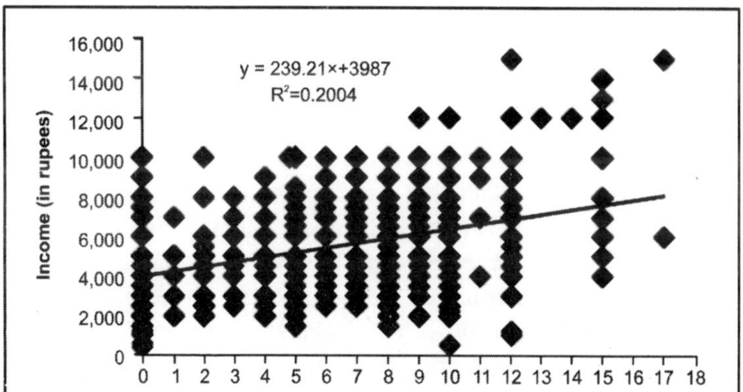

increases, the per capita income also increases. With a post-graduation degree, a worker can earn around fifteen thousand rupees or sometimes more in the city.

Association of Type of Work and Socio-economic Characteristics of the Respondents

Women workers are engaged more in construction related/domestic works since such a work does not require any special skills. It should be noted that an overwhelming majority of women is either uneducated or has low educational attainment. Thus, women in construction work as helpers carry stones, bricks and supply cement, etc., to the construction site. This is the reason why women workers have positive correlation with the construction/domestic jobs and it is statistically significant. On the contrary, male workers generally have better skills and better education and, therefore, the number of male workers engaged in construction/domestic work is small. Most of the workers in the construction sector are married. There is no scope for the children to work on the construction sites in the city since child labour is banned by law and it is strictly abided by construction workers now. Moreover, children may have a low work capacity which further reduces the possibility of them getting a job in construction. Therefore, married workers are positively correlated and statistically significant. Age of the workers is negatively associated with construction workers as compared to the workers of the regular jobs. This is because construction work requires more physical strength as compared to regular jobs. Young workers work efficiently on construction sites and this could be one of the reasons why lower age is positively and significantly associated with construction work. On the other hand, educational attainment of the workers is negatively associated with construction work. It could be due to the fact that workers in construction require less education because it is an unskilled job. Most of the workers have low educational achievement and they work for small wages. The income of the construction workers is less as compared to the regular workers, and it is statistically significant. It is mainly because poor skills and uncertain job fetches lower salary to these workers. Household size among the construction workers is larger as compared to the workers with a regular job. Due to lower educational achievement and small income, most of the workers do not have knowledge of family planning methods. Moreover, high infant mortality and lack of healthcare availability may be other factors behind large family sizes they have. Most of the workers of the construction sector do not receive treatment from public healthcare facility in case of illness. It should be noted that it could be due to the fact that most of the public healthcare facilities in the city are over crowded and visiting such healthcare facilities requires a worker to take a day off from job and stand in a long queue in order to get prescription and treatment. Therefore, repetitive visits to public healthcare facilities are impossible in the city. Most of the workers are removed from informal jobs if they remain absent from their job for a considerable period of time. This, perhaps, explains as to why healthcare access and medical treatment are negatively correlated with construction workers.

Most of the construction workers spend a sizeable amount of their income on purchasing fuel, necessary for cooking, from market. They either buy wood or kerosene from the private market. Although, government does provide kerosene at subsidized rate, it is often sold in black market at higher rates due to high demand. They have no other option than to buy fuel at higher rates. Therefore, it is positively correlated and statistically significant. The expenditure on clothing is statistically significant and negatively correlated. Construction workers may be spending less on their clothing as they earn less and spend a large part of their salary on their basic needs. The expenditure on the medical services is positively co-related to workers of the construction sector. They work for more hours with maximum physical strength. Due to work pressure, low hygiene and poor food quality in terms of nutritional content affect their day-to-day life and they possibly fall sick more often than others do. Due to overburdened public healthcare facilities, they have to visit the private healthcare facilities where they have to pay more in lieu of services with less/no waiting time. In such a situation, falling ill might lead to unbearable expenditure on the medical services. The expenditure on the *paan* and *bidi* is generally more among construction workers because they generally develop a habit of such items in their peer group, the possibility of usage of such substances is usually less in other kind of works. Hence, the spending on such items is comparatively higher among those who work as construction workers. They also spend significantly more on telephone. It is mainly because they may have to call their relative and friends back home or often make calls in search of new jobs. It is also possible that at lower income, the per cent of money spent on telephone shows more weight. Therefore, it is statistically significant and positive.

Self-employment workers are compared with regular workers, and the results are explained as follows. There are a few female self-employed workers. This is probably because they do not prefer to take risks and society usually does not support women's engagement in self-employment. In the self-employment category, most of the workers are married; therefore, it is statistically significant and positive. Perhaps, young workers take more risk and start business. In the self-employment category, most of the workers are less educated. It is mainly those individuals with less education who do not find a regular job and decide to start their own businesses or small enterprises. Those who are highly educated usually get regular jobs. Therefore, education is negatively correlated to the workers of the self-employed category but positively correlated in the case of workers who take up regular jobs.

The income earned is negatively associated with self-employed workers. It is mainly because at the initial stages, there is more investment and less returns in self-employment. Secondly, it may also be the case that they might have cited their income less than what they actually earn. They sometimes have to invest again to earn a profit. Therefore, while calculating income, it is not added as a source of income. Self-employed workers may have to fetch water from long distances as most of them are poor. They have no water facility in the premises. Similarly, it is seen that most of self-employed workers do not have a latrine in their house or premises. They have to use the public toilet which is usually at a distance from their houses. The poor usually live in very small huts where water supply connection and toilet facility are almost impossible to have. They have to use public taps and toilets. The expenditure on fuel is statistically significant and positively associated with the type of employment. The expenditure on clothing is negatively associated possibly because they do not purchase their clothes frequently due to smaller incomes.

Table 6 *Multinomial Logit Regression Results for Different Types of Workers*

Variables	*Construction/Domestic Work*		*Self-employment*	
	Co-efficient	*T-statistics*	*Co-efficient*	*T-statistics*
Sex of Worker	0.68**(0.21)	3.21	–0.3,926	–5.9
Married	2.30*(0.32)	7.21	1.84*(0.30)	6.00
Age	–0.02**(0.00)	–2.04	–0.02**(0.00)	–2.42
Body Mass Index	–0.02(0.02)	–1.31	–0.01(0.01)	–1.28
Education	–0.003(0.00)	–7.27	–0.05**(0.20)	–2.52
Income	0.00(0.00)	–9.98	0.00(0.00)	–3.58
Household Members	0.24***(0.14)	1.71	0.20(0.14)	1.42
Treatment Taken	–0.30***(0.16)	–1.81	0.10(0.15)	0.69
Water Carried (minutes)	–0.00(0.01)	–0.62	0.02***(0.01)	1.78
Latrine Facility	–0.01(0.36)	–0.04	–1.27**(0.43)	–2.92
Fuel Expenditure	0.00**(0.00)	2.05	0.00**(0.00)	2.81
Expenditure on Clothing	0.00(0.00)	–4.06	0.00(0.00)	–4.12
Education	0.00(0.00)	0.75	0.00**(0.00)	2.01
Medical Services	0.00*(0.00)	3.83	0.00*(0.00)	4.91
Pulses	0.00(0.00)	0.9	–0.00**(0.00)	–2.11
Eggs	0.00(0.00)	1.09	0.00**(0.00)	2.05
Paan/Tobacco	0.00**(0.00)	2.03	0.00(0.00)	1.36
Telephone	0.00**(0.00)	2.56	0.00**(0.00)	2.99
Constant	1.76(0.81)	2.16	–0.38(0.79)	0.48
LR chi^2=1,355.09 Prob. >chi^2=0.00, Log likelihood = –1,314.49 Pseudo R^2=0.340				

*Significant at 1 per cent, **Significant at 5 per cent, ***Significant at 10 per cent

In Mumbai, the changes in class relations, increasing inequality and development of new lifestyles and patterns of living among the urban middle class have resulted in the growth of services. Illiteracy, low caste and migrant status, lack of alternative employment opportunities, dependency on placement agencies and so on make domestic workers vulnerable to various exploitations. Long working hours, low pay, absence of job security and low social status characterize their occupation. Although these are the characteristics of many informal sector occupations, the absence of legal protection makes domestic workers, particularly, vulnerable to many labour market exploitations (Neetha, 2009). However, there is no law or regulatory body to monitor the wages, work hours and holidays of informal sector workers. Most of the workers in the city work for a long period of time in the informal sector without any kind of social security.

Conclusion

In the city of Mumbai, there is a high demand for skilled and unskilled labour in manufacturing, services and construction sector and that could be one of the basic reasons behind large-scale migration to the city from rural areas. The present study finds that the workers engaged in construction and self-employment have lower educational attainment which ultimately later translates into lower income. A female worker with lower education either ends up in construction sector or work as domestic help. Low level of educational attainment and smaller income affect the standards of living among these workers. Most of the workers do not have access to basic infrastructural facilities such as electricity, water supply, sanitation and healthcare. Most of the women and children have to fetch water from long distances. The time spent in carrying water has a high opportunity cost. Healthcare facilities are overcrowded in the city and, thus, direct and indirect cost of medical care is very high for causal workers.

In order to overcome various issues raised in this paper, the Government of Maharashtra should provide technical training to informal sector workers. The female workers should also be given training. Training programmes will enhance skills among women (Anupama, 2008). Empowerment of the poor cannot be a turnkey job. What is even more important to realize is that empowerment of the poor not only needs changes in the poor and their environment but also requires changes in the mainstream institutions in order to make them poor-friendly and supportive of intensive growth (Rao, 2009).

Microfinance facility could help them start their own small-scale businesses and some technical skills could help them improve the productivity, production and income. Since most of the workers are causal workers; visiting healthcare facility in case of even not-very-serious illnesses may forego their daily wages. Government must provide them either with health check-up facilities at their workplaces or compensation for foregone wages. Morning and evening camps across the slums in Mumbai city could also be a useful strategy to provide healthcare access to workers and their children. It might help reduce their economic burden by waving off the amount they pay for private healthcare facilities. Government must provide water taps at the doorstep of each household in the slums of Mumbai as it not only helps reducing the physical and economic burden on the slum households but also makes sure that they get good quality potable water. Children can spend such time to study or play. Women can work more in labour market and earn more income. Female workers involved in the informal sector do not get maternity leave. However, female workers should be entitled to maternity benefits, extra leaves in conformity with their biological cycle and crèche facilities for nursing mothers. The equation of equality and equal opportunity needs to be legally resolved (Chandra, 2009). The non-governmental organizations and government institutions should work in this direction.

Households in the slums generally purchase food and fuel from the market. They spend a significant portion of their income on such items but their incomes are irregular and seasonal in nature. If government provides fuel and food through a public distribution system, then standard of living could improve to a large extent as it would save a considerable amount of money spent on these items. Although city's growth is fuelled by the cheap labour migrants, that is slum and pavement dwellers, there is no provision to plan for their housing. However, when the poor build houses in the empty spaces that they can find, a city deems these as an illegal encroachment upon land and demolishes such structures. Thus, a constant war of attrition continues while the city demands the poor's economic participation. It refuses to recognize them as legitimate urban citizens who are included in the development plans. This results in the mushrooming of slums (Burra and Mahadevan, 2005). Overall, government policies towards slums are doubtful. Most of the slums are declared illegal in the city and regularly demolished. Owing to their illegal status there settlements are not provided with the basic infrastructural facilities that other areas of the city get.

Although the slums and migrant workers are integral parts of the city environment, the workers are expected only to work and not to ask for basic facilities in their community. Government should change its stand about the slum households. More slum redevelopment schemes, affordable and rental housing can help improve the standard of living of the people of the slums. Since this workforce is contributing to the economic growth of city in a big way, denying basic facilities for their settlement is unethical. Government must ensure a decent work environment for workers and secure a better standard of living and respectable life (Choudhury, 2005). After all, the city of Mumbai also works as an engine of economic growth for India. Every worker is contributing to district, state and national domestic product but in return, they also expect the basic amenities be provided to them.

References

Absar, S. (2002). 'Women Garment Workers in Bangladesh'. *Economic and Political Weekly*, July 20: 3012–16.

Anupama, D. (2008). 'Globalization and Employment of Women Workers in the Unorganized Manufacturing Sectors in India'. *The Indian Journal of Labour Economics*, 51 (4): 687–700.

Beneria, L. (2001). *Changing Employment Patterns and the Informalisation of Jobs: General Trends and Gender Dimensions*. Geneva: ILO.

Burra, S. and Devika Mahadevan (2005). 'Making Markets Work for the Poor: The Small Investors Fund'. *Economic and Political Weekly*, July: 3245–49.

Chakravarty, D. (2004). 'Expansion of Markets and Women Workers: Case Study of Garment Manufacturing in India'. *Economic and Political Weekly*, 39 (45): 4910–16.

Chandra, N. (2009). 'Labor Rights and the Working Poor'. *The Journal of Labour Economics*, 52 (3): 471–88.

Greene, W. (2003). *Econometric Analysis*. Delhi, India: Pearson.

Choudhury, R. (2005). 'Labour Activism and Women in the Unorganized Sector: Garment Export Industry in Bangalore'. *Economic and Political Weekly*, May 28–June 4.

ILO (2002). *Decent Work and the Informal Economy: Sixth Item on the Agenda Report VI*. International Labor Conference 90th Session, Geneva: ILO.

Kusum, D. and K. Gunajit (2009). 'Are Labor Intensive Industries Generating Employment in India? Evidence from Firm Level Survey'. *The Journal of Labour Economics*, 52 (3): 411–32.

Neetha, N. (2009). 'Contours of Domestic Services: Characteristics, Work Relations and Regulation'. *The Journal of Labour Economics*, 52 (3): 489–506.

Ruffer, T. and J. Knight (2007). *Informal Sector Labor Markets in Developing Countries*. Oxford: Oxford Policy Management.

Rao, V. (2009). 'Promoting Self Employment among the Rural Poor: Experiences and Lessons from India'. *The Indian Journal of Labour Economics*, 52 (3): 387–410.

Topala, T. (2009). 'India: Growing Fast but also Needs to Industrialize'. *The Journal of Labour Economics*, 52 (1): 57–70.

Unni, J. (2002). *Size, Contribution and Characteristics of Informal Employment in India*. Ahmedabad: The Gujarat Institute of Development Research.

Appendix

Selected Slums in Urban Area (2011)

Area	*Households*	*Per cent*
Jogeshwari	34	3.2
Malad	21	2.0
Chembur	63	6.0
Mankhurd	60	5.7
Kurla	74	7.1
Lower Parel	64	6.1
Dadar	111	10.6
Matunga	61	5.8
Bandra	59	5.6
Goregaon	60	5.7
Mazgaon	126	12.0
Govandi	76	7.2
Dahisar	122	11.6
Kandivali	109	10.4
Borivali	10	1.0
Total	1,050	100.0

In our sample, we selected households from the eastern suburbs such as Chembur, Mankhurd, Kurla, Dadar, Govandi. From the western suburb, we selected households of Malad, Jogeshwari, Lower Parel, Matunga, Bandra, Goregaon, Mazgaon, Kandivali and Borivali, etc. The survey was undertaken in May–June 2011.

9 Disparities in Healthcare in Slums of Mumbai

Atul Jaiswal and Shikha Gupta

India is one of the rapidly urbanizing countries in the world. Around 30 per cent of its population lives in urban areas. The decadal population growth in urban areas during 1991 to 2001 was about 31 per cent – higher than population growth rate (17%) in rural areas. The United Nations has projected that by 2030, more than half of the world population will find its habitats in urban areas. One of the major concerns arising out of this rapid population growth is that this might lead to the growth of poorly settled population clusters within the city usually known as 'slums'. The economic growth and rapid urbanization in India are bringing with it an expected health transition. By 2021, over 143 million people in the country will be above 60 years of age and the number of towns with million-plus population will increase, creating a necessity for country's healthcare landscape to constantly evolve and mature (Agarwal and Sangar, 2005).

The Census of India conducted in 2001 adopts a very clear definition for designating an urban settlement a 'slum'. The slums, according to the Census of India, are densely packed areas with population of around 300 (60–70 households), living in congested, dense and unhygienic environment. The housing infrastructure is mostly *kutcha* or semi-*pucca* without inbuilt sanitary or drinking water facilities. Urban slum dwellers leave their ancestral homes in rural areas and migrate to cities with dreams of better education, employment and a better quality of life but the present set of conditions poses a picture of a nightmare for them. Slums, in most of the cases, are unauthorized colonies, which gradually come up along the railway tracks, industrial areas or commercial factories, construction sites, etc., where basic facilities like water, electricity, sanitation and health services are not formally established. Moreover, these areas mostly serve as dumping grounds for the city where various hazardous or non-hazardous wastes are dumped from all over the residential or non-residential areas. The health care utilization in the population residing in such conditions is severely hit by multiple factors originated from poverty, illiteracy and poor environmental conditions. Additionally, their rural values, traditional beliefs and practices, including status of women in their society, factors related to migration and mobility, etc., also act as one of the determining factors affecting health status and health service utilization (Madhiwala, 2007).

It is a general conception that urban areas have better health facilities and, hence, urban population has a better health status. However, if we look into differentials apart from average figures, the poor health conditions in urban slums get uncovered. The most common diseases in these areas are communicable diseases that spread mainly due to unhygienic environmental conditions, lack of safe drinking water and improved sanitation. More serious forms of communicable diseases such as tuberculosis, worm infestations, skin diseases, acute respiratory disorders, etc., are also likely to spread due to overcrowding and congestion. Due to multiple deprivations, including malnutrition, the immunity decreases and people become more and more prone to infections. Incomplete immunization can lead to vaccine-preventable diseases like measles, diphtheria and whooping cough. As most of the houses are located along big '*nalaas*' flooded with infectious garbage which lead to breeding of mosquitoes, the spread of vector borne diseases such malaria, dengue, chickengunia is not uncommon. Stagnation of water in soak away pits, ditches, ponds or open latrines lead to spread of many water, food and air borne diseases in such locations (Sclar et al., 2005).

The review of existing literature suggests that despite a wide network of primary health services, there are multiple challenges from both sides – provider and beneficiary – hampering optimum utilization of these services. Although, the public health services are cheaper than the private ones, they, nevertheless, remain underutilized and people prefer to go to private health facilities in case of sickness or illness. Therefore, this study tries to examine the multitude of factors that determine the utilization of services provided to slum population from the perspective of both, the service providers and the community members, as there is a need to re-orient the national health polices and priorities with a specific focus on the context of slums.

Review of Literature

The slum population of Mumbai has been growing rapidly, especially in peripheral areas of the city, in recent decades. Agarwal et al. (2007) in their study 'Urbanization, Urban Poverty and Health of the Urban Poor: Status, Challenges and the Way Forward' have highlighted the fact that the slums represent the fastest growing areas of the city with a growth rate of about 5–6 per cent per annum which is double the growth rate of the overall urban population. Most of slum inhabitants have low socio-economic status due to which they cannot afford to build private toilets or other sanitation facilities. Among these lower socio-economic status communities, there are further categories of people who earn lesser than the least with income even less than ₹ 60 a day and, hence, these slums shows multiple layers of poverty.

Due to the illegal characteristic of these settlements, the enumeration of the slum population remains mostly underestimated. Moreover, these are settled in small pockets having population less than 5,000, which remain out of the counting most of the times. There are some states, which do not count and enumerate slum population at all because these areas are unlisted in official records. Hence, they remain out of reach of all government schemes, benefits and services.

'Urban poverty' manifests itself in various forms such as propagation of slums and squatters, fast growth of the informal sector in labour market, increasing casualization of labour and increasing school drop-outs and catastrophic health expenditures. The problem of urban poverty is a manifestation of the higher incidence of marginal and low income employment in the informal sector because of which vulnerability of a household to be poor increases manifold. 'Housing vulnerability' is one of the most common issues in which the slum dweller suffers from lack of safe tenure, shelter without ownership rights, no access to individual water connection/toilets and insanitary living conditions. The next big hit is 'economic vulnerability' in the form of irregular/casual employment, low paid work, lack of access to credit on reasonable terms, exposure to the hazardous occupation, lack of access to formal safety net programmes and legal constraints to self-employment. 'Social vulnerability' include low education, lack of skills, low social status, inadequate access to food security programmes, lack of access to health services and exclusion from local institutions, which make them outliers among the inhabitants of the city. Finally, a hidden and very often neglected vulnerability that affects people considerably is 'personal vulnerability' which includes proneness to violence or coercion, especially women, children, the elderly, disabled and destitute, belonging to low castes and minority groups, lack of information about the rights and lack of access to justice.

In other words, there are four groups of factors that lead to the harmful effects on the health of the urban poor. The first includes the direct effects of poverty, that is low income, limited education and insufficient diet. The second factor relates to the man-made conditions of the living environment, including poor housing, overcrowding, pollution and an increased exposure to infectious diseases. The third factor involves social and psychological problems encompassing instability and insecurity. The last factor at the macro level is lack of evidence based policy and poor implementation of policy initiatives due to lack of resources or enthusiasm by service providers.

Pal and Pal (2009) emphasized that the health problems of the urban poor are related to a multifarious mesh of causation. Some inherent characteristics of the urban slums that pose challenges for evolving a plan for a primary healthcare provision in the set-up is the heterogeneous character of the population that makes it difficult to define 'the community' in urban slums. A majority of the population in the slums has migrated and, hence, is in a socio-cultural transition raising the risks of mal-adaptation.

The pregnant women are sent to their native villages because of very common perception among slum dwellers that the delivery at home in presence of traditional *dai* will be the best option for her. In due course, that lady remains in her native village for some time and gets deprived of the essential modern medical care at the time and even after few months of delivery. Apart from this, the regular inflow of these migrated populations to their native areas leads to discontinuity of treatment and spread of infections contributing to the failure of the public health services. Mumbai city officials estimate 2–3 million floating population special during *kumbh melas, Magh mela, Besakhi* and *Ardh kumbh melas* (Kausar, Griffiths and Matthews, 1999).

The urban slums are represented mainly by the poor and middle class and the slum dwellers are either self-employed or engaged in labour which makes it difficult to contact them at fixed times. The economic pressures are such that anyone who can work is employed, making it difficult to get a purely voluntary worker in urban slums. As compared to rural areas, the pollution levels in these urban agglomerations from industrial, vehicular and domestic sources are very high. Due to lack of a proper solid and biological waste management system, the areas where formal residential settlements are not established become the dumping grounds and places for slum's formation.

There is an established dependence on curative services among the urban masses, especially from the private service providers making it difficult for the primary healthcare approach to achieve quick and instant credibility. Considering the high density of the population, the geographic distribution of the health centres also poses a challenge. Slums are located near waste disposal sites, large open drains and cluster of pigs and vultures. People living in such areas mainly constitute construction site workers, workers of small-scale or commercial industries or brick-kiln workers residing along with their families. All these factors contribute to increasing risk of infection (Pardeshi and Kakrani, 2006).

Kapadia-Kundu and Kanitkar (2002) highlighted that the appointment of the Krishnan Committee acted as a major milestone in an implementation programme for the provision of primary health care in urban areas in the sixth five-year plan in 1982, which highlights the need and importance of health services for the urban slum dwellers. One of the suggestions was to establish an urban health post run by a doctor, a Public Health Nurse (PHN), four

ANM, four multipurpose workers and 25 Community Health Workers (CHWs) for a population of 50,000. The report also recommended that the health post staff should reach out to the community and involve the community in the implementation of the primary health care programme. The implementation of these recommendations has been far from satisfactory. Reach of health services in the slum areas has been inadequate as evident from the current health situation of these areas. Factors such as indiscretion, social elimination of slums, hidden slum pockets, lacking coordination among various stakeholders, lack of interest of influential and powerful people in the welfare of these sections of society and neglected political consciousness has led to a great challenge for developmental thinkers and policy planners to formulate and implement a strategy for these groups. Therefore, with this background, this paper tries to uncover the various dimensions of urban poverty with their manifestations and effects on the various components of health and life of urban slum dwellers.

Objectives of the Study

- To get an understanding of the social, cultural, political and economic factors associated with healthcare service delivery and its utilization in the L-ward slum.
- To identify challenges and barriers faced by the healthcare service providers in providing healthcare services to the people living in slum areas of L-ward.
- To identify ways to maximize utilization pattern of healthcare service by the people in slums and strengthen the healthcare service delivery system.

Methodology

Descriptive research design, mixed method research approach (quantitative and qualitative) is used to understand the challenges faced by community people and service providers to attain equitable healthcare, and the factors associated with it and the required feasible interventions. For sampling, the universe was the community of L-ward and public healthcare service providers of Brihanmumbai Municipal Corporation (BMC) serving in the same ward. The area of study – L-ward of Mumbai – included Chunabhatti and Qureshi Nagar areas. Multi-stage cluster sampling for quantitative data and purposive sampling for qualitative data was used to identify a reasonably representative sample. Sample size comprised 150 respondents. Out of which, there was one primary group of 125 people from Chunabhatti, Qureshi Nagar and Kurla station areas and a secondary sample comprised 25 BMC Public healthcare service providers (1 MOH, 2 MOs, 2 PHNs, 8 ANMs, 8 CHVs, 3 Malaria Investigators and one DOTS organizer). Primary data collection is accomplished by taking structured interviews, semi-structured interviews and focus group discussions from the sample population (primary and secondary). Secondary data is obtained from reports of government and non-governmental agencies, journals, articles, books and other e-resources. Data is analysed using quantitative and qualitative data analysis methods.

Introduction to Study Area and Available Health Services

The study population was selected from three sections of the L-ward, namely, Qureshi Nagar, Rahul Nagar, two near Priyadarshini, Swadeshi Mill Chawl near Chunabhatti. The area of L-ward is about 16 square kilometres and, as per 2011 Census of India, the population is 8,92,278. In these slum areas, the population density is above 49,000 inhabitants per square kilometres. A large majority of population resides in the various slums and six villages included in this study. Both private and municipal health services are present but government health services are lacking. There is one major municipal hospital called Kurla Bhabha Hospital catering to this large population. Additionally, there are 11 dispensaries and 13 health posts in the study ward. There is only one maternity home and one laboratory along with Chunabhatti health post. The public health services are not utilized properly. Private medical practitioners (PMPs) are present in good number which is the major factor determining increased utilization of private health services by the slum population. Lack of safe drinking water and poor sanitation are two basic public health challenges in this area. Out of total 10 public toilets, only two are functioning.

Demographic Profile of Study Population

About 66 per cent of population in the study area was between 8 to 35 years of age. There seems to be no sex imbalance in the population as measured by sex ratio. Hindu Marathis (88%) is the largest group followed by Muslims and Buddhists. About 63 per cent of the sample population belongs to Scheduled Castes (SCs)/Scheduled Tribes (STs)/Other Backward Classes (OBCs) and about 33 per cent were from general category. As for educational status of the community, about 52 per cent of the population was educated till 5th class and about 23 per cent of the population was educated till 8th to 10th class. The average income of the families (55% of the sample population) ranged from ₹ 5,000 to ₹ 10,000. The majority of the population was found to be engaged in private sector (52%) and informal employment (26%) characterized by no fixed and regular income. The major occupations among population were daily wage labourers, private company labourers, vendors, drivers, clerks and, small businesses like tea or *bhajia* stall. A large portion of population mainly comprising housewives, elderly population and non-school-going children was non-working workforce (64%).

The average food expenditure of the household was about ₹ 3,500. About 74 per cent of households spent ₹ 100 to ₹ 500 on minor illnesses monthly. Similarly, about 53 per cent of households spent ₹ 100 to ₹ 500 monthly on education of their children. Most of the sample houses were semi-*pucca* or *pucca* houses (78%). More than 99 per cent of people use public toilets. Public (33%) and individual taps (67%) are the main sources of drinking water. The major diseases are upper respiratory tract infections, fever and gastroenteritis. In monsoon season, there is a significant burden of malaria cases too.

Findings and Discussion

Utilization of healthcare services is a multidimensional concept. Anderson's framework of utilization of services describes certain enabling, predisposing and need factors that influence utilization of healthcare. These factors may be regrouped as socio-demographic, economic, community beliefs and practices, health status and perception of health, and healthcare system related factors (Anderson, 1973). The pattern of utilization can hint at probable gaps in the provisioning of healthcare from the user's perspective as well as provider perspective. This can eventually form a base for policy change towards more user friendly, appropriate, accessible, acceptable and better quality services. The utilization of BMC health services is reported to be 50 per cent. Therefore, this study, which includes the views of providers and beneficiaries, has resulted in some key findings which are divided as individual, societal and service system factors and described in the following paragraphs (Figure 1).

Individual Factors

The religious beliefs and misconceptions are always reported to have significant effects on the perception of illness as well as health seeking behaviour. The interviews taken from Auxiliary Nurse Midwives (ANMs) of Qureshi Nagar revealed that the majority of Muslim females were unwilling to go for institutional deliveries as their husbands did not allow the females from their family to go in front of male doctors. Most of them do not accept family planning methods also, especially terminal method of contraception as they consider vasectomy religiously unacceptable. Moreover, they consider children the 'gift of God'.

Most of the slum population in Qureshi Nagar is Muslim and have been found to have misconceptions regarding the Oral Polio Vaccine (OPV). They do not let ANMs or immunizers to administer OPV to their children stating that it will make their child infertile or disable. They also allege that by administering OPVs to their children, the majority (Hindu community members) want to reduce the numbers of their ethnicity. According to WHO (2011), almost all the AFP cases found between 2002 and 2008 in Mumbai were Muslims and mothers of those patients did not provide their children, not a single dose of polio vaccine. Moreover, it has also been reported there have been cases where males in Muslim families have divorced to their wives when they are found to be affected from tuberculosis (TB).

Results from the discussions with health providers of Qureshi Nagar also revealed that ignorance towards health as well as diseases and illnesses has hampered the compliance with healthy behaviour as well as with the treatment. Most of the slum population does not accept that they have suffered from some health problem or a major disease and try to avoid revealing their illness. In case of TB and malaria, there are very high drop-out rates as they are ignorant about their health and hygienic practices.

There are huge opportunity costs which they have to bear if they visit public health facility. The majority of the population was found to be engaged in informal employment having no fixed and regular income. Most of the household's income was seasonal. The major occupations which were found are daily wage labours, private company labour, vendors, drivers, clerks, or running small business like tea or *bhajia* stall. They cannot afford to visit the health facility due to time constraints because OPDs of dispensaries or health posts remain open only between 10 am to 4 pm. These hours are the peak working hours for the labourers. Health providers also mentioned that due to time constraints, the community people visit PMPs which prescribe irrational medicines.

Another contributing factor to poor health among the slum dwellers is the low awareness and practice of recommended health practices. Other practices among the urban poor such as hygiene and sanitation are sub-optimal. Illiteracy and the lack of awareness about healthy behaviours as well as availability of health services leads to the poor responsiveness of slum dwellers to the available health services to them. They also do not keep the health cards or immunization cards with them which leads to difficulty in keeping and maintain records of the treatment provided to them.

Around 50 to 60 per cent of population of L-ward has migrated from the states of Uttar Pradesh and Bihar. One of the main reasons that were found responsible for the dropouts for ANC care, institutional deliveries or compliance with DOTS is frequent movement and displacement of the people to their native villages. Along with this, there is the issue of floating population (seasonal workers) which keeps on moving from one place of their livelihoods to another, depending on the season of their work or place of work like construction workers due to which dropout rates further increase. These people are hard to trace and maintaining their records pose difficulty to the providers. Most often diagnosis of tuberculosis and appropriate treatment is generally delayed in these groups because of ignorance, poverty and variety of social economic and cultural reasons.

Women living along with their husbands in such hazardous settlements face the double burden of health risks. They are posed to triple responsibilities, which are looking after household chores, looking after children and doing labour work along with their husbands to earn and fill the mouth of their children. Because of their social and economic roles, they are exposed to a greater number of environmental, biological and physical hazards. At the time of pregnancy and child birth, these burdens get multiplied and make them susceptible to various diseases. The immunity which is already burdened during pregnancy gets further weak due to poor nutrition, poor care and multiple mental, social and biological stresses.

As observed, nearly two-third of women reported that it was not necessary to deliver in hospitals may be due to either no pregnancy complication felt by the women themselves or their other family members. Nearly 20 per cent of Muslim and 35 per cent of Hindu women elicited economic and infrastructural reasons. Among Muslim women, nearly 10 per cent reported that husband or family did not allow them to go to a health facility for institutional delivery. Some women have recently migrated from rural areas and many belong to linguistic groups that do not enable them to communicate with service providers.

The work participation rate are low among these groups which could be one of the factors contributing significantly to the poor status of the slum community. In terms of household size, Muslim households were little more than one member than Hindu households. Dependency ratio indicates larger dependency among child age population which is likely to result due to higher fertility in Muslim slum community. On the other side, in communities other than Muslims, it has been reported that women in poor households are engaged in some informal work like collecting garbage, etc., due to which she neglects the health and hygiene of herself as well as the child.

Service System Related Factors

Reasons Highlighted by Beneficiaries

Distance to services, time and the behaviour of providers play a major role in making the urban poor's decision to seek health services. Dissatisfaction of government services due to rude and improper behaviour by the health workers/staff (48%) especially in maternity homes, staff shortages (40%) especially doctors and specialists, and lack of supplies and drugs (60%) was found as the major factor which has resulted in the low utilization of health post services and need to be considered for better coverage and effectiveness of services. Results highlighted that community people preferred private doctors as compared to public health practitioners of BMC. About 56 per cent of slum population turned to private practitioners for OPD care because public health services are too far from their community which means distance is a major barrier (32%). Apart from that, waiting time to meet doctor and get prescription from the doctor (36%) is too long (Figure 2). However for inpatient care, the poor seek out public facilities (70%) mainly Kurla Bhabha and Sion hospital which are the nearest municipal hospitals in the L-ward.

The main reasons for low utilization of public health services found in the study were the loss of wages (88%), overcrowding and long queues in municipal hospitals (72%), unfavourable attitude of providers (44%) and instant relief (68%) from private providers. The main categories which were found under the broad head of private practitioners were MBBS doctors practicing allopathy, AYUSH practitioners, naturopathists, local healers, pharmacists and quacks with other irrational degrees (Figure 3).

The public hospitals, like Sion Hospital and Kurla Bhabha Hospital which are overcrowded, cater to a large population (8 to 10 lakhs) (approximately one bed for 2,500 people) and suffer from severe resource crunch are, thus, unable to deliver the expected quality of services. The scheme of urban health centres called as Urban Health Posts was introduced in 1983 with a view to provide outreach health services, basic primary healthcare services, family welfare and maternal and child health (MCH) services as close as possible to the people to make the healthcare accessible and available at easily affordable costs in urban areas. These health posts are categorized according to the population covered by each health. 'Type A' covers areas with less than 5,000 population, 'Type B' covers areas with 5,000–10,000 population, 'Type C' is for areas with population 10,000–25,000 and 'Type D' is for areas with population 25,000–50,000. Now, the point which draws the attention of health planners and public health professionals are that population has amplified manifolds but the revision of the required number of facilities has not been done since then.

Interrelated factors such as underdevelopment and poor condition of dispensaries and health posts, inequitable distribution of primary healthcare services according to the population norms, poor referral systems, inadequate inter-sectoral and interdepartmental linkages such as with water department, pest-control department or food and drugs administration department, vertical programming of AIDS/HIV or TB, human-resource availability and dedication, attitudinal and administration challenges, and incompetence of data management systems were also identified as supply side shortcomings which poses major challenges in effective delivery of health services in slum areas.

Figure 1 *Reasons for Low Utilization of Public Health Services*

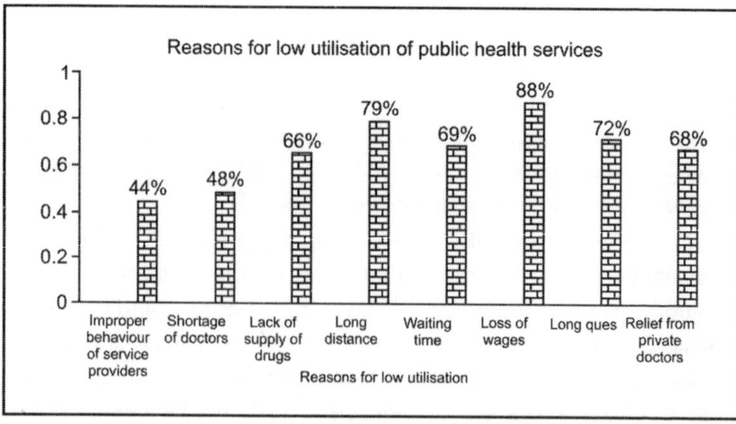

Societal Factors

Factors Highlighted by Health Providers

Access to health services for the urban slum poor is a challenge for a variety of social reasons also. The first and leading is the rapid growth of slum population (68%) which renders the meagre health infrastructure poor and deficient. The space crunch in the urban areas, majorly in slums, has resulted in a very high spread of infections like TB as most of the families have five to six members living in small common rooms. Most of the houses have not more than one to two rooms of size 10 feet by 10 feet (Table 1).

Table 1 *Challenges Faced by Service Providers in Slums*

Challenges Faced by Service Providers in Slums	*Number of Providers (in %)*
Loss of Wages of Working Population	22 (88%)
Overcrowding and Very High Population Density in Slums	20 (80%)
Poor Hygienic Practices	18 (72%)
Ignorance	19 (76%)
Misconceptions and Religious Beliefs	15 (60%)
Illiteracy and Lack of Awareness	16 (64%)
High Drop-out Rates	10 (40%)
Lack of Basic Amenities	18 (72%)
Poverty	12 (48%)
Expanding Population	17 (68%)
Migration and Mobility	12 (48%)
Work Participation of Women	10 (40%)

The small congested room with very high population density (80%) has increased the spread of infections manifold. Moreover, due to vicious effects of poverty (48%), poor nutrition also contributes to poor health of these populations. About 80 per cent of the diseases which are prevalent in these areas are communicable diseases, which spread due to an inadequate provision of water and sanitation including diarrhoeal diseases and worm infections.

Figure 2 *Challenges Faced by Service Providers in Slums*

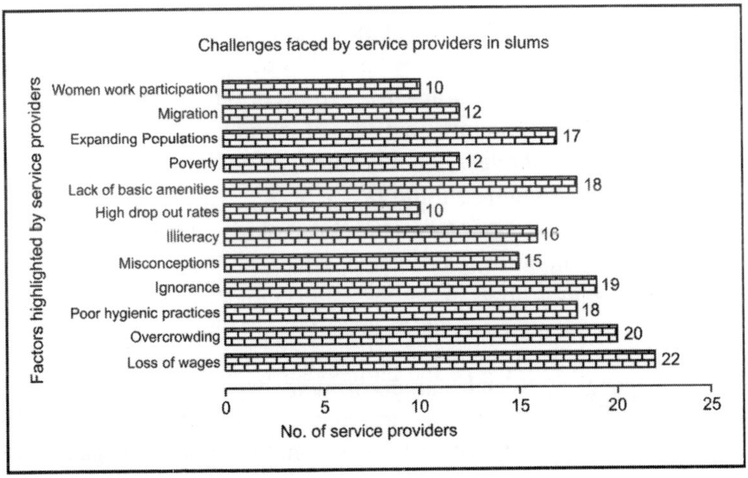

The lists of households with the ward office or health posts do not include illegal slums or people living on pavements or footpaths or near railway tracks. Moreover, the lists do not get updated frequently. The lack of an index for identifying the poor makes the process more difficult. New migrant groups and squatters that form slum groups with a high degree of mobility remain deprived of the services (Figure 2). Socio-economic analysis of households reveal that still nearly 80 per cent household has no access to toilet facility especially in slums like Qureshi Nagar, Priyadarshini, Rahul Nagar 2 and Kasaiwada and people use open spaces/fields or community toilets which are few in number. The provision of basic amenities for slum and slum-like populations is inadequate.

Recommendations

This study conducted with both the providers as well as beneficiaries has highlighted the complex web of causation which includes a multitude of social, economic, environmental, individual and health system related factors. There are also various issues mentioned by both the community and service providers that were important. Therefore, considering all the challenges identified, the following recommendations could help in solving some of the issues and contribute in future policy making, especially concerning to slum population.

1. An integrated multi-sectoral approach is appropriate to ensure coordination between ranges of activities. As the various socio-economic factors make the slum population vulnerable and deprived of basic amenities, providing them facilities such as toilet, safe drinking water and housing through coordinated efforts and collaboration is required. The community development component consisting of income generation activities, pre-school services, establishment of community councils and security of tenure should take a lead.
2. Coordination among various stakeholders: There is a scope for strengthening the coordination among different stakeholders for optimal utilization of scarce resources. For enhancing the reach to the urban poor, it is important to utilize resources from different departments. For example, regular coordination and meetings between health department, department of urban development, non-profit organizations, ministry of women and child welfare, municipal corporation, community-based organizations

and local representatives to ensure the maximum coverage and better utilisation of resources.

3. The main reason resulting in poor utilization of public services which has been highlighted from both the beneficiaries and health providers is the loss of wages due to visit to public health facility. Most of the study population has been engaged in informal work such as daily wage labourers or contract workers who cannot afford to lose their working hours even for a day. Therefore, the timings of the health post and dispensaries should be made flexible, and more outreach services can be arranged for them.
4. An in-built health information system should be evolved in which each family should have an up-to-date family folder. Monthly reporting system by the Urban Health Centre should be scheduled. The urban slums are prone to outbreaks, disasters and accidents. A sensitive surveillance system should be designed, which will include private practitioners and be able to detect problems at the earliest. Information technology can be of great value in maintaining, analysing and interpreting the enormous data generated through active efforts.
5. The ignorance, illiteracy and lack of awareness among slum population are found to be a main barrier to the success of any health programme or service, therefore rigorous integrated implementation of information education and communication (IEC) activities, including all the community members like school teachers, *mahila mandals*, religious leaders and youth groups, can be used as the strategy to spread awareness in a more effective manner. Amongst the adolescent group, those from the urban slum are all the more vulnerable. They can be contacted through schools, *balika mandals* linked to *anganwadis,* youth clubs, etc. The health check-ups and IEC activities can be conducted for them. The opportunities for vocational training and healthy recreational activities should be planned. Counsellors to guide the adolescents should make their services available to them when indicated. Peer to peer education techniques can be used effectively to spread the messages.
6. Community mapping, participatory rural appraisal techniques and micro-planning using community members can be effective in better planning and implementation of activities at local-levels.

7. A surveillance system should be strengthened for pavement dwellers to ensure early detection of epidemic outbreaks and to formulate provision of basic health services for this highly vulnerable group.
8. The working group in urban slums is often engaged in hazardous occupation. The employers should be involved in implementing organized schemes for the provision of health services to the working group. For example, regular health check-ups, provision of safe housing, water and sanitation to the labourers.
9. Nutrition component is completely being avoided by the BMC health service system. Nutrition education to the mothers should be given more importance as most of the mothers as well as children of slum areas are found severely malnourished. Moreover, the urban slum dwellers can purchase food at subsidized rates through the Public Distribution System (PDS). The quality of food distributed under PDS has been reported of very poor quality due to which they have to buy it from private shops and outlets at higher rates. Therefore, the quality of food needs to be improved.
10. Going beyond the notified slums to find out the urban poor, a comprehensive planning is required in urban development with DUDA (Department of Urban Development Authority) to ensure that unlisted and invisible urban poor clusters or slums are reached. Since urban health services should become mobile, flexible in timings and availability will lead to better coverage and decrease in drop-outs from treatment. Official slum lists also need to be updated to make the services reach the interiors of the slum areas so that no one remains deprived of benefits of government facilities.

Conclusion

It is evident from the results of the study that health is multidimensional and multi-factorial. There are wide disparities not only in the health status of the community but in their economic status, education and the conditions under which they live, grow, eat and work. Therefore, a comprehensive inter-sectoral approach is required to achieve social and health equity through the action on 'Social Determinants of Health'. Only through the action on these determinants, both for vulnerable groups and the entire population, inclusive, equitable, economically productive and healthy societies can be attained. As the health inequity is the shared responsibility, therefore, it requires engagement of all sectors of the government with all sections of the society. Achieving the ultimate goal of health equity is dependent on the involvement of and dialogue with other sectors and actors who are main stakeholders determining the other determinants such as education, employment, housing, access to food and safe drinking water. In conclusion, we can summarize that improving the daily living conditions and considering the inequitable distribution of power, money and resources can effectively tackle this challenge of providing health services to the vulnerable section of the society at the macro level in the long run.

References

Agarwal, S. et al. (2007). 'Urbanization, Urban Poverty and Health of the Urban Poor: Status, Challenges and the Way Forward'. *Demography India*, 36: 121–34.

Agarwal, S. and K. Sangar (2005). 'Need for Dedicated Focus on Urban Health within National Rural Health Mission'. *Indian Journal of Public Health*, 49 (3).

Kapadia-Kundu, N. and T. Kanitkar (2002). 'Primary Healthcare in Urban Slums'. *Economic and Political Weekly*, 37 (51): 5086–89.

Kausar, F., P. Griffiths and Z. Matthews (1999). 'Poverty and Maternal Health Care Utilisation in Maharashtra: Associated Influences on Infant Mortality and Morbidity'. Opportunities and Choices Working Paper No. 20, Department of Social Statistics, University of Southampton, UK.

Madhiwala, N. (2007). 'Healthcare in Urban Slums in India'. *The National Medical Journal of India*, 20 (3): 113–14.

Pal, R. and S. Pal (2009). 'Primary Health Care and Public-private Partnership: An Indian Perspective'. *Ann Trop Med Public Health*, 2: 46–52.

Pardeshi, G. and V. Kakrani (2006). 'Challenges and Options for the Delivery of Primary Health Care in Disadvantaged Urban Areas'. *Indian Journal of Community Medicine*, 31 (3).

Sclar, Elliott D. et al. (2005). 'The 21st Century Health Challenge of Slums and Cities'. *Task Force 8: Improving the Lives of Slum Dwellers*, 365 (9,462): 901–03.

10 Beyond the Definitional Paradox and the Legal Arbitrariness

Towards a Comprehensive and Operational Definition of Begging

Olivier Brito

This paper contributes to the quest for an operational definition of begging. Researchers and policy makers examining begging suffer from definitional shortcomings. Social scientists generally provide a minimalistic and paradoxical definition of begging. Begging is indeed, simultaneously considered as a productive activity and as a non-reciprocated gift. Among law and policy makers, there is no consensus on a definition of begging. Begging can be defined broadly or narrowly, it can be considered as acceptable or be criminalized. In order to illustrate the need for an operational definition of begging, we will review the legal definition of begging enacted in the Bombay Prevention of Begging Act as well as theoretical definitions of begging. We will then propose an operational definition of begging in which we distinguish begging policies, begging strategies and begging technics.

Begging can be considered as universal and ageless activity (Goyal, 2005). Analyzing begging is particularly interesting for social scientists. Not only does it represent the most tangible expression of contemporary poverty. It also highlights social, cultural and structural inequalities (Gilliard, 2005). Begging has been exhaustively documented and analysed through a range of paradigmatic and disciplinary lenses, including law (Goel, 2010; Mukherjee, 2008), history (Baker, 2009), linguistics (Makri-Tsilipakou, 1997), economics (Dean and Melrose, 1999), geography (Swanson, 2010a), sociology (Lee and Farrell, 2003), population sciences (Ballet et al., 2010) and anthropology (Williams, 1995).

A considerable amount of studies is based on the particularities born of historical, social and cultural legacies. Researchers, as well as law and policy makers have often debated begging in the light of local contexts. These focuses on the local context can, perhaps, explain why begging, unlike other informal street activities such as prostitution or street vending, has not been conceptualized and theorized. This lack of conceptualization is particularly visible when we consider the definition of begging.

Social scientists and policy makers studying begging suffer from definitional shortcomings. The former tend to define begging in a minimalist approach in which it is impossible to differentiate begging from labour. Among policy and law makers, there is no consensus as to what constitutes begging. Begging can be criminalized or be considered as an acceptable activity. It can be defined narrowly as well as broadly. There has been a striking lack of consistency in this complicated definitional task. This heterogeneity raises both conceptual and operative ambiguities. This paper offers an operational definition of begging. Our objective is to help researchers and policy makers observe and identify begging, share an understanding of begging and communicate about their concepts. Our concern for operationalization encourages us to examine begging under a set of measureable operations. Our hypothesis is that begging systematically relies on range of mechanisms that we have identified as begging policies, begging strategies and begging technics. These three levels of analysis found units of measurement.

Before presenting our operational definition, we attempt to disentangle some of the definitional questions that arise. The broad legal definition of begging of the city of Mumbai will first be examined. Thereafter, we will review the recent begging literature surrounding the definition of begging. This literature is regarded as particularly paradoxical. We will then review some of the existing definitions and illustrate how they are contradictory.

Beyond the Arbitrariness of Legal Definition: The Case of Mumbai

Begging is considered as a criminal offense in several Indian states. In Delhi and Mumbai, this ban is regulated by the Bombay Prevention Begging Act (BPBA), established in 1959 and until now unmodified. The penalties for begging in public spaces range from 2 to 10 years of imprisonment (Mukherjee, 2008). The BPBA offers a broad definition of begging as it does not only focus on the people asking for alms but extends to a range of street activities such as vending or performing. In the BPBA, begging is defined as:

(a) soliciting or receiving alms in public place, whether or not under any presence such as singing, dancing, fortune-telling, performing, or offering any articles for sale,
(b) entering on any premises for the purpose of soliciting or receiving alms,
(c) exposing or exhibiting, with the object of obtaining or extorting alms, any sore, wound, injury, deformity or disease, whether of a human being or animal,
(d) having no visible means of subsistence and, when during about or remaining in the public space in such condition or manner, as makes it likely that a person doing so exist by soliciting or receiving alms, and
(e) allowing oneself to be used as an exhibit for the purpose of soliciting or receiving alms; but does not include soliciting or receiving money or food or gifts for the purpose authorized by the law, or authorized in the manner prescribed by the Deputy Commissioner or such officer as may be specified in his behalf of the Chief Commissioner.

This act is often perceived as particularly harsh as it extends to a wide range of vulnerable populations. People can legally be arrested under the BPBA for being homeless, or for working in the streets. In the past decade, the BPBA has been at the centre of several controversies. According to Mukherjee (2008), the BPBA can be questioned for assimilating vending, dancing, fortune-telling and performing to begging. Indeed, in the aforementioned activities, a service or a good is offered in return of the financial transaction. The BPBA also fails to distinguish begging from charity. People receiving religious charity can be considered as beggars under this legal definition (ibid.).

The BPBA has also been criticized for being arbitrary, disproportional and discriminatory (Goel, 2010). The act gives full powers to policemen as they can arrest and detain anyone falling under the BPBA begging definition. Moreover, the court's decisions often only rely on single policeman's testimony. Citizens who were not begging have sometimes been detained for begging (ibid.). Under the BPBA individuals who simply look poor can be incriminated for begging. In other words, the BPBA, provides a legal basis for criminalizing ostensible poverty (Ramanathan, 2008).

The act has also been contested on legal and constitutional grounds (Goel, 2010). The criminalization of poor people based on their appearance of poverty seems to be contrary to several rules of law. The criminalizing people for what they look like rather for what they do is precisely contrary to the principle *reus non facit reum nisi mens sit rea* according to which *the intent, and the act must both concur to constitute the crime.*' The act has also been criticized because it leads to an unreasonable prohibition of rights. The act deprives beggars from the freedom of speech and expression as well as the right to life and liberty, respectively, guaranteed under the articles 19 (1)(a) and 21 of the Indian Constitution. The 1959 Act also appears to be contrary to the article 19 (2) of the Indian Constitution according to which restrictions on liberty must be justified by the compelling state's interest, and be rationally related to the objectives it purports to serve. The 1959 Act does not fulfill these obligations. On the one hand, peaceful begging cannot be considered as a menace to state's interests and on the other hand, the prohibition of begging can be perceived as unreasonable since beggars are deprived of resources. Finally, the 1959 Act appears to be contrary to the void for vagueness constitutional principle. According to the doctrine of the void for vagueness, average citizens should always be able to understand the laws and should all be able to determine the conducts regulated and prohibited. Under the broad definition of begging provided in the 1959 Act, the boundaries between informal street activities, religious charity and begging are blurred. The citizens are, therefore, not able to determine whether their activities are prohibited or not. Under the BPBA, in a country like India where over 70 per cent of the population lives below the poverty line, a huge number of individuals looking ostensibly poor could be equated with beggars.

Beyond the Theoretical Paradoxes

The Traditional Minimalistic Definition of Begging

Among researchers, there seems to be an agreement on a minimalist definition of begging articulated around few attributes. Begging itself generally refers to a public request for money, food, or other goods, with little or nothing of value given in return (Lankenau, 1999a, 1999b; Snow and Anderson, 1993; Van Houcke, 2005). It is also generally agreed that this non-reciprocated gift, situates the beggar outside the gift-exchange theory structure (Swanson, 2007). This asymmetrical relationship places the beggar in an awkward position. Indeed, giving is often associated with goodness while receiving is perceived as an immoral act (Erskine and McIntosh, 1999) which raises suspicions (Johnson, 2007) and stigma (Jones, 1999). Though it is admitted that begging offers nothing in return, beggars are paradoxically often considered as productive economic agents. Indeed, being based on a monetary relation, begging is considered as a street level economic activity (Dean, 1999). Moreover, some researchers explicitly assimilate begging to labour (Ballet et al., 2010), in a similar vein, policy-makers have proposed to use the terminology 'professional beggars' (Dean, 1999). Finally, beggars often consider their own activity as work (Damon, 1998; Kassah, 2008; Swanson, 2010b).

This traditional minimalistic definition highlights two major assumptions that we have entitled the 'unreciprocated-gift hypothesis' and the 'productive begging hypothesis'. These assumptions are inadequate to fully address the complexity of begging. On the one hand, the two major suppositions are paradoxical as the unreciprocated-gift paradigm is explicitly opposed to productive logic. On the other hand, the 'unreciprocated-gift hypothesis' as well as the 'productive begging hypothesis' suffers from serious definitional flaws that we will now try to bring forth.

Do Beggars Offer Anything in Return? Re-examining the Non-reciprocated Gift Hypothesis

The minimalist definition considers that beggars have nothing to offer in return of the alms-giver's gift. This statement doesn't appear to be that obvious. This exemption of the counter-gift logic can first be questioned because it is not easy to assess. Indeed, on a pragmatic ground, the boundaries between work and begging are not always clearly defined (Baumohl, 2004). An individual vending or performing on the streets will, for example, be considered as a worker if he has a licence, and perceived as a beggar if he doesn't carry an authorization. The confines between begging and working can sometimes be blurred by the beggars themselves who can simulate vending or performing in order not to be disturbed in their begging activities (Dean, 1999). If we consider the immaterial scopes of begging, the 'unreciprocated-gift hypothesis' appears to be uncertain. While focusing on the symbolic dimensions, some researchers have considered begging as a win-win scenario between the alms-giver and the receiver (Abebe, 2008; Kassah, 2005). Beggars can for example have something to return on the religious ground by permitting givers to complete an action they perceive as an obligation (Kassah, 2005). Begging can also have a social function by allowing givers to build a positive image and legitimize their privileged social positions (Gilliard, 2005; Swanson, 2007). In a similar logic, researchers have considered that donations to beggars could strengthen convictions of citizenship (Abebe, 2008; Nieuwenhuys, 2001).

Recognizing the Non-productive Nature of Begging

The second assumption of the traditional minimalistic definition considers begging as a productive activity. This statement directly implies that begging can be assimilated to labour and work. We believe this assertion should be nuanced. Begging deserves to be differentiated from work and labour on various levels. In the first place, unlike the majority of economic activities offering a linear relationship to time, begging is modelled by a circular relationship to time that does not allow oneself to project into the future (Murray, 1984). Beyond this difference which may seem anecdotal, we also consider that begging should be discerned from labour and work on a definitional ground. By examining the standard definitions of work and labour one can rapidly realize these definitions do not suit to begging. Indeed, it is widely agreed to define work and labour as the production of a good or service (OCDE, 2008; Reskin, 2000). On the same basis, informal work can be defined as the production of goods and services relying on a low level of organization (BIT, 1993).

Whether it is formal or informal, work and labour are intrinsically associated to production. Yet, production is a missing element in the begging activity if we confine to the material dimension.

Therefore, in order to better examine begging, another possible perspective would be to focus on the core element of begging, which is the gift. This suggestion could lead us to move towards fields and disciplines familiar with assessing non-reciprocated gifts. In such a process, we may venture to compare begging with politics and religions. This comparison can be considered as exaggerated at first sight. However, these three activities share common features. They all consist of sending a message to an audience by raising social and societal issues. Moreover, the begging repertoires are often heavily embedded in the political and religious dimensions. The comparison between begging, religion and politics can be pushed to a further step. In a functionalist perspective, it is possible to consider that begging, just like religion and politics, can be as beneficial to the community (Waldron, 2000).

The first valuable feature of begging is to inform the society. Indeed, beggars send out a message of social distress to the whole society which highlights the failure of public policy and the existence of deep social problems (Moon, 2000). Begging can, therefore, produce understanding and awareness among people of the mainstream who might otherwise never think about the vulnerable people (Hershkoff and Cohen, 1991). Considering that citizens have the right to be informed on the social inequalities and the right to draw their own conclusions, begging can be perceived as an indirect contribution to the democratic process.

Finally, we may wonder if begging can induce to move from information to action. It is well-known that political and religious messages can have an impact of human behaviour; it would also be interesting to examine the potential of the begging message and see whether it can lead to concrete actions beneficial to the welfare of the community. This rapprochement with politics and religion, offers a perspective to not only consider begging through financial lenses, but also help researchers widen the scope of their analysis.

Towards an Operational Definition of Begging

The conceptual and theoretical debates around begging seem to be endless. We argue that an operational definition is necessary to provide empirical meaning of begging. Our operational definition is built around a coherent set of operations that systematically compose begging. We clearly identify three levels of begging, namely, begging policies, begging strategies, and begging technics.

Begging Policies

Definition

A begging policy can be defined as the set of basic principles and associated guidelines of begging. These global guidelines determine the mode of begging and direct and limit the beggar's decision-making and actions. In other words, the begging policy can be defined as the statement of intent of begging imbricated in a set of urban mechanisms intended to provoke the passer-by's donation. In order to reveal the begging policy, it is necessary to focus on the beggar's discourse or on the setting sent out to the potential donors. We distinguish three types of begging policies namely primary begging policy, secondary begging policy and tertiary begging policy.

Primary Begging Policy

The beggars engaging with a primarily begging policy will build their discourse or setting in order to convey the idea that the passer-by's gift is intended to satisfy a basic need requiring to be immediately fulfilled. In other words, the donations will be subjectively perceived as crucial to the beggar's survival as they will allow him to be housed, to eat, to take care of his health, to protect himself from the cold, or to ensure his physical safety. We can also note that the primary begging policy is paired with a direct or indirect message related to the dysfunctions of the society.

Secondary Begging Policy

The secondary begging policy is built around the idea that the passer-by's donation will allow the beggar to satisfy a secondary need. Secondary needs are those necessary for human survival without being vital. Primary needs whose satisfaction is not urgent may be perceived as secondary needs. These needs can be very diverse in nature: clothing, educating, moving... . The secondary begging policy will not systematically carry a message challenging the dysfunctional society.

There is no objective boundary between what might be considered as a primary or a secondary need. To illustrate the complexity of classifying, we can take the example of the need for housing. A shelter can be considered a basic need. However, according to the beggar's setting and discourse, this need can be perceived differently. A beggar asking for money to pay for his hotel room stresses on an emergency. If the latter fails to pay for his hotel room, he will be forced to sleep in the streets. It's, therefore, highly probable that bystanders perceived the beggar's request as related to a primary need. In contrast, a beggar asking for money to pay his rent at the end of the month can be considered differently. Though he is trying to fulfill the same need for shelter, he theoretically has a range of solutions that can prevent him from being homeless (earn more money, find a cheaper housing...). It is, therefore, likely that in the eyes of many people, his request is perceived as related to a secondary need.

Tertiary Begging Policy

A begging discourse or setting conveying the idea that the passer-by's gift will satisfy a non-vital and non-crucial need can be considered as a tertiary begging policy. This 'tertiary need' can allow fulfilling special or unconventional lifestyles. The donation will, therefore, be considered as a support to this particular lifestyle. Tertiary begging policies are diverse. They can be equally related to religious or hedonistic purposes.

A Terminology which Extends to Donors

It is perfectly possible to apply this classification to donors. Individuals more inclined to primary policy begging could be named primary donors. For the latter, begging is a legitimate activity when the objective is to fulfill basic needs, begging should be the last resort. Primary donors will, thereby, tend to give money for food or clothing. On the other hand, secondary donors are those who are less sensitive to the level of distress of the beggars but who remain sensitive to poverty. Finally, the tertiary donor's gift will not be associated with poverty.

Begging Strategies

Definition

A begging strategy can be defined as the ability to coordinate and prioritize multiple tasks aimed at obtaining donations. The objective of a begging strategy is to best exploit emerging possibilities maximizing the beggar's assets and minimizing the various constraints. The strategy will, therefore, be determined on an estimate of the cost of begging and the resources necessary for getting donations. The beggar's strategic thinking will coherently organize the individual and collective resources.

Street life being difficult to predict, the begging strategies are more about a set of options than a fixed plan. Beggars must be able to deal with their uncertain environment and think through a range of solutions to determine the best way to get the passer-by's donation. The main issue of a begging strategy will be to predict the human behaviour in public spaces and choose between ranges of options.

The Coercion Strategy

The coercion begging strategy relies on persuasion. The objective will be to force the passer-by to change behaviours towards begging by compelling them to give though they initially had no intention to. The coercion begging strategy is not based on the use of physical force. However, a threat to use physical force can be suggested. This approach mainly relies on a psychological pressure that includes threats and intimidation. A beggar's aim will be to bring the passer-by to a psychological breaking point beyond which he would rather give money to the beggar than continue to suffer the inconvenience created by the begging. A beggar's task will be to erode the passer-by's motivation not to give by demonstrating resolution and willingness to escalate to high levels of harassment. This refined psychological approach can also be considered as bargaining strategy forcing the passer-by to prevent an unwanted intimation escalation.

The Routine Strategy

The routine strategy mainly takes place in environments where begging is a common and ordinary activity. Begging will, therefore, flow with the everyday life scenes. Giving to beggars is perceived an ordinary activity. Though it is conventional by nature, the routine strategy should be considered as a true strategy as it relies on collective and social constructs situated beyond individual skills. Beggars must be able to conform to the social normality, but also stick to their begging discourses and settings and be capable of repeating their performances.

The Surprise Strategy

The objective of the surprise strategy is to catch attention. Beggars seek to cause surprise or disorientation in order to interrupt the passer-by's ongoing activities and contrast with the immediate surroundings. In this situation, begging can be considered as a stimuli resulting in heightened consciousness of the surprising begging. The challenge will be to keep the bystander's attention long enough to encourage gifts. In some case, the surprise can be built around unexpected occurrences. These approaches will work well, but will only work once. Therefore, beggars will constantly try to update their attention-catching strategies. In other cases, this begging can rely on dramatically and radical staged begging. The human body will often be used for this purpose (mutilated bodies, extreme submissive position, etc.).

Diversionary Strategies

The diversionary strategy relies on the illusory production of goods or services. The beggar will publicly try to demonstrate that his actions are designed to provide benefits to the bystanders and, therefore, do not directly and immediately fall under begging. The bystander's gifts are presented by the beggar as a payment for services or goods though they could not claim to be compensated in ordinary situations. This strategy often involves street performers who's performances could not really qualify for a financial compensation. The distinction between begging and work is prone to a subjective interpretation. A musician playing on the public space can, for instance, be considered as an artist by some bystanders, while others see him as a beggar.

The Rational Persuasion Strategy

In the rational persuasion strategy, the beggars will offer the passers-by an opportunity to assess the begging's legitimacy. This strategy assumes that the potential donors are inherently rational and are guided by reason in deciding whether or not do they support the beggars. The latter will, therefore, provide information to the givers, so they can evaluate through a range of rational arguments the begging's authenticity. The beggars will communicate through objective information and empirical support. This rational donation is internalized and does not result in persuasion.

Begging Techniques

Definition

The begging techniques refer to the manner and ability with which the beggars employ their skills to perform tasks associated with the begging policies and strategies. These specific begging skills and abilities will result in the achievement of the beggar/bystander interaction.

Passive Techniques

Passive begging techniques are characterized by a low level of action. In this approach, the verbal and physical traits of begging tend to be motionless. The passive begging techniques are often arrayed in a static posture. The beggar, who merely begs sitting behind a cup, is a perfect example of passive begging.

Active Techniques

Active begging techniques rely on a great number of body and verbal actions. These approaches involve physical mobility and/or verbal vitality.

Aggressive Techniques

The begging techniques imposing physical, verbal of psychological nuisances to individuals wishing to avoid them, can be considered as aggressive. The more difficult it is to avoid the nuisance caused by begging, the more aggressive the begging will be considered. The aggressive techniques, designed to compel the bystanders to donate, can be considered as instrumental. In contrast, an aggressive begging can be considered as peripheral, when it is not expected to directly lead to a gift.

References

Abebe, T. (2008). 'Earning a Living on the Margins: Begging, Street Work and the Socio-spatial Experiences of Children in Addis Ababa'. *Human Geography*, 90 (3): 271–84.

Baker, D.J. (2009). 'A Critical Evaluation of the Historical and Contemporary Justifications for Criminalising Begging'. *Journal of Criminal Law*, 73 (3): 212–40. doi: 10.1350/jcla.2009.73.3.570

Ballet, J. et al. (2010). 'Les enfants mendiants à Antananarivo: quelles logiques familiales sont à l'œuvre?'. *Population*, 65 (4): 801–19.

Baumohl, J. (2004). 'Panhandling'. In D. Levinson (ed.), *Encyclopedia of Homelessness*. London: Sage.

BIT (1993). *Rapport de la Conférence, Rapport pour la XVème Conférence Internationale des Statisticiens du Travail*. Genève: BIT.

Damon, J. (1998). *Vagabondage et mendicité*. Paris: Flammarion.

Dean, H. (1999). *Begging Questions: Street-level Economic Activity and Social Policy Failure*. Bristol: Policy Press.

Dean, H. and M. Melrose (1999). 'Easy Pickings or Hard Profession? Begging as an Economic Activity'. In H. Dean (ed.), *Begging Questions: Street-level Economic Activity and Social Policy Failure*. Bristol: Policy Press, pp. 63–82.

Erskine, A. and I. McIntosh (1999). 'Why Begging Offends: Historical Perspectives and Continuities'. In H. Dean (ed.), *Begging Questions: Street-level Economic Activity and Social Policy Failure*. Bristol: Policy Press.

Gilliard, P. (2005). *L'extrême pauvreté au Niger: Mendier ou mourir*. Paris: Karthala.

Goel, A. (2010). 'Indian Anti-Beggary Laws and their Constitutionality through the Prism of Fundamental Rights, with Special Reference to Ram Lakhan V. State'. *Asia-Pacific Journal on Human Rights and the Law*, 11 (1): 23–38. doi: 10.1163/157181510793468653

Goyal, O.P. (2005). *Anti-social Patterns of Begging and Beggars*. Delhi: Isha Books.

Hershkoff, H. and A. Cohen (1991). 'Begging to Differ: The First Amendment and the Right to Beg'. *Harvard Law Review*, 104 (4): 896. Retrieved from: http://search.ebscohost.com/login.aspx?direct=true&db=bth&an=7736255&lang=fr&site=ehost-live

Johnson, K.S. (2007). *The Fear of Beggars: Stewardship and Poverty in Christian Ethics*. Grand Rapids, Mich.: William B. Eerdmans Pub.

Jones, J. (1999). 'Begging in Time and Space: 'Shadow Work' and the Rural Context'. In H. Dean (ed.), *Begging Questions: Street-level Economic Activity and Social Policy Failure*. Bristol: Policy Press, pp. 63–82.

Kassah, A.K. (2005). *Begging as a Way of Life*. Baltimore: PublishAmerica.

——. (2008). 'Begging as Work: A Study of People with Mobility Difficulties in Accra, Ghana'. *Disability and Society*, 23: 163–70.

Lankenau, S.E. (1999a). 'Panhandling Repertoires and Routines for Overcoming the Nonperson Treatment'. *Deviant Behavior*, 20 (2): 183–206. doi: 10.1080/016396299266551

——. (1999b). 'Stronger than Dirt: Public Humiliation and Status Enhancement among Panhandlers'. *Journal of Contemporary Ethnography*, 28 (3): 288–318. doi: 10.1177/089124199129023451

Lee, B. and C. Farrell (2003). 'Buddy, Can You Spare a Dime?'. *Urban Affairs Review*, 38 (3): 299–324. doi: citeulike-article-id:7152514

Makri-Tsilipakou, M. (1997). 'Gendered Panhandling?'. *International Journal of the Sociology of Language*, 126: 123–43. Retrieved from: http://search.ebscohost.com/login.aspx?direct=true&db=sih&an=10516277&lang=fr&site=ehost-live

Moon, R. (2000). 'Begging to Differ'. *Constitutional Forum*, 11 (2): 41–49.

Mukherjee, D. (2008). 'Laws for Beggars, Justice for Whom?: A Critical Review of the Bombay Prevention of Begging Act 1959'. *The International Journal of Human Rights*, 12 (2): 279–88.

Murray, H. (1984). 'Time in the Streets'. *Human Organisation*, 43 (2): 154. Retrieved from: http://search.ebscohost.com/login.aspx?direct=true&db=bth&an=5206836&lang=fr&site=ehost-live

Nieuwenhuys, O. (2001). 'By the Sweat of their Brow? Street Children, NGOs and Children's Rights in Addis Ababa'. *Africa*, 71 (4): 539. Retrieved from: http://search.ebscohost.com/login.aspx?direct=true&db=aph&an=6656730&lang=fr&site=ehost-live

OCDE (2008). *OECD Glossary of Statistical Terms*. Éditions OCDE. Retrieved from: content/book/9789264055087-en

Ramanathan, U. (2008). 'Ostensible Poverty, Beggary and the Law'. *Economic and Political Weekly*, 43 (44): 33–44.

Reskin, B. (2000). 'Work and Occupations'. In E.F. Borgatta and R.J.V. Montgomery (eds), *Encyclopedia of Sociology*. New York: Macmillan Reference USA.

Snow, D. and L. Anderson (1993). *Down on their Luck?: A Study of Homeless Street People*. Berkeley: University of California Press.

Swanson, K. (2007). ''Bad Mothers' and 'Delinquent Children': Unravelling Anti-begging Rhetoric in the Ecuadorian Andes'. *Gender, Place and Culture: A Journal of Feminist Geography*, 14 (6): 703–20. doi: 10.1080/09663690701659150

——. (2010a). *Begging as a Path to Progress: Indigenous Women and Children and the Struggle for Ecuador's Urban Spaces*. Athens: University of Georgia Press.

——. (2010b). 'Revanchist Urbanism Heads South: The Regulation of Indigenous Beggars and Street Vendors in Ecuador'. *Antipode*, 39 (4): 708–28. Retrieved from: http://eprints.gla.ac.uk/15317/

Van Houcke, F. (2005). *Recherche d'une réponse sociale à la mendicité des mineurs*. Bruxelles: CODE.

Waldron, J. (2000). 'Homelessness and Community'. *University of Toronto Law Journal*, 50.

Williams, B.F. (1995). 'The Public I/eye: Conducting Fieldwork to do Homework on Homelessness and Begging in Two US Cities'. *Current Anthropology*, 36 (1): 25–51. doi: 10.1086/204340

Index

Rajeshwar